Jeff Bagwell in Connecticut, a consistent lad in the land of steady habits.
Edited by Karl Cicitto, Leonard Levin, and Bill Nowlin

Copyright 2019 Society for American Baseball Research, Inc.

Cover and book design by Gilly Rosenthol

ISBN 978-1-943816-97-2
ebook ISBN 978-1-943816-96-5

All rights reserved. No part of this book may be reproduced in whole or in part without written permission from the publisher, except by reviewers who may quote brief excerpts in connection with a review in a newspaper, magazine or electronic publication; nor may any part of this book be reproduced, stored in a retrieval system, or transmitted in any form or by any means electronic, mechanical, photocopying, recording, or other, without written permission from the publisher.

Society for American Baseball Research
Cronkite School at ASU
555 N. Central Ave. #416
Phoenix, AZ 85004

Phone: (602) 496-1460
Web: www.sabr.org
Facebook: Society for American Baseball Research
Twitter: @SABR
Printed in the United States of America

Jeff Bagwell in Connecticut

A consistent lad in the land of steady habits

Edited by Karl Cicitto, Leonard Levin, and Bill Nowlin

Thank you...

To Janice Bagwell for her kindness and positive energy

To The University of Hartford

To Xavier High School

To American Legion Post 75 and The Middletown Sports Hall of Fame

To Brian Crowley, for his patience, time and generosity of spirit

To David Sizemore for his detailed memory and kind support

To Gerry Berthiaume, Dan Gooley, and George Grande who joined Mr. Crowley and Mr. Sizemore on our Bagwell panel

To Jim Keener, for shining the light on Todd Reynolds and the University of Hartford Hawks.

To Philip Cacciola, Ed Wilcox and Dave Darling.

To David Eustis, Jr., Matt Conway, Jeff Otterbein, Rich Magner and Tony Jaskot

To Brian P. Wood for determined fact checking and vital suggestions

In memory of...

Greg Erion and Jim Bransfield, who contributed to this book before their passing.

Contents

Introduction 1

Panel Discussion *by Karl Cicitto* 3

Jeff Bagwell, a concise biography *by Greg Erion* 25

The High School Years

All District, All State & Undrafted at Xavier
by George Pawlush 41

Coach Terry Garstka *by William J. Ryczek* 57

American Legion: Emerging Excellence *by George Pawlush* 63

A Palmer Field history *by Jim Bransfield* 77

The College Years

Soaring like a Hawk at the University of Hartford
by Pete Zanardi 87

Beyond Expectations: the 1988 Hartford Hawks
by Karl Cicitto 107

Todd Reynolds *by Jim Keener* 125

Cape League *by Andrew Blume* 131

Dan Gooley *by Pete Zanardi* 141

Randy Lavigne and Moe Morhardt *by Jim Keener* 147

Bill Denehy *by Alan Cohen* 155

Gary DiSarcina Recalls Bagwell, College Foe *by Bill Nowlin* 171

Freshman Bagwell Had Remlinger's Number *by Alan Cohen* 173

New Britain Red Sox

New Britain Red Sox *by Alan Cohen* 177

New Britain Red Sox Game Log *by Alan Cohen* 185

Butch Hobson: Manager, 1990 New Britain Red Sox
by Andrew Blume 191

Beehive Stadium: Grand Canyon East *by Stan Dziurgot* 199

Statistics

Bagwell's Statistical Legacy *by Steve Krevisky* 209

Stats *by Tom Monitto* 212

Contributors 233

Introduction

"I'm a kid from Connecticut."

Getting to the essence of a local player is a task the Connecticut Smoky Joe Wood Chapter of S.A.B.R., with much assistance from SABR-at-large, is uniquely qualified to accomplish.

Jeff Bagwell grew up in Connecticut. He played high school, American Legion, college and professional baseball in the Nutmeg State for teams in Middletown, West Hartford and New Britain. CT SABR's researchers and writers are local, determined and experienced.

After a year of research and the writing of 65,000 words you may well ask what sort of person SABR researchers found Jeff to be.

Jeff was an intelligent player. His American Legion coach, Dave Darling, said that Jeff might make a mistake on the diamond but he won't make the same one twice.

Jeff is loyal. He paid direct tribute to his University of Hartford coach, Bill Denehy, after Bill's ignominious fall.

Jeff was ready for a big moment at any time, worked hard and maintained humility according to Rich Magner, Terry Garstka and Tony Jaskot, his coaches at Xavier High School.

Beyond those particulars there is an under-the-radar quality to Bagwell. He is regular, even vanilla, and markedly so for a baseball star.

One of our writers commented after interviewing one of Jeff's coaches: "He didn't have one good story about Jeff. Not much color there."

Jeff seems genuinely humble. Reacting to the news in 2007 that the City of Houston was going to have a Jeff Bagwell Day, Jeff was quoted in the 1-27-07 *Houston Chronicle* as saying, "Having a Jeff Bagwell Day throughout the city is something that's hard for me to comprehend just being a ballplayer."

The unassuming Bagwell admits to having worked very hard. As is evidenced by the statistical chapter of this book, he became really good at hitting a baseball, fielding his position, and running the bases, especially for a self-confessed non-speedster.

His demeanor and countenance didn't portend his offensive capabilities. The late, great columnist Jim Murray took note of this.

JEFF BAGWELL IN CONNECTICUT

In the May 12, 1994 *LA Times*, Murray, who is also from Connecticut, warned that Jeff Bagwell was not what he appeared to be: "First of all, he's averaged sized for baseball, only 6 feet, 195 pounds. You look at his statistics and picture a 6-foot-5 giant with a blue-black beard, a chaw of tobacco in his cheek and a perpetual snarl. Jeff Bagwell looks as if he is going to sell you a vacuum cleaner. He's almost baby faced. You imagine Billy the Kid looked like this. Until he drew."

Another Murray pearl about JB: "He is like the choir boy who turns out to be a serial killer."

And then there is this inferiority inducing blow from Murray: "You get ball players from Texas, California, Florida or one or all of the Caribbean islands. You don't get them from Connecticut."

It is no surprise that a ballplayer who doesn't act like he is God's gift passed on millions out of loyalty.

On Dec. 12, 2000, David Barron wrote in the *Houston Chronicle* that Bagwell, coming off a 2000 slash line of .310/47/142, left millions of free agency dollars on the table by signing a contract with the Astros. "I'm very proud that I'm going to finish my career as a Houston Astro," Bagwell said.

In 2003, local chapters of the Baseball Writers' Association of America gave the first annual Darryl Kile Awards to Jeff and Mike Matheny. The Kile Awards honor the Astro and Cardinal who best exemplify Kile's traits of a good teammate, a great friend, a fine father and a humble man." (www.baseball-almanac.com).

As Bagwell ended his MLB career, he was praised for many qualities, including some not detected in a ballgame. On 12-16-06, John Lopez, writing in the *Houston Chronicle* offered: "I doubt I will ever come across an athlete as humble, gifted, clever on the field and off, candid and likeable. I doubt I will ever see an athlete wear the burden and privilege of being a sports hero so well. I doubt I will ever see someone as honest and respectful with the guy at the bar, the kid in a wheelchair, the reporter asking the tough questions and everyone he came across."

In these ways it seems that Bagwell personally revised Xavier High School's motto of "Be a man" into *Be a good man*.

He may belong to the Houston community but Connecticut baseball fans claim him, too, and always will.

19 minutes and 13 seconds into his HOF acceptance speech, Jeff prefaced his thoughts about friendship by saying," As I said, Baseball is about relationships and I want to say one thing: I'm a kid from Connecticut....".

Karl Cicitto
CT Chapter, Society For American Baseball Research
West Suffield, CT
Sept. 27, 2018

Connecticut Men Recall Bagwell

By Karl Cicitto

On March 25, 2017, the Smoky Joe Wood (Connecticut) chapter of SABR hosted a panel discussion at Quinnipiac University in honor of Jeff Bagwell's induction into the National Baseball Hall of Fame. The panelists included Gerry Berthiaume, General Manager of the New Britain Red Sox during Bagwell's 1990 season; George Grande, ESPN, Fox, and WTNH broadcaster and journalist who closely followed Bagwell's career; Brian Crowley, Bagwell's teammate and hard-hitting right fielder at the University of Hartford; Dan Gooley, Bagwell's college baseball coach in his sophomore and junior seasons; and David Sizemore, goalkeeper and teammate on Bagwell's soccer team at Xavier High School.

Moderator Karl Cicitto introduced the panelists, who were asked to take turns telling about their experience with Bagwell. An audience Q & A followed.

Please note that these shared memories were recalled with the intention of accuracy but human memory is not perfect or fixed. It is fluid. In fact it has been termed "… the ghost in the neural machine, a widely distributed, continually changing, multidimensional conversation among cells."[1]

So, dear reader, enjoy this oral history knowing that the details have been recalled to the best of the panelists' abilities, and that only the anecdote here about a baseball and a pig at the University of Vermont intentionally veered into hyperbole.

Here follows the transcript of the voice recording.[2]

BRIAN CROWLEY:

Jeff was not the most gifted athlete to play baseball at University of Hartford. He didn't have the strongest arm. He wasn't the fastest or quickest. He didn't have great lateral movement. He had limited range. I recall when our trainer (at the U. of H.), Dick Cote, was doing conditioning with jump ropes and Jeff just could not jump rope. He was very frustrated and it was very funny. But a couple of weeks later he had gotten the gist of it. Having said that, Jeff Bagwell could do one thing exceptionally well and that was hit. When he came to Hartford he was a skinny shortstop with a stand-up stance. He had a slight head tilt. (Brian demonstrates Jeff's early stance).

He had just a little tilt of the head. I couldn't understand how he could see the ball that way but Jeff made it work. By the spring of his freshman year he was thicker, he had spread out his stance, pulled his hands up nearer his ears, and tilted his head even more. Which kind of looked like this. (Brian gets into the Bagwell scrunch.) It was odd to say the least. I don't know how he hit out of that stance. He almost looked like a fighting scorpion, or like a scorpion holding a bat. This worked for him. He hit for the cycle against St. Leo's in his first game, but he hit in every game that we played that season — and in every season that followed.

We faced a young prospect named Pete Harnisch who would play with Jeff later in his major league career. Jeff was unfazed by Pete and got multiple hits off of him. He also hit Dartmouth star and future MLB pitcher Mike Remlinger; he hit him like he was a seasoned veteran. With Remlinger, the ball came out of nowhere and he threw 93 or 94 miles per hour. You really couldn't see his release. Remlinger two-hit us that day and Jeff got both hits. We were at McKenna Field. He hit one off Remlinger that I think is still traveling. I mean the ball had backspin, it had carry, it was sick to watch. When the rest of us faced these elite guys we just went up to the plate, put our spikes down, watched three pitches go by and then headed back to the dugout. Jeff could just flat out hit.

Another game that comes to mind was when we were playing Yale in a doubleheader. He hit two home runs (nods to Gooley); you were coaching at the time and one of Jeff's homers won the game. Yale Field is a big field and it has that big backdrop with the clock. Jeff hit a ball that went over that highest part of the fence and then soon after hit another ball that probably went 500 feet and hit our bus. The big joke was whether we were going to be able to start the bus and go home - or if had Jeff broken it. It was a majestic shot.

Then there was a game against CCSU. A pretty good pitcher who would spend some time in the minor leagues faced us. The wind was blowing in about 40 mph. It was freezing. Bottom of the seventh inning, or later perhaps, the guy throws Jeff a fastball on a day when nobody-but-nobody is going to hit the ball out of the park. The wind is just ripping. As soon as the ball hit the bat we jumped out of the dugout and ran to homeplate. It was an incredible sight to see. Jeff had a flair for the dramatic.

Above our lockers we all had motivational sayings. Some people had references to working harder or the draft that was coming in June. Jeff had one word. I remember this well. It was on a white piece of athletic tape. It just said CONSISTENCY. A simple word. CONSISTENCY. And boy was he consistent. He wasn't the most athletic player as I mentioned before. The difference? He was consistent while the rest of us were inconsistently consistent.

Jeff also had a bit of lady luck on his side. One game comes to mind. Try to follow along here. We are playing at University of Vermont. We're playing at an old minor-league stadium. They don't have a minor-league team there anymore. There was a wooden fence and it had rotted and it had blown down in a storm. So there was no fence in left field. There was fence in left-center and center and right field. So we're playing UVM and Jeff hits a ball that would have been over the fence but the fence wasn't there. And out in left field there's a barn yard. There are all sorts of animals milling around. And they could not find the ball so they go out there and the umpire is fishing around looking for the ball and they see a pig — choking on the ball. The pig is spitting out pieces of leather and he's spitting out laces and everything. There's no call by the umps so Jeff doesn't know what to do right away, but he circles the bases and steps on home plate. The umpires convene and finally one ump said, "OK, we're going to call that an inside-the-pork home run."

(applause and laughter.)

Obviously that's a made-up story — but — Jeff could hit the ball.

Jeff stepped on the University of Hartford campus as a kid and left as a man amongst boys. The rest, as they say, is history. He was not only a great player but he was loyal and never forgot his roots. After he won the Rookie of the Year in 1991 he came back to Connecticut for a card signing. Me, Jeff, and some former teammates concocted a plan to have a home-run hitting contest at our old stomping grounds, McKenna Field. This is a true story. There's no pig involved in this one. We jumped the fence because it was locked. We had a 30-pack of beer. Me, Jeff, Petey, and a couple of other guys. It was 40 degrees, wind blowing in. So who do you think won the home-run hitting contest? Jeff won it — with one home run. The wind had something to do with it; you couldn't feel your hands, but, Jeff was and still is the real deal.

Although I won't be able to attend his HOF induction, I will always be able to say that I played with the best baseball player that New England ever produced. As great of a player as he was, he was a better person. He was hard-working, dedicated, and serious in a funny way. His loyalty to his friends and his family remains fierce to this day. His consistent personality, humility, and baseball skills are second to none. Playing with Jeff Bagwell not only made me a better player, it made me a better person. Of all the uncertainties in life I am certainly glad that I was born when I was, that I attended U of H when I did, and that I can say that Jeff Bagwell was my teammate.

DAN GOOLEY:

Before I start I'd like to thank everyone for coming here today. Karl, thanks a million for having us.

CICITTO:

Thanks for coming.

GOOLEY:

There are three guys in this room that are very special to me. And a couple I haven't seen in a long time. In fact when I drove in today one almost hit me with his car. I haven't seen him in a long, long time. He is one of the finest sportswriters in the history of Connecticut. He was with us with the *New Haven Register* and he was telling me his daughter is now a doctor and she teaches at the University of Vermont. One of the all-time favorite friends in my life—Pete Zanardi. (applause.) Another fellow that is here today is someone I haven't seen in a few years. He was our sports information director at the University of Hartford. He was in charge of our scoreboard. We used to run a couple of plays and all of a sudden the scoreboard would get dark with balls and strikes. It was very well coordinated. He is the Director of Development at the University of Hartford—Jim Keener. (applause.) The last guy I'll mention, I am convinced if he was not here at this University when I started to go to school here (at Quinnipiac) in 1966 I am sure I couldn't have made it through without his help in getting me to understand the philosophies of education. He was the key guy who got me to graduate from this university and also the key guy at SABR who helped me get in here with you guys—Larry Levine. Larry, thanks. (applause.) This is a SABRmetric group. And he is a little bit modest but I have to tell you something about Brian Crowley. Not only was he one of our captains that year we went to the ECAC championship with Jeff, he also did something I have never seen before. And you ladies and gentlemen in SABR will appreciate this. We played at the University of Maine. It's a freezing cold day. It was a brutal day to play but I saw the greatest hitting feat at any level I've ever been at. I saw Brian Crowley in a nine-inning game hit four consecutive home runs on seven pitches. Now I don't know percentages but if you're going to get seven pitches and out of those seven pitches you take four out of a legitimate stadium - that's outstanding. Brian, that's outstanding.

(applause)

CROWLEY:

The last one I don't really remember. You know the saying every dog has its day? A guy by the name of Gary LeBlanc—he got drafted—he was a heavier guy—he threw in the 90's and when he threw down here nobody had any right touching him, including me, and I just did what Mo Morhardt said, "drop the barrel and close your eyes." And as soon as I hit it I said, wow, that ball is going a long distance and it's like you're walking on air. It was one of those surreal events that, you know, I never did even in softball. Thank you very much.

A CONSISTENT LAD IN THE LAND OF STEADY HABITS

GOOLEY:

When I went up to (become the coach at) the University of Hartford, on my first day there, four guys walked into my office. A young kid, the late Todd Reynolds, his nickname was Scrap Iron, Brian Crowley, Chris Peterson, and Jeff Bagwell. I was overwhelmed by their size and their strength. I shook hands with them and it was like shaking hands with blacksmiths. They were the guys who were the heart and soul of our club. Brian was right about the kid Bagwell. He had this little stance. He put his hands near his head and he opened his stance. He was a pull hitter. Pull, pull, pull. Everything he did was pull. Outside pitches were pulled down the third-base line, a pitcher further outside he'd pull closer to second base. I had two great assistants during my five years. One was a young guy by the name of Randy Levigne, who was a UConn graduate who played basketball and baseball at UConn. He played five years of minor-league baseball, got to AA with the Iowa Cubs. The other gentleman is probably the finest baseball guy I've ever been around in my entire life, his name is Mo Morhardt. Mo is from Winsted, Connecticut. He was an All-American soccer and baseball player, he played 34 games with the Chicago Cubs and played with Ernie Banks. He came to me and said I have an idea. I'd like to change Bagwell's approach to hitting. I said, hold on a second. We have a great hitter here. What are we going to do? He said, I am going to introduce centerfield to Jeff Bagwell. And so he did. And Bagwell who loved to pull, pull, pull all of a sudden by the end of his sophomore year has now changed and is attacking right-center field. In his junior year in college he hit above .400, and was by far the most dominant college baseball hitter I have ever seen in my life, he makes the All-New England team as a junior and we go to Fenway Park for the All-Star Game. I'll never forget this. This is a few days before the major-league draft. Bagwell goes to take b.p. at Fenway. Ever major-league scouting director and all the cross-checkers in the country are there to see different players. Bagwell puts on a show, this is a legitimate treat to watch, he hits four or five balls into the net, but what he does that's so impressive is that he hits line drives off the Green Monster that are ricocheting back into the infield. Do you have any idea how strong you have to be to hit a line drive off the Green Monster and have it ricochet back into the infield? It doesn't happen. Later, Jeff goes in the fifth round to the Red Sox, and of course the rest is history. And the next piece is a very interesting piece. Jeff is a very special guy, everybody knows him as a baseball player and a great teammate, a guy with a loyalty factor, what people don't realize is how important he's been to the city of Houston and his foundation has been involved there. This year he got a volunteer award from the Houston School System; he's a big-league player but more importantly he's a great human being, I really am very happy for him.

You know, you are going to come (to a place) in your lifetime, maybe a point in your coaching lifetime when you…you have a young guy…who makes it to the big

leagues and plays one day there…and gets released. Maybe he gets an at-bat, maybe he plays an inning in the infield or outfield, but in my coaching career I'm fortunate that I've had two guys get to the big leagues. One was Turk Wendell, who played 10 years in the big leagues. Another one is a young guy like Jeff Bagwell, who I had for two years and who went on to play 15 years in the big leagues and on January the 18th (Hall of Fame announcement day) he becomes an immortal of baseball. How does that happen in your coaching career? It doesn't. People say, "You did a good job with him." I didn't do a good job with him. I kept out of his way. I let Mo Morhardt teach him how to attack left centerfield. Which opened up everything. It was very special. I'm very proud of Jeff Bagwell. Thank you.
(applause.)

DAVID SIZEMORE:

You know we're at a university here and I feel like there's a test question: Which of the five doesn't belong on this panel? (laughter.) In terms of baseball, I mean, obviously I am not a baseball player, although I'm a big baseball fan. I actually got to know Jeff before any of these guys (on the panel) and bring a different kind of perspective. Last night and this morning I was preparing my remarks for today and I decided to go with a thematic approach. And I'll share with you some different elements of my interaction with you about Jeff. I actually came up with nine characteristics, like the nine innings of baseball. Jeff also wore the number nine. I know some people will say he was number five in Houston, but he wore the number nine in soccer and in highschool at Xavier. I know he wore the number nine for the New Britain Red Sox and I believe the story is that he really wanted number nine with Houston but a guy named Ken Caminiti was the number nine guy and he was the veteran so Jeff had to take the next-best number. And I'm sure Bagwell would have taken the number 2009 if he had to.

So, I came up with nine characteristics. The first one is *reliable*. You have heard the stories about Jeff being a great soccer player. And as Karl mentioned at the beginning, he scored 35 goals. I am not sure how much you know about soccer. That record will never be broken as a season record. That is unheard of. It's like Dan's story about Jeff hitting balls off the wall at Fenway. We had a magical year our senior year. We actually started the year by tying in our first game and we then actually won 17 straight before losing in the state semifinal. Thirty-five goals sounds great enough but the reason that I say he is reliable, and you've got to listen to this, is that not only did we as a team not get shut out that year, but Jeff didn't get shut out that year. He scored in every single game, all 19 games. That is unheard of. But given what these other gentlemen have already said, it's probably not surprising.

The second thing I would say about Jeff is that he is *unassuming*. Every time he scored a goal, and for those who have seen some soccer on TV, every time a goal is scored—what does the player do? He takes his shirt off, waves it around, runs to the flag pole, does a little dance, and he and his teammates all jump on one another. That was not Jeff. When Bagwell scored, he acted as if he had done it many times before, which of course he did. There was only one time when I ever saw Jeff cheer for a goal. And it was for good reason. We are down 3 to 1 in what ultimately was our last game when we lost in the state semifinals, 5 to 3. Here's a picture of him (holds picture up) and I have more artifacts I'll hold up later, this is how he reacted and it was unusual for him, the reason he reacted this way was that he was trying to cheer us on and the season was on the line, the only time ever in terms of showing emotion after he scored a goal in a soccer game. He was just unassuming. Jeff was modest. He gave far more credit to his team mates than he would take on himself. I mean he obviously got quoted a lot in the papers, but he would actually say that he was the third best forward on the team. Not the first best or second best, but third best. We actually had two wingers who were better than Jeff, and the right winger who eventually became center forward later on, actually outscored him. I mean Bagwell scored 58 and he's only second in the history of Xavier Soccer—the gentleman that beat him, Jim Foley, scored 65, a Guilford kid who ultimately played for the Columbus Crew of the MLS. But Jeff knew that even back then.

Jeff could be *forceful*. It wasn't necessarily a big part of his personality but when he was he would tell you exactly how he was feeling. There's a story that comes to mind. I don't care how big your school is but there is never enough space at a high school. For soccer we had to train on the outfield of the baseball field. We were not allowed to touch what was called the Main Field. We had a Brother back in those days at Xavier, Brother Houlihan, who would always yell "GET OFF MY GRASS!"—and he wanted us to play like the Jetsons, six feet above the ground. So we could never really be on that field except for game day, so we were fortunate to have Middlesex Community College up the street. We were divided into three teams and one team always had to practice at Middlesex. So one day there are two teams, the varsity and the freshmen. The Jayvees were up at Middlesex. Set up for training…and Jeff saw one freshman player really giving it to the freshman goal keeper. He was laughing at him and teasing him because the ball slipped through his hands or he got "megged," short for "nutmegged," meaning the ball went through his legs, which is embarrassing. So Jeff went over to that kid who was doing the teasing and chewed him out something good, but that wasn't the funny part. Knowing that the kid was a freshman and was going to listen to someone like Jeff Bagwell, he told him, "You get in the goal, I want to start shooting on you." You didn't want to take one trying to catch a shot off of Bagwell. So…Jeff could be forceful, but again, very rarely did he have to be.

Jeff was *multi-talented*. You've heard the stories today about all the soccer goals he scored and what he did in baseball, but just a couple of other stories. Number one, in his senior year Jeff tried out and made the basketball team because he just wanted one more opportunity to play. He knew he wasn't going to continue to play basketball in college. I was the sixth man on the basketball team. He was the seventh. He was content just being on the court competing with the guys. He didn't have to score X amount of points. He just wanted to be part of the team. And the other thing he would do was he would play pranks for fun. One day after practice Jeff and another teammate snuck on the main football field to have a field goal kicking competition, against Brother Houlihan's rules. They start kicking them from 35 and 40 yards. The guy he was kicking with missed from 40 and Bagwell kept kicking. He hit one from 45 and just missed one from 50 yards. Think about this. You just don't pull out a football, decide to kick field goals, and kick one from 45 yards. I saw this with my own eyes. You don't just do that. I was a goal keeper. I could punt the ball. But I was never great about kicking it so I didn't dare go into a competition with him. It would not have been pretty.

Jeff was also *witty*. I have one G-rated story to share. As Brian mentioned, Jeff wasn't the best athlete. He certainly didn't like to run. I took a lot of pride in running because there was always that myth that the goalkeepers were out of shape, so we used to do sprints, and what was called a Cooper Test, which means you had to do two miles in under 12 minutes. Well, I was always first or second. I would always pride myself. But Jeff would dog it, he didn't put that much effort into it. But then in practice there's always this emotional part at the end when the coach would have us do sprints up a really tall hill at the apex of the campus, so especially the day before a game there would be a lot of loud clapping and cheering and I would always be the cheerleader. I would say, "Let's Go X!"- and they would cheer. And I would say, "I can't hear you!" and I used to really go crazy like that. This particular day it was late in the season and people were getting sick of hearing my voice all the time as captain, so Bagwell was (mocking me) with a weak "I can't hear you guys," and there was just this small moment of levity that made me realize that maybe I was being too serious about the game. Jeff knew how to do that.

He could be *self-deprecating*. One day we were playing St. Bernard's. We were winning the game, 4 to 1. And he was about to come out of the game, but we had one more scoring change. St Bernard's actually had a female player. They didn't have a girls team at the time. She was a defender. So Bagwell gets the ball and everybody thinks he is going to blow by this girl and score another goal. Well, normally as a defender sometimes your plan is to backpedal a little bit, and I think Jeff was expecting her to do that. But instead she went at him. Just as he was about to touch the ball both his foot and the girl's foot hit the ball at the same time. Well, guess who won that battle?

The girl did. Jeff goes flying over her and hits the turf and we are dying laughing and we will never let him forget that he got slide-tackled by a girl.

The eighth thing is that Jeff was very *perceptive*. He had a knack for being at the right place at the right time. Back in those days, again in soccer we played four defenders, three mid-fielders and three forwards. He was the center forward. So the balls were always fed into him from the wings. He knew that. He knew that his role was to stay in the center of the field and not waste energy coming all the way back to track back and be a defender. So the balls were fed to him and that's why he scored as many goals as he did. He scored probably six goals by his head. He scored goals right foot, left foot, and I think there was one time he just threw his body at the ball and it went in like a guy rushing a hockey goalie. But he also had 27 assists so he also was perceptive to help a teammate. He wasn't just about him scoring. If somebody else could score in his place he would definitely do that.

The last story that I have is about Jeff just being *in the zone*. My fondest memory of the team is actually the very last game we played on our field. It was the first formal round of the State Tournament. We had a bye and we were the number one ranked team in (Class) LL. We had home field advantage and hosted the game against Simsbury. It was a 1–1 tie at the end of regulation and at the end of overtime. It went to penalty kicks and there were actually 18 penalty kicks. So typically (with penalty kicks) you do five and five, and then if it is still tied you do another one, so it goes six-and-six (kicks) and seven-and-seven, and eight-and-eight. I mean for me it was definitely my highlight as an athlete. I'm the goalie. The crowd is cheering and I still get goosebumps about it in terms of everyone supporting me and encouraging me to make the save. So I actually saved the 17th kick and we won on the 18th kick. The place went nuts. There were about 400 or 500 kids there. The principal actually let school out early that day so kids could attend. Many stayed and watched the (entire) game. But what I remember is that a little while later when the euphoria had worn off a little later that night, the football team was playing Notre Dame at Quigley Stadium. We had just had a little time to process what had happened at our game. And I said hey, Bags, what do you think? And I remember Bagwell saying, "I am floating." And I'll never forget that he said that.

So, those are a few of the anecdotal stories about him as a soccer player. I have recently been in touch with his Mom. She couldn't make it today…I know she is thrilled that this event is going on today. We are hoping to get him up (in Connecticut) in May (2017) to recognize him again. We (Xavier) have already had a banner made in his honor and we're going to have that on display. So certainly if that does come to pass I'm going to let Karl know. It would be a game at Palmer Field and certainly you guys would be welcome, if that does happen. I know Jeff has heard about this (panel discussion). I know his Mom told him about this event today and I know he was very pleased that we were doing this.

Thank you for having me today.

(applause.)

QUESTION FROM A PANELIST (unidentified):

How could he score so many goals but he couldn't jump rope?

SIZEMORE:

I know! And he only played soccer three months out of the year. He would just lace them up and he was on auto-pilot. Then as soon as soccer was over the cleats were put away. He wasn't necessarily the best athlete but he was good at what he did.

CROWLEY:

That's THE X-Factor. It's just something that you don't know why it is what it is—it just is.

SIZEMORE:

That's so true.

CICITTO:

Gerry (Berthiaume), would you like to begin?

BERTHIAUME:

First of all I'd like to thank you for the opportunity to allow me to be here. And if there is anybody here who feels he is truly out-of-place—it's me. You guys have had such closeness with Jeff over the years as team mate, coach, friend. I do have to correct Karl on one issue (from his introduction). I did not attend the University of Maine, that's a Division I school. I went to the University of Maine at Portland Gorham, an NAIA School...

(On getting into team management) I went to the Baseball winter meetings in 1981...rented a Gremlin...met Joe Buzas at the meetings. In January of 1982 I found myself at Muzzy Field, working for the Bristol Red Sox. Being from Maine... (I rooted for the) Red Sox/Patriots/Bruins/Celtics...and so being a part of the Bristol Red Sox was for me a dream come true. Making $500 a month for Joe Buzas. Living on Summer Street in Bristol. My wife and I were married on March 27, 1982, celebrating our 35th wedding anniversary this coming Monday...I was loving life and back in baseball with Ed Kenney, Jr. at the helm. We were a two-person operation. (I) popped popcorn before the games, served beer to the unruly crowds on beer nights. And just watched our team play. As you all know the team moved from Bristol in 1982 to Bee Hive Field in 1983. We had Steve Lyons on that club in 1983. A young man by the name of Roger Clemens joined our staff in August of 1983. On September 10, 1983, we won the Eastern League Championship with Roger Clemens on the hill. (I have) an Eastern League Championship ring that I still wear today. After that (1983) season Ed Kenney, Jr. went up to Boston to sit near his father, Ed Kenney, Sr., who was the farm director for the Red Sox. Literally since we were still a two man operation Joe Buzas handed me the keys to Bee Hive Field and said, "Congratulations, kid. You're my new GM."

From that moment on it was the kid from Biddeford, Maine being the GM of a Double-A club in New Britain, Connecticut. It doesn't get any better than that. And with players like Johnny Valentin and Mo Vaughn, Sam Horn, et cetera, et cetera, you really get a chance to see some great players—when you knew—when Roger Clemens pitched—as soon as the ball left his hand you knew Roger Clemens wasn't (going to be) hanging around in the minor leagues. Even some folks with no baseball experience could see that.

CROWLEY:

So on that team the pitching coach was Bill Denehy. Who was actually the head coach who recruited Jeff Bagwell to Hartford. So it's just funny how that all connects.

BERTHIAUME:

But we (the New Britain Red Sox) are (at that time) hearing about Jeff. He's close by at Xavier and then playing at the University of Hartford. We're hearing all the scuttlebutt about what's going on with this kid Jeff Bagwell. The draft comes and the Red Sox take him in 1989. We get him in 1990.

He was just a baseball player, really. You know, every once in a while I would get a player that would act as a union rep…for the clubhouse, you know how someone in the clubhouse would come in every once in a while and say the guys need this and the guys need that…Todd Pratt was one of those guys…Curt Schilling was one of those guys…but Jeff was just so unassuming. We had a manager at that time by the name of Butch Hobson. You could see that there was some synergy between Butch and Jeff. When you came to the ballpark at 1 o'clock or 2 o'clock in the afternoon, there was probably one guy on the field and that guy was Jeff Bagwell. At third base. Taking ground balls. Day after day after day. Now everybody knew Beehive was like Death Valley to power hitters. Jeff Ledbetter, who had led all the NCAA in HRs one year, comes to the New Britain Red Sox and hits .190 with two home runs. It just got into guys' heads that you just couldn't hit a ball out of Beehive. But here comes Jeff

Bagwell. Hitting to right-center field. And hitting line drives. You didn't need to hit the ball over the fence to make an impression. And when he did hit the ball he hit it with authority. It was always going to right center, doubles all the time. It was so much fun to watch this kid.

One of the great stories that I have happened in 1990. The All-Star Game was in London, Ontario, Canada. With me in a white van, a big-ass van, and with the Joe Buzas school of thinking (financially), we had to drive from New Britain, Connecticut to London, Ontario, Canada…In the van with me were Mike Kelly, an outfielder, Jeff Plympton, who pitched in the big leagues, Kevin Morton, who pitched a seven-inning perfect game on August 25, 1990, kid from Norwalk, Connecticut, a little lefty pitcher, (and) Eric Wedge, our catcher (who later) managed clubs with Cleveland, Seattle, Toronto, our manager Butch Hobson, our trainer, Gordon Hurlburt, who was from Connecticut…and Jeff Bagwell.

So we get up to London, Ontario…we're at the All-Star Game and Jeff gets a hit, a double. I get to my hotel room later, it's about 11:30, and I hear a knock on the door. It's Butch. He wants to know what I'm doing. I tell him I'm going to bed because I have to drive you and the players to the airport and then I drive back to New Britain. Butch said: "You're going (out) with us." So we end up going to some bar in London with all these guys including Jeff. And what I saw there was the real bond between Butch and Jeff. It was big brother and little brother. Knocking each other around (physically) in the bar. And when the tab came, everybody got up and walked out. I was the guy left with the $277 bill.

But that's OK. So as I'm walking back to the hotel, in the streets of London, Ontario, here are Jeff Bagwell and Butch Hobson wrestling in the middle of the road. The next morning we get up. I've had four cups of coffee by 8 A.M. These guys get in the van about 10 minutes after waking up. And now I'm driving to the Buffalo, New York area. So before anyone can fall asleep in the van I say, "If we see Niagara Falls—that means we're lost." We're driving and I see Niagara Falls. The first guy to (really) wake up is Bagwell and he says, "Hey, Ger, how we doing, man?" And I say, "Jeff, we are lost, brother."

We find our way to Buffalo airport where of course the (team) plane (to the next game) was late. The guys were laying out in the airport. I said I'm going back to New Britain. And eventually everyone got to where they were supposed to be.

I'll always remember that story because of the bond between Jeff and Butch.

Jeff just worked hard. He was so humble about it. Never said a word about it. Never came into our offices. The one place he went to was the field—and that is why he did so well.

So, at the time, he's doing well and leading the Eastern League in hitting, and we are about to clinch a spot in the Eastern League playoffs down the stretch, and I am at home and the team is in Albany and I get a call from a Hartford Courant reporter asking me what I thought of the trade. It's 6 P.M. on August 31 and I said—*what trade?* I was told the Red Sox had just traded Jeff Bagwell to the Houston Astros for Larry Andersen. And my reaction was, "WHO IS LARRY ANDERSEN?"

I asked if the reporter was kidding me. She said she wasn't. And all I could think about was Butch Hobson having to break that news to Jeff (on the road) in Albany.

Now typically when a major-league player gets traded for a minor-league player, it usually is published in the transaction column as something like Larry Andersen is traded to the Red Sox by the Astros for a player to be named later. Which typically means the trade was for a minor-league player. And then they let that minor-league player play in the minors to finish the season. But not in this case.

Jeff was told that he couldn't play (any more in New Britain). And that decision wasn't from the Houston Astros. I tracked down the Astros' scout—who will remain anonymous—and I asked what happened. He said the Red Sox had Scott Cooper and Jeff Bagwell on the (trade) table. And since I (the scout) had been following Jeff in the Eastern League I knew there was only one play to make. Grab Jeff. I then asked why Jeff wasn't being allowed to play out the season in New Britain. The scout said that was the decision of the Red Sox, (that) they did not want Jeff to play at the end of the season even though you were in the playoffs—and we told them that. We (Astros) even said we'll write you a letter and even if Jeff gets hurt during the playoffs we will still take Jeff Bagwell.

And the Red Sox said no.

So we made the playoffs. And we played against the London Tigers who had a first baseman named Rico Brogna from Waterbury. During the playoffs—and this was a killer—Jeff would come to the park, and could not come into the clubhouse, and literally had to watch the game from the stands with his mother. I wish his mother was here today—because it was his mother who walked in wearing a Houston Astros hat—every game that we played.

We lost that series to the London Tigers. As it turns out, the New Britain Red Sox did not get another chance to win the Eastern League playoffs. Jeff led the league in hitting that year with .333. And for Jeff, a diehard Red Sox fan, this still turned out to be the best thing that ever happened to him, with him winning the NL Rookie of the Year as an Astro, and so forth.

Jeff would speak at the Middlesex Chamber every once in a while. I had a nice conversation with Larry McHugh of the Chamber a couple of days ago. I would literally take my kids out of school because I wanted my sons Joe and Jordan to meet Jeff. And Jeff would sign all this stuff for us. He signed an Astros bat, and a black bat, 'To Joe and Jordan." He was such a good guy. And a heckuva player.

This is the 35th consecutive year of professional baseball in New Britain, and I am happy to be back as the GM of the New Britain Bees Baseball Club.

Over those 35 years, Jeff is our first player to be inducted into the Hall of Fame, which is wonderful. Certainly David Ortiz, who played in New Britain in 1997, will most likely be the second to be inducted. Unless they erase the PED considerations and then we may see Roger Clemens in the Hall of Fame next.

As someone on this panel who has had a little bit of time with Jeff I will say he was certainly someone to watch. I am so happy and proud to have Jeff Bagwell be the first in New Britain baseball history to make it.

Thank you very much.

(applause.)

GEORGE GRANDE:

I'll give you a quick synopsis and then go to questions.

Just to reaffirm what all these guys have said, I've known Bags since he was in high school and throughout his professional career. Whenever we are together he cherishes not his major-league years or what ballclub he's with or what his numbers are, he cherishes each step along the road that you have heard about here today. Most of the time we would get together and he'd talk about his time with Dan Gooley. He'd talk about his days at Xavier. He talked about his days with New Britain. He talked about his team mates. That's the kind of guy Jeff Bagwell is.

I first got to know Bags when he was at Xavier. Joey Tonelli and I were watching a Xavier baseball game against Notre Dame of West Haven. The eyes popped out of both of our heads. I went to a U.S.C. and Tonelli went to a (different) U.S.C.—I went to the University of Southern California. He was the captain of their Baseball team at University of South Carolina. Joey knew baseball. From the first time (you saw) Jeff you knew he was something special. He wasn't fast, as Brian said he wasn't the best (big) athlete in terms of being 6' 5", and the scouts in that era looked for the 6' 5" guys—guys like Gene Bennett who ran all those major-league tryout camps. Those guys would not have looked at Jeff and said he was going to be a major leaguer. Unless you knew him.

We talked about Jeff's previous coach. When Bags went to Hartford he was a shortstop. After making a couple of errors, that coach ridiculed Bags, moved him to third base, and said you'll never play short for me.

Bags was sensitive. We all know that. He doesn't show that to many people. It hurt him. When Dan Gooley came to Hartford to coach, he gave Jeff the strength to hold those feelings from other people. So he never complained, never said boo, never talked about the way he was treated. To this day, Bags says Gooley's was still the best curveball he ever had to face—giving him one curve after another in BP—Gooley told him he believed in him, showed him that he cared about him, that had a lot to do with Jeff Bagwell and his growth. Danny, you had something to do with his going to Cooperstown.

(applause.)

Ed Kenney, Jr. and Ed Kenney Sr. —I was at Fenway Park the day the trade went down. I was there to talk to Ed. I was there to do some interviews with the Red Sox. Mary Jane, the secretary, sat right outside his door. I'm there at noon when the trade goes down. Ed comes ripping out of the office and says, "Mary Jane, I'm leaving. And I may never come back again." That was the reaction that Ed Kenney had. The entire baseball organization and the minor-league organization were against this deal. Look at what the Red Sox did this year (2017). They traded some of their best minor-league prospects because they wanted Chris Sale. It was the same kind of thing. They thought Larry Andersen was one of the best relief pitchers in the game at that time and could get them a championship. When you're the general manager you will expend the capital you have, which are your minor league players. But everybody to a man—scouts, coaches, and everyone else involved—was against that trade. They were irate! The whole office took off … and never went back (that day). Ed was flushed red coming out of that office.

A couple of brief stories. Jeff gets traded to Houston. You mentioned number 9 and number 5. Ken Caminiti was #9. He was the emotional leader of the Houston Astros. Bagwell comes to camp as a third baseman, which he was throughout his minor-league career. Caminiti was not leaving. He was the leader. They go to spring training and they saw the way Bags could hit. The Astros hadn't seen a lot of him in person.

I called him the day that Bags got into the Hall of Fame. Second such call I've made in recent years.

Matt Galante, who went to St. Johns and was a minor-league coach, helped Jeff Bagwell. He helped Craig Biggio. Biggio was a catcher. He moved him to second base, hit ground ball after ground ball to make him a passable second baseman. That summer I remember sitting in the stands (waiting) for them to finish. Galante's hitting ground ball after ground ball to Bagwell at first base. They knew he wasn't going to play third but they wanted his bat in the lineup. And Matty kept hammering groundballs at him. It started then. And for every year he was in the major leagues he was Jeff's personal groundball guru. I'm sure he'll mention his name at his Hall of Fame induction. Matty Galante had a lot to do with that move to first.

He did it (the adjustment to first base) in one spring. It wasn't like he played first for two or three years. He did it in three weeks. Makes the major leagues, one of the moments that touch me more than anything, was when his Mom was there, when he made his first appearance as a major-league baseball player. I still see the look on her face. A special lady. Talk about a competitor. That's where he gets it from.

JEFF BAGWELL IN CONNECTICUT

The day he hit the upper deck in Pittsburgh - which was one of the first upper-deck home runs ever hit in Pittsburgh by a right-handed batter, I remember walking into the clubhouse afterward and looking at him, saying, "Now they know who Jeff Bagwell is!" He had a big smile.

Let's go from there to his MVP year. MVP-SchwemVeePee! He was (still) the same guy. Never changed one iota all the way through. He ends up, as most of you know, Biggio-Bagwell-Ausmus. Brad Ausmus was, of course, another Connecticut product. Those three guys ran the Houston clubhouse. I went in one day and they had one of the most bright hitting prospects in all of baseball coming up. But the guy was a foul ball. The guy was a pain in the neck. He was big league-ing everybody. We were sitting and they had little stools in the Houston clubhouse, the three of those guys were always together: Biggio, Bagwell, Ausmus. Bags looks at Beej (and) says, "You want to straighten this guy out? Or you want me to do it?" Bags said, "I'll take him." Next day, he takes him out to breakfast and reads the riot act to him. If you want to be a part of our team, if you want to be a Houston Astro, these are the things you have to do. Needless to say, the kid never did it. A year or two later…(he was) gone. Another part of this story (is) when the Astros traded Brad Ausmus to the Detroit Tigers. At that point in time both Biggio and Bagwell's contracts were coming up, they told the front office—the front office was trying to sign both of them (because) they were the lynchpins of the Astros organization—(and) they both said, "We're not signing—unless you bring Ausmus back." They brought Ausmus back.

That was leverage. You don't see that very often today. I was sitting with a major-league manager the year after Bags left, and Biggio and Ausmus left…we looked at the team that the Astros had on the field and it was pretty good, and I asked the manager, "What's wrong with this Astros team?"…He said, "No Biggio, no Bagwell, no Ausmus."

They brought something that—Brian (to Crowley), you try to bring to your (Southington High School) club everyday—and that's leadership and people caring about each other, people that want to do the right thing, people that aren't afraid to get in somebody's face and tell them, "We do this, we don't do that. We're major leaguers. We win like major leaguers. We lose like major leaguers. We have to believe in each other."

Those three fellows did that. That was the heart and soul of the Astros organization. That's why they went from where they were—to the bottom of the heap (after the three players left). Talent wise they (new Astros) had great talent. But they never had the heart and soul those three guys brought.

One quick funny story. Bagwell has always had a great personality. We (the Reds) had a pitcher named Scott Sullivan. A righty, almost a side-armer, Sully would come to town and Bags was 0-for-22 against Scott Sullivan. And every time I'd come to town

I'd walk out for batting practice and Bags would say, "George, did you trade Sullivan yet?" (laughter.) And "Did he get hurt this week?" (more laughter.)

And then he'd hug Sully. I'll give you another example of the type of person he is. Tommy McGraw was a hitting instructor for the Astros for half a year. As Brian was saying, when he (Bags) was in high school he was like this (batting scrunch). As a hitter, he did a couple of things that no one else does. He went backwards and he went up—that's the way he started his swing. People tried to change him all throughout his career. Tommy McGraw was an outstanding major-league hitting instructor. He came in for the last three months of the season. We had the last series of the season. I'm sitting near Bags's locker on the last day of the season and Tommy comes over and gives him a hug and says, "Bags, it's been great working with you but I gotta tell you, I didn't help you a lick because I don't know how the hell you hit! I don't know how you do it."

And Bags said, "Thank you, Tommy, you gave me what I needed."

That was Bags. He is a special individual. A leader. A man who cares about his team mates. Who cares about the people around him. And as everybody has said here, a special person. Yes a great baseball player, but more importantly a special person. I think all of us are going to have a big smile on our faces when he goes into Cooperstown, and justifiably so. It's well deserved. I think we've all been pretty fortunate to have known him and been around him all these years.

(Applause.)

CICITTO:

We are going to open it up to questions now.

AUDIENCE (unidentified):

Lou Gorman wrote the book, *One Pitch From Glory*, in which he mentioned the Bagwell-Andersen deal. He continued to defend it up until he died. Have you ever spoken to him about what his reasoning was?

BERTHIAUME:

At the time, Joe (Buzas) had been with the Red Sox (as a minor-league owner) since 1955. He bought the club in Allentown, Pennsylvania for $25,000. That (trade) hurt Joe. It hurt us. I didn't realize how bad that affected the Red Sox. You are right. Lou Gorman defended that for years.

GRANDE:

You got to understand: Lou was under pressure from the major-league staff. The genesis of that deal came from the fact the Sox had a weak bullpen. He wanted to win in the same way the Red Sox want to win now. At the major-league level you use the capital that you have, which is the minor-league talent. But he was under a lot of pressure from his major-league people to get a reliever at the deadline.

AUDIENCE (unidentified):

As a fan you can question what happened. You're seeing it from a fan's perspective. Knowing that when that happened the Oakland A's had won the AL West and were a much more powerful team than the Red Sox, even though they had won the (East) division, and even with that trade I wasn't confident that the Red Sox would be able to beat Oakland, so from a staff position it would be different, I guess.

GRANDE:

You kind of live in a little nutshell. The pressure that is going on internally sometimes (makes) you lose sense of reality. You also are looking (toward) today. Not tomorrow. Not next year. Not up the road.

AUDIENCE (Marc Wise):

I personally went to my first Red Sox game in 1980. August 31, 1980. As it turned out 10 years later to the day I was back at Fenway Park, August 31, 1990. Maybe George can attest to this because he was probably there when they announced that trade. I swear to God when they announced that trade there was an audible groan throughout the ballpark…the reaction was so strong…My God we gave up Bagwell!

BERTHIAUME:

Again, I never really talked to Butch about it. Butch had to make that announcement…Butch had to be the one to make that (trade known) to Jeff and he called into the (team) office from Albany, New York, because that is where the team was. I never really asked him how that (talk) was, that meeting between him and Jeff.

SIZEMORE:

I think can tell you that Jeff was extremely disappointed and frustrated. I had seen him the next day or soon thereafter because he came to my house for a cookout. He was bitter. I saw the big picture and I said Jeff this is the best thing that ever happened to you. You are behind Scott Cooper, Tim Naehring, and at least one more guy, you have a logjam at third base. The rest of course worked out.

AUDIENCE (Steve Krevisky):

A couple of things related to that but in a different vein…I sometimes think that Bagwell in Houston might not have been appreciated enough in the sense that he went as a consequence of the trade that you are all talking about, from a hitter's park to one of THE ultimate pitcher's parks…And you look at the numbers that he put up there for most of his career and it seems to me he was actually better than his numbers indicated. (To David Sizemore)…when you were at Xavier…did you get sense of how good of a baseball player he was then, and also—for George: in the early years after that trade, did the Reds ever try to get Jeff?

GRANDE:

From the Reds' standpoint, there was always an interest but there was never ever a wavering on the Astros organization because they knew what they had. They were building for the future. We (the Reds) came close to making a couple of deals with the Astros over the years—most recently Hunter Pence, when he was available, but they (the Astros) never wavered and they were smart in that respect. Tal Smith (Astros GM), who at one time was a Reds front office guy, knew full well what they were building for the future (in Houston) so there was never a chance. Jeff was supremely respected in every clubhouse he went to, I'll give you one quick example. Bags got hit a number of times on the left hand…because of the way he set up people had to pitch him inside. By his locker he had a box…it contained 87 different hand protectors they made him…and he learned to live with one that was comfortable. We (the Reds) had Aaron Boone, who had been hit…and Barry Larkin got hit a couple of times…and he (Bagwell) went over and said, "I don't want you guys to lose (playing) time…because I know what happened to me—I lost half a season one year." He invited them in and said, "Try these on, take one home with you, and our guy will make them for you." That's the kind of guy he was…I mean we were in the middle of the Central Division race every year but he didn't want Boone to get hurt, Larkin to get hurt because they were getting pitched inside as well. As it turned out neither one of them ever felt comfortable (with a hand protector). It took Bags a long time to be comfortable with that guard. He hated it. But he realized he had to do it.

CROWLEY:

I'll add on to that…and then I'll answer that other question. I played in the Hartford Twilight League while Bags was in the big leagues and I broke my hand and Jeff sent ME a glove! I get a glove (from him) with what looks like a stack of cards (built) on it to protect him. That's the type of person that he is.

SIZEMORE:

As far as knowing in high school the first time that any of us remotely thought he was big-league material was when, as I mentioned before, he played basketball, we played basketball together senior year, and there's always this confluence, again, for those of you who know Connecticut High School sports, the basketball tournament had just wrapped up last weekend which was the week before pitchers and catchers reported. So we were still playing, we were .500, I remember we had a (basketball) practice and as soon as it was over Bags immediately started throwing because it was the first day for pitchers and catchers. I think I went to one baseball game but to actually see him up close throwing hard, he actually pitched for us (Xavier), as many good baseball players do for their high-school teams, (Sizemore looks at the other athletes on panel) you probably pitched too. Jeff threw a no-hitter, by the way in high school and people were (then) talking, yeah, Bagwell's got a (professional) shot...and I said *really*? And I didn't say it because I doubted him.

I knew how good of a soccer player he was and he was being recruited in soccer by Joe Marone at UConn, and UConn soccer back in those days was big time. They are still very good. But in those days before UConn had the basketball (success), UConn soccer won a National Championship in 1981. I remember the fact that we made the (soccer) team as freshmen (and) that our coach took us to a UConn (soccer) game. We might as well have gone to a Super Bowl. That was such a big deal (as freshmen) being invited to go with the varsity guys to see UConn soccer play.

The fact that Bagwell was being recruited in soccer (was what seemed defining). But Jeff did the calculus pretty easily. There was no professional soccer league at the time. The NASL had disbanded. The MLS was still 10-plus years away. Clearly it was going to be baseball. But the buzz started the spring of my senior year that he had a chance to play (baseball) at the professional level. Again, I was saying, really? And I was also saying, well, maybe just maybe. He played Legion ball too, he played in the Cape Cod League, he had a lot of different experiences to get him ready for the majors. But I have to say, I definitely think soccer played a part, to some degree, in his development.

GRANDE:

Quick trivia question: Who are the three MLB players who were All-State Soccer players in Connecticut? You know one of them. Name me two more. (Wrong answers spoken.) Rob Dibble. He was an All-State sweeper. And Ronny Wotus who is the bench coach for Bruce Bochy in San Francisco.

AUDIENCE (Larry Levine):

There is no doubt that Jeff Bagwell's path from Xavier to big leagues was unstoppable. But I think he was lucky to have the kind of coach that Dan Gooley is. I've had the opportunity to have many of his players through the years in my classes. I can tell you without any question. The affection that his players have for this coach, the support that he gives them, the love that he bestows upon them is a very special kind of thing. Coaching is important at every level. Bagwell's talent was going to carry him through. But I consider him lucky to have had Dan Gooley as his coach…
(applause.)

GRANDE:

He does, too. Bags does, too.

AUDIENCE (unidentified):

Had Jeff Bagwell not been traded…..

BERTHIAUME:

…We would have won the Eastern League Championship in 1990…

AUDIENCE (unidentified):

…how long do you think it might have been before he had the opportunity to be a regular player for the Red Sox?

BERTHIAUME:

That's a really good question. Some players know that they are going someplace. Personally, I didn't see that in Jeff. He really didn't seem to make a lot of noise. But these guys (the Astros) knew what kind of talent he had. I saw him for five months. We had heard about him (before New Britain). He hit .333 and was the Eastern League batting champion at that time. But I'm not sure that because of the backlog (at third base) that they had at that time at Fenway….George, maybe you could answer that.

GRANDE:

This goes to your question about Lou's reaction and the major-league staff. Tim Naehring was the hot item. (He was) big, strong, majestic. And Scott Cooper could hit. Everybody knew that. They put Bags third on that list in terms of who would be the next good hitter to come up, the next best player to play third base. First base was another story, too. They (Sox) put him second or third for every position they looked at. From Lou Gorman's standpoint, not the minor-league standpoint, he was looking at two other guys he thought might be better.

AUDIENCE (Unidentified):

Naehring didn't really last. He didn't live up to that potential.

GOOLEY:

I'll tell you just a quick one. It was in 1990 when Jeff gets traded, from the Red Sox to the Astros, I'm sitting in my office at the U. of H., and the late Ed Buckey, who is the Astro scout that was involved in this trade, is with Tom Mooney…the northeast regional scout for the Astros…they are sitting in my office and I'll never forget this, my right hand to God, George….it's spring training, the Astros' Ken Caminiti is having a great spring. Jeff is having a great spring. I said (to Buckey and Mooney), "What are you guys going to do with the kid, Bagwell?" They said, "We don't know what we are going to do with Bagwell." I said this in passing now, but I did mean it. I said, "You guys must know this kid was an All-State soccer player." They said, "We do." I said, "Well if this kid can catch a damn ball with his feet he can catch a base with his feet." I said it half-heartedly with a chuckle. Two days later they moved Bagwell to first base. I'll never forget that. Bagwell called me up and said, "Dammit, what did you tell these guys?" I said, "I told them the truth." So now Bagwell's at first base and I said, "Oh my God."

CICITTO:

On that note I'm going to cut it. We're a little bit over. You were all fantastic. Thank you so much.

NOTES

1   Benedict Leery, *New York Times*, February 12, 2018
2   I-Audio recording by Karl Cicitto, SABR general meeting, at Quinnipiac University, March 25, 2017.

Jeff Bagwell, a concise biography

By Greg Erion

Jeff Bagwell was a dominant player in the National League for most of his 15-year career. Eight seasons he drove in more than 100 runs. Nine times he hit 31 or more home runs and scored over 100 runs. In 1994 he was unanimously selected as the Most Valuable Player. Despite these and other accomplishments, Bagwell's career was shadowed by controversy because he played during the steroid era and his reputation, justified or not, was marred by that juxtaposition of timing.[1]

Many felt this issue played a substantial role in his being delayed selection to the Hall of Fame during his first six years of eligibility. While conclusive evidence never surfaced that Bagwell used steroids, his reputation seemed to rest with the concept of inductive reasoning expressed by the old phrase, "If it looks like a duck, swims like a duck, and quacks like a duck, then it probably is a duck." His election to the Hall in 2017 went a long way toward dissipating the cloud over his reputation.

Jeffery Robert Bagwell was born in Boston, Massachusetts on May 27, 1968, the only child of Robert and Janice Bagwell. Baseball entered his life early: His father had pitched in college at Northwestern University and subsequently on a semiprofessional basis.[2] Janice, who eventually became a police officer, played softball into her 20s. She later recalled that Jeff "could throw a ball before he could walk. When he was six months old, we'd throw a ball to him and he would throw it back."

Bagwell attended Xavier High School in Middletown, Connecticut, and although playing shortstop for the school, his main sport was soccer. Soccer notwithstanding, he received a baseball scholarship to attend the University of Hartford and came under the tutelage of Coach Bill Denehy. Denehy, a former major league pitcher, soon realized Bagwell's potential, converting him into a third baseman that quickly became a team star.[3]

While Bagwell performed well for Hartford, he thought major league scouts noticed his playing summer ball. He recalled, "I got my chance in the Cape Cod League. ... A lot of players from the best programs in the summer came to play there. Albert Belle was playing there. Frank Thomas. I only hit about .205 that year, but I looked at those guys and decided I could play with them." Next year he hit over .300, and Boston selected him in the fourth round of the 1989 amateur draft.⁴

Assigned to the Class A Winter Haven Red Sox in the Florida State League he batted .310, exhibiting little of his eventual power, collecting just two home runs. His performance still earned him promotion to New Britain, the Red Sox Class AA team in the Eastern League. There Bagwell hit .333 to win the batting title and was named the league's MVP. Again, he generated little power with only four home runs on the year.

As the season ended, word came out of Boston on August 30, 1990, that the 22-year-old Bagwell had been traded to the Houston Astros for Larry Andersen, a 37-year-old relief pitcher. It was then and still is, considered one of the worst trades in baseball history. Red Sox General Manager Lou Gorman, who received the bulk of criticism for this transaction, spent many of his ensuing years explaining his reasons for trading Bagwell.

In a tight pennant race as the 1990 season entered its final month, Boston needed bullpen help badly after their best reliever Jeff Reardon was lost for several weeks due to surgery. Andersen looked like the best potential available help, but Houston wanted a minor league prospect in return.

Bagwell had shown potential at third, but he was at the end of the queue for the position in the Red Sox system. Gorman felt he could fill a yawning hole for Boston to "win now" without much sacrifice.⁵ Years later, Bagwell commented on the trade from his perspective. The Red Sox were in a pennant race. They needed help. I was third on their chart at third base. They had Wade Boggs. They had Scott Cooper at Pawtucket. You look at that, and you look at their situation—they bring in free agents all the time."

At the time, the trade devastated Bagwell: "I was one of the saddest guys you'll ever see. All my life everything had been Boston. I was born in Boston. My father was from Watertown; my mother was from Newton, both outside Boston. . . . our house was one of those places where you couldn't mention the word Yankees. . . . Every weekend the television would be tuned to . . . [t]he Red Sox. No other games. My grandmother Alice Hare, she's 81 years old, she still lives in Newton, and she can tell you anything . . . about the Red Sox. I called her to tell her the news. She started crying."⁶

Andersen pitched well the last month of the season. In 15 games he posted a 1.23 ERA helping Boston to secure a division championship. As a free agent during the winter, he eventually signed with the San Diego Padres. Those 15 games do not begin to match against Bagwell's spectacular career with Houston.⁷

Although he no longer had to compete against Cooper or Boggs, Bagwell still had to contend with Ken Caminiti, well entrenched at third for the Astros. Bagwell came to spring training expecting to be assigned to Houston's farm club in Tucson. But his play so impressed the Astros that two weeks before the season opener, Houston decided to bring him to the majors—as a first baseman. Bagwell went through a crash course learning how to play the position. In the time remaining until Opening Day he manned first in minor league games during the morning and for the Astros in the afternoon. *The Sporting News* put it succinctly: "Rookie Jeff Bagwell never played first base before this spring, but the position is his to lose. It's up to his bat."[8]

But that put him in a tenuous position, because Bagwell started slowly, hitting just .100 early in the season. But when he came up to bat in a tie game against the Braves, his first major league home run won the game. The next day he homered again. By the end of April his average had improved to a more respectable .254. And he continued to hit well, finishing the year at .294 with 15 home runs and 82 RBIs, winning the Rookie of the Year Award in a romp with 23 of the 24 first place votes.[9]

Bagwell's power numbers surprised baseball observers. During his two Double A minor league seasons, he hit six home runs in 932 at bats—or one for every 155 at bats. His 15 home runs for Houston came at the rate of one every 36.9 at-bats. Bagwell's home run total was all the more impressive for having been amassed in the cavernous Astrodome. He also exhibited unique plate discipline for a rookie, gathering 75 walks, 10th in the league. This contributed to a .387 OBP, fifth in the league. Both his power and patience at the plate would improve over the years, each becoming a signature part of his game.

Houston finished last in the NL West in 1991 at 65-97, tying a franchise record for futility. Since winning the division championship in 1986, they had descended into consistent mediocrity. In place of such departed luminaries as Jose Cruz, Glenn Davis and Nolan Ryan, Craig Biggio and Bagwell were coming on board. And they would anchor a team that made the 1990s the most successful decade in Houston's franchise history.

While the season had not been successful for Houston, Bagwell immediately sensed a key difference from the minor leagues. "I'll tell you what made the greatest impression on me during the whole year. We were in Atlanta when the Braves clinched the pennant. We'd played them early in the season, and maybe 10,000 people were at the game ... at the end of the season, the place was filled every night. All these people were singing and cheering, celebrating. It made you think. You play in the minor leagues and it's all individual, really.... everybody is always looking up, trying to figure where he's going to go next." In "major league baseball [, t]he individual didn't matter. Winning mattered. I watched the Braves, and everything came into focus for me: This is what I want for us."[10]

Bagwell successfully avoided the sophomore jinx in 1992. Playing in all 162 scheduled games, his home run total increased to 18. While his average dipped to .273, a careful review of his performance indicated a more disciplined hitter. Strikeouts decreased from 116 to 97 and walks increased to 84, seventh in the league. Part of Bagwell's success may well have involved his unique batting stance.

Numerous unusual batting styles pepper baseball's history. Mel Ott's lifting his right leg, a "foot-in-the-bucket" stance as he began his swing or Stan Musial's "peeking around the corner" approach come distinctly to mind.[11] Bagwell's was equally unique. It has been described as a "crouching-tiger, hidden dragon" batting stance or more indelicately, "like he is sitting on the john." He stood in the batter's box with his legs spread wider than his shoulders in an exaggerated crouch.[12] With his bottom hand over the knob of the bat, he lifted his left foot a few inches and unleashed a forceful uppercut swing. "That wide stance keeps him from over striding," Joe Torre observed, "which can be your biggest problem when you're trying to hit for power." Despite his odd stance, Bagwell still hit with authority.[13] And as unorthodox as his stance appeared, it served another purpose, minimizing Bagwell's strike zone, a factor in his ability to coax a walk.

His unique stance caused Bagwell repeated injuries three consecutive seasons beginning in 1993. That year he began to come into his own. Batting .320 with 20 home runs and 88 RBIs in mid-September, Bagwell broke his hand on a pitch from the Phils' Ben Rivera. His next two seasons ended prematurely for the same reason. An examination of his swing indicated Bagwell's hands dipped into the strike zone making them vulnerable to injury. After his third broken hand in 1995, he began wearing a protective pad over his batting glove.[14]

While the season ended early for Bagwell, it marked Houston's steady improvement. After having finished last in 1991, the Astros progressed to fourth in 1992 and third in 1993. Bagwell as well as players like Craig Biggio, Caminiti, and Luis Gonzalez were improving. Pitcher Darryl Kile blossomed in 1993 going 15-8. In the strike-shortened 1994 season, both Bagwell and the Astros improved markedly.

In just 400 at bats, Bagwell scored 104 runs and drove in a league-leading 116. He hit .368, second behind Tony Gwynn's .394, but what really caught everyone's breath was his .750 slugging percentage. At the time it ranked seventh highest all-time in a season, second best in the NL, just behind Rogers Hornsby's .756 in 1925. On June 24, he hit three home runs in a game against the Dodgers, two coming in the sixth inning. Indeed, between May 16 and July 24 Bagwell hit two or more home runs in a game five times. "Crazy stuff happened that year," Bagwell recalled. "Every pitch that I was looking for, I got. And when I got it, I didn't miss it. It was ridiculous."[15] Lost amidst Bagwell's hitting exploits was his receiving the NL Gold Glove Award at first base, a testament to his well-rounded abilities.

Unfortunately the 1994 season ended when players went on strike in mid-August due to acrimonious disputes with team owners over several issues. Houston trailed Cincinnati by half a game when the strike took effect. Whether the Astros could have continued to hold their own in the race was problematic though. Because the day before the strike commenced, Bagwell was hit by a pitch from San Diego's Andy Benes that broke the fourth metacarpal on his left hand, the same bone he broke a year earlier. "I can't believe this happened to me two years in a row" he said after X-rays confirmed he would be out several weeks—essentially until the end of the season.[16] But a day later the season ended anyway. Paradoxically, timing of the strike benefitted Bagwell in ways unforeseen at the time.

Despite the truncated season, players were still selected to receive individual awards. The BBWAA unanimously choose Bagwell as the National League's MVP. He was only the 11th player and fourth National Leaguer to win every writer's first place votes. "It's very flattering. It means more to me than you can possibly imagine."[17]

Strong conjecture had it that if the season had continued with Bagwell sidelined the award might have gone elsewhere. Matt Williams of the San Francisco Giants who finished second in the MVP voting had 43 home runs when the strike started and on a pace to hit over 60. With the Giants in the thick of the pennant race he could well have supplanted Bagwell in the voting. Bagwell did win the award however, the first and only Astro through 2016 to do so. Despite his spectacular year however, Bagwell's achievement is always less lustrous because it happened in the "strike shortened season."

Once play resumed in 1995, Houston was expected to contend as they had in 1994. Bagwell and Biggio began dominating the Astros' offense, and within a year they gained a nickname, "The Killer B's." Over the years other "B's"—Derek Bell, Carlos Beltran, and Lance Berkman—came to prominence, but Bagwell and Biggio remained constants.

The team performed well; on July 30 they were just 3½ games behind the Reds when Bagwell was hit on his left hand by San Diego's Brian Williams, taking him out of the lineup for several weeks. "I was getting it X-rayed and I was moving it pretty good," said a frustrated Bagwell. "I thought, O.K. it's probably going to be O.K. That's the same thing I said last year, and that's the same result. I don't know whether to change my stance. I've taken all the precautions."[18] Of the pennant race, he noted: "I can't tell you how sad I am about this right now because...we're playing great baseball. We've still got a great team and everything, but I know my production was helping, at least."[19] From then on a special pad protected Bagwell's batting glove, and he never suffered this injury again.

Bagwell proved prescient. The team had gone 9-21 in his absence and was 13½ games behind the Reds, well out of the race. He had started the season slowly, hitting just .183 at the end of May, but in the next two months he had improved to .283 and was on a batting spree. Bagwell finished at .290 with 21 home runs. A fall off from

1994, but he would more than make up for it the next several seasons as his and the Astros' potential came to full fruition.

Bagwell undertook a rigorous training program after the 1995 season. He gained 20 pounds and enhanced his endurance for the rigors of grueling seasons by a concentrated period of weight lifting, change of diet, plus the use of creatine and androstenedione.[20] In later years those entering the Astros' gym were welcomed by a banner reading, "Bagwell's Gym. Work Hard. Play Hard. Or Leave," a testament to his intense work ethic. "It's pretty impressive when you watch a guy like him," observed Geoff Blum, a later teammate. He "knows what he has to do, and he puts his mind to it and he does it."[21] While successful in the short term, Bagwell later came to feel his regimen shortened his career, that his muscular buildup contributed greatly to shoulder problems forcing his retirement in 2005 at age 37.[22]

By the start of 1996, Bagwell was one of the senior members on the Astros if not by age then by tenure. He had become a forceful influence on how Houston prepared for games, i.e., with maximum effort and players held accountable for their actions. Discipline fostered camaraderie, and Bagwell made sure everyone on the team was part of the team.[23] His and Biggio's leadership propelled the Astros to new levels of play.

His workout regimen generated tremendous results. The 1996 season began a run of performances that established Bagwell's reputation as one of the most dominant players of his era. That year he batted .315, hit 31 home runs, drove in 120 runs, and led the league with 48 doubles. It was the first of six consecutive seasons where Bagwell scored and drove in at least 100 runs, averaging 128 runs scored and 126 RBIs per year during this stretch.

Some of the numbers he put up were spectacular. In 1999 Bagwell drew 149 walks (including a major league record six in one game), at the time the third highest single season total in the National League. Twice that year he hit three home runs in one game. The following year he launched a career-high 47 homers and scored 152 runs, fourth highest in the NL since 1900.

Bagwell had become a complete ballplayer. In 1997 he stole 31 bases and hit 43 home runs. In 1999, 30 stolen bases and 42 homers. One of only 13 major league players to have accomplished 30 home runs and steals in a season more than once, Bagwell and Joe Carter remain the only first basemen to reach the 30-30 club through 2014. While Bagwell was at the peak of his career Houston took division championships in 1997, 1998, 1999, and 2001, the best run in franchise history. Of the 13 games played in the four post-season series however, Houston managed but a single 5-4 victory over San Diego in 1998. Unfortunately in the other three series Houston confronted the Atlanta Braves and their buzz-saw starting rotation of Tom Glavine, Greg Maddux, and John Smoltz. Bagwell's performance in these series was equally dismal, just .174 with no extra base hits and just four RBIs.

A CONSISTENT LAD IN THE LAND OF STEADY HABITS

In 2002 and 2003 both Bagwell and his team declined. Houston finished second both years but failed to make postseason competition. Bagwell's run of 100 RBI seasons ended with 98 in 2002. He achieved an even hundred RBIs in 2003, but his peak-year production had waned. His slugging averages dipped into the low .500s, well below what had become customary for him. Still a strong hitter, at 35 years old he no longer dominated as he once had.

Beginning in 2001 pain began flaring in his left shoulder. He underwent surgery in the offseason to extract bone spurs and restore a torn labrum.[24] Eventually he developed arthritis in the other shoulder, an affliction that worsened over time.[25] By 2004, his career entered the twilight: Bagwell's average fell to .266 with "only" 27 home runs and 89 RBIs. His defense suffered too. The first baseman who could whip a ball to third on bunts eventually got to the point where he had trouble merely throwing to infielders between innings.[26] Ironically, he had the best post-season of his career in a seven game series that St. Louis ultimately won. Bagwell hit .318 with two home runs, the second helping break open the fifth game.

As the 2005 season began, Bagwell played through April until the pain in his right shoulder became intolerable. On May 4, after going 0-5 in a loss to Pittsburgh he was hitting just .250 with only 3 home runs in 88 at-bats. The next day he asked Astros' manager Phil Garner to be pulled from the lineup. "I couldn't hit, I couldn't throw, if I played, I'd just be hurting the team."[27] By September, following shoulder surgery, he was well enough to join an Astros team contending for a wild card spot in the standings. Playing exclusively as a pinch hitter he drove in his last major league run on a ground out against the Cubs, providing an insurance run in a critical 3-1 win. For Houston's win that day and the next allowed them to finish one game ahead of the Phillies for the wild card position.

The Astros finally beat their longtime nemesis Atlanta Braves to win the Division Series then defeated the Cardinals to win the NL pennant. But the Chicago White Sox swept them in four straight games in the World Series. Bagwell went 1 for 8 as a DH and pinch hitter, just one of many Astros stymied by Chicago's pitching in a closely played series. Bagwell's ground out as a pinch hitter in the fourth game proved his last major league appearance.

Bagwell went to spring training in 2006 to see if he could still contribute on the field. But legal issues, specifically who was going to pay Bagwell's estimated $15.6 million salary for the year, muted Houston's welcome. The situation was awkward. The Astros had obtained a disability insurance policy on Bagwell when he had signed a multi-year contract in 2001. And at this point the team essentially had to prove that Bagwell became disabled between the end of 2005 and January 31, 2006, when the policy expired. So Bagwell's appearance in camp threw Houston's claim that he was disabled into question. Amid the legal maneuvering, it was revealed that a physical examination of Bagwell in January 2006 concluded he could only throw a ball 35 mph, and then only for short distances.[28] Based on that assessment, the attending physician declared Bagwell totally disabled.[29]

Bagwell appeared in a few practice games but had to quit several when his shoulder became too sore to continue. He was hitting just .219, but the major obstacle to continued play remained his arm. He simply could not throw a ball to meet major league standards. The chances of additional surgery succeeding were minimal. The conclusion was obvious.

Bagwell had given it all to come back. "You have to do everything you can to try and play. If not you'll be kicking yourself." Houston placed him on the DL, and Bagwell recognized the reality: "I may never play again."[30] He was right. A few months after the 2006 season ended, he officially retired from the game.[31] "[I]t's been a great ride," he said. "I wish I could still play and try to win a World Series here in Houston but I'm not physically able to do that anymore. I'm OK with that."[32]

Bagwell's lifetime stats are impressive: .297 batting average, 449 home runs, 1,529 RBIs, 79.6 WAR, and .948 OPS. But there was more to Bagwell than robust numbers. He was a role model in the clubhouse, a "consummate professional" who, along with Biggio set the bar for how an Astro approached the game. Some of Houston's best years remain the heart of the "Killer B" years (1996-2001) during which the Astros won four of six division championships, .

The Astros wanted Bagwell to stay connected with the organization and so signed him to a personal services contract through 2009, mostly to spend time working in player development. Bagwell's post playing career has been largely low key and private. Although he has had intermittent assignments with the team, Bagwell's aversion to travel and devotion to his family have been his guiding principles.

He did not totally avoid the limelight however. On June 28, 2007, his longtime teammate and friend Craig Biggio singled against the Colorado Rockies to get his 3,000 hit. Biggio's family joined him on the field, and he insisted Bagwell come out to be with him as well. It was Bagwell's first appearance before Houston's fans since he retired.[33] A few months later Houston retired his Number 5 before Bagwell, his family, and more than 42,000 onlookers.

In mid-season 2010, the Astros asked Bagwell to become their batting coach. Last in hitting, the team hoped his expertise and rapport with players could improve their output. Their hitting did improve over what remained of the season, but Bagwell, citing family obligations, turned down a proffered two-year contract to continue the job. "My decision came down to the times that these coaches put in, the effort they put in, and my family."[34] He returned to his personal services agreement occasionally spending time with the club, usually in spring training helping younger players.

In 2011 Bagwell became eligible for induction into the Hall of Fame. More than anything else this has kept his name in the media and before fans over the years. The first year he was eligible he received 41.7 percent of the writer's votes for induction. Every year since he consistently received over 50 percent of the vote with a high of 59.6 in the 2013 election.

Whether he deserved induction was a controversial subject over the years. Several factors delayed his induction. On a few occasions, most recently in 2015, he was up against a crowded field of worthy candidates, which tended to concentrate votes on first-time eligible players.[35] A second and more serious consideration is that Bagwell's career peaked in the late 1990s coinciding with what has become known as baseball's steroid era. One of the major side effects of this period was to cast a pall of suspicion over virtually all its players, including high performers like Bagwell.

Several aspects of Bagwell's career prompted questions about steroid use. Ken Caminiti, one of his teammates and close friend on the Astros, publicly admitted he took steroids during his career, a fact dramatically underscored when he died of a drug overdose at the age of 41, just three years after retiring from the game. For Bagwell it suggested guilt by association.[36]

His physical growth led to further conjecture. The slim 185-pound minor league third baseman grew to 220 at the peak of his career. Creation of a bodybuilder's physique and its subsequent reduction in size as a career waned was "typical" of players found to have used steroids—and another factor fueling speculation about Bagwell's career.[37]

These perceptions seemed relevant because of the curve of that career. He started out with just six home runs in two minor league seasons and averaged fewer than 20 per year during his first three years in the majors. At the top of his game he had successive seasons of 31, 43, 34, 42, 47 and 39 home runs. Bagwell surged almost simultaneously with Mark McGwire and Sammy Sosa, two sluggers whose drug use subsequently sullied their career reputations. Their and others' accomplishments generated questions about the proliferation of home runs hit during this period. It became a centerpiece of suspicion that something might be amiss.[38]

These sorts of associative considerations fueled speculation that Bagwell used steroids or PEDs. He was never linked to use of drugs, however, either through the drug testing policy, various investigations, or legal actions. Bagwell consistently denied employing drugs or steroids on numerous occasions. But he has come to believe that whatever he says will not matter. In a 2009 interview, Bagwell observed that his is a no-win situation. "I know what I did; I know how hard I worked. If someone thinks I took crap because I was in that era, what am I going to do to show them I didn't? I can't go take a blood test now."[39]

Bruce Jenkins, Senior Sports Editor of the *San Francisco Chronicle*, acknowledges that while steroid suspicion was a factor for several voters, there is another point of consideration. "I certainly can't speak for the bulk of national baseball writers, but I know that many are suspicious of Bagwell—without proof, as you say. I've always voted for the best players—Bonds, McGwire, Clemens, etc.—so that's not a factor for me. I always found Bagwell just a bit short of Hall of Fame material. Heck of a player, I don't mean to knock him, just my personal opinion. And I do know that some other writers feel that way, as well."[40, 41]

Because of the controversy over drugs, Bagwell increasingly showed ambivalence about getting into the Hall because even if elected, it would be an empty accomplishment. Induction into the Hall is not what defines him, "I keep telling people this and people don't understand it. . . . Baseball does not define me as a person. It's what I do with my kids, and as a husband, that's going to define me. It'd be an honor, don't get me wrong, but I've got other things to do in my life too."[42, 43]

Amid the discussions, Bagwell went on with his life. Twice divorced, he remarried in August 2014. He and his wife Rachel have five children in their blended family.[44] He lives in the Houston area and occasionally works with the Astros, most recently spending several days with them in the spring of 2015 as a special instructor.[45]

Just when it seemed Bagwell would stay in a Hall of Fame netherworld, a change took place in how players were selected for induction. A rules change in voter eligibility seemed to generate greater support for his induction. Beginning with balloting in 2016, voters were required to have ten years of continuous membership in the Baseball Writers Association of America as well as be active members or been active members in the Association in the ten years prior to balloting. This had a practical effect of removing more than 100 voters from the process, many of whose careers paralleled the steroids era. The elimination of this bloc of voters seemed to signal a more tolerant perspective of players from that time frame.

It was reflected in a change of voter patterns. Mike Piazza, thrice denied induction was selected with the 2016 vote. Players suspected of steroid use such as Barry Bonds, Roger Clemens and Curt Schilling saw their support increase. Bagwell received 71.6 percent of the vote, missing election by 15 out of the 440 votes counted.

That trend continued for many of these players in 2017, most dramatically for Bagwell who was selected for induction receiving more than 82 percent of the votes, higher than anyone else on the ballot. He was formally inducted into the Hall of Fame on July 30, 2017 surrounded by family, friends, fans—and teammates. Most prominent of these was Craig Biggio.

While Bagwell's credentials were questioned for years there was never any question how his teammates viewed him. Astros pitcher Mike Hampton once called Bagwell "the ultimate teammate," in an interview. "Bagwell and Biggio let it be known that there was an Astros way of doing things. The Bagwell and Biggio way was to demand accountability, starting with themselves. Bagwell was particularly quick to deflect credit for his success, explaining 'that's my job,' and to readily accept blame—often for the failures that weren't even his. His ability to connect with teammates knew no barriers, racial or otherwise."[46]

This description, echoed by many, more than any outside voting process reflected the highest compliment a player can receive. It speaks well of a one-time skinny Red Sox prospect who indeed had "a great ride."

NOTES

1. The author would like to express his appreciation for Mr. Bill Francis at the Baseball Hall of Fame (HoF) who provided a copy of material from Jeff Bagwell's HoF file for this article and to Tom Schott for his editorial skills in improving this piece.

2. Bill Ryan, "Sergeant, Mom, Her Dream is Still Fenway Park," *New York Times*, August 28, 1994, A1.

3. Ibid.

4. Leigh Montville, "Trade Deficit Jeff Bagwell Has Proved by Trading him to the Astros, the Red Sox Made a Ruthian Blunder," *Sports Illustrated*, Vol. 79, No. 4, July 26, 1993: 44-48.

5. Lou Gorman, *One Pitch From Glory: One Decade of Running the Red Sox*, (Champaign, IL: Sports Publishing L.L.C., 2005), 137-39.

6. Montville, "Trade Deficit Jeff Bagwell."

7. See, for example, "The List: Readers Pick Most Lopsided Trades," http://espn.go.com/page2/s/readers/worstdeals.html

8. "Rolling the Dice," *The Sporting News*, April 15, 1991, 10.

9. Pittsburgh first baseman Orlando Merced received the other first place vote.

10. Montville, "Trade Deficit Jeff Bagwell."

11. See Alfred M. Martin, *Mel Ott, The Gentle Giant*, (Lanham MD: The Scarecrow Press, 2003), 23-25, and James M. Giglio, *Musial: From Stash to Stan The Man*, (Columbia, MO: University of Missouri Press, 2001), xi.

12. Steve Campbell, "Jeff Bagwell knows he did things the right way in a Cooperstown-worthy career. But if the Hall doesn't call the former Killer B? 'I'm good' he says," *Houston Chronicle* clipping, July 28, 2009. Bagwell's HoF file; Tom Verducci, "One of a Kind—A self made slugger with a screwy stance," *Sports Illustrated*, Vol. 91, No. 3, July 19, 1999: 56-61.

13. Tim Windal, "The Swing is the Thing," *USA Today Baseball Weekly*, July 27-August 2, 1994, 36.

14. Verducci, "One of a Kind."

15. Ibid.

16. "Benes Pitch Breaks Bagwell's Hand," *The Washington Post*, August 11, 1994, D4.

17. Robert Mcg. Thomas Jr., "Bagwell's Latest Stat: All the M.V.P. Votes," *New York Times*, October 28, 1994, B13.

18. Murray Chass, "Different Departures for Bagwell and Kruk," ibid., July 31, 1995, C3.

19 "Astros Lose Games but lose Bagwell," *The Washington Post*, July 31, 1995, B7.

20 Verducci, "One of a Kind."

21 Jose De Jesus Ortiz, "Bagwell turns to weight room to regain shoulder strength," *Houston Chronicle*, November 26, 2002.Bagwell's HoF file.

22 Jerry Crasnick, "Jeff Bagwell Tires of Steroid Talk," *ESPN.com*, December 29, 2010,http://sports.espn.go.com/mlb/hof11/columns/story?columnist=crasnick_jerry&id=5963276.

23 See, for example, Campbell's "Jeff Bagwell knows he did things the right way in a Cooperstown-worthy career. But if the Hall doesn't call the former Killer B?" and John Smith, "Stats alone no measure of this man," *Houston Chronicle*, December 16, 2006, sports section, 1.

24 Ortiz, "Bagwell turns to weight room."

25 Richard Justice, "Bagwell reaches limit of pain," *Houston Chronicle* clipping, May 10, 2005, from Bagwell's HoF file.

26 ESPN.com News Service, "Bagwell acknowledges he might ever play again," March 26, 2006.

27 Richard Justice, "Bagwell reaches limit of pain," *Houston Chronicle* clipping, May 10, 2005, Bagwell's HoF file.

28 Jose De Jesus Ortiz, "Bagwell insurance claim denied," *Houston Chronicle* clipping, March 28, 2006 from Bagwell's HoF file.

29 The Houston Astros and Connecticut General would eventually settle the matter in a confidential agreement in December 2006. See Brian McTaggart, "Insurance Settlement Reached," *Houston Chronicle*, December 2006, from Bagwell's HoF file.

30 Jason Stark, "Bagwell acknowledges he might never play again.'" *ESPN.com News Service*, March 26, 2006.

31 A private settlement was reached on the Astro's insurance claim in December 2006. Alyson Footer, "Report: Astros settle insurance claim," MLB.com, December 15, 2006.

32 Brian McTaggart, "Bagwell retires, remembers 'great ride,'" *Houston Chronicle* clipping, December 2006, Bagwell's HoF file.

33 "Biggio Gets His 3,000 Hit in Houston," *New York Times*, June 29, 2007, D4.

34 Zachary Levine, "Bagwell cites family reasons," *Houston Chronicle* clipping, October 28, 2010, Bagwell's HoF file.

35 The 2015 HoF selectees were: Bagwell's teammate Craig Biggio, Randy Johnson, Pedro Martinez, and John Smoltz.

36 See for example Asher B. Chancey, "The Bagwell Conspiracy,"http://baseballevolution.com/asher/bagwell-conspiracy.html or Harold Friend, "Jeff Bagwell is Guilty Until Proven Innocent," April 20, 2012,http://bleacherreport.com/articles/1153441-jeff-bagwell-is-guilty-until-proved-innocent-of-steroid-use or Adam Spolane, "If Frank Thomas is a Hall of Famer Jeff Bagwell Should Be Too, January 8, 2014,http://houston.cbslocal.com/2014/01/08/if-frank-thomas-is-a-hall-of-famer-jeff-bagwell-should-be-too/ for several online articles concerning Bagwell and Caminiti.

37 See http://houston.cbslocal.com/2014/01/08/if-frank-thomas-is-a-hall-of-famer-jeff-bagwell-should-be-too/ and Richard Justice, "Steroids? Not me, says Bagwell," *Houston Chronicle* clipping, February 25, 2004,Bagwell'sHoF file.

38 One measure of this phenomenon: In the 1980s, just 13 major leaguers hit 40 or more home runs in a season. In the 1990s, 71 players did it, and more than 60 homers in a season happened four times. During the previous 90-plus years only Babe Ruth (in 1927) and Maris (in 1961) achieved this mark.

39 Steve Campbell, 'B' all, end Hall?" *Houston Chronicle*, July 28, 2009 from Bagwell's HoF file.
40 Email, Bruce Jenkins to author, July 19, 2015.
41 For a dissenting view to Jenkins', see Dayn Perry, "Hall of Fame candidate breakdown: Jeff Bagwell," August 27, 2015, http://www.cbssports.com/mlb/eye-on-baseball/24906915/hall-of-fame-candidate-breakdown-jeff-bagwell.
42 Ted Berg, "New Astros instructor Jeff Bagwell on his Hall of Fame case: "I don't expect to get in," *USA Sports Today*, March 10, 2015, http://ftw.usatoday.com/2015/03/jeff-bagwell-houston-astros-hall-of-fame-spring-training-instructor-mlb.
43 Jerry Crasnick, "Jeff Bagwell Tires of Steroid Talk," ESPN.com, December 29, 2010.http://sports.espn.go.com/mlb/hof11/columns/story?id=5963276
44 The author wishes to thank Bob Dorrill of the SABR Houston/Larry Dierker Chapter for information on Bagwell's post-career life.
45 Evan Drellich, "Jeff Bagwell takes small step back into baseball with the Astros," March 10, 2015, http://blog.chron.com/ultimateastros/2015/03/10/jeff-bagwell-takes-small-step-back-into-baseball-with-astros/#30721101=0
46 Steve Campbell, 'B' all, end Hall?" For others' views on Bagwell, see Richard Justice, "Astros retire Bagwell's No. 5," *Houston Chronicle*, August 26, 2007, and Tom Haudricourt, "Biggio, Bagwell finally there," *Milwaukee Journal Sentinel*, Oct. 20, 2005.

Jeffery Robert Bagwell, the only child of Robert and Janice Bagwell, beams for the camera. (Courtesy of University of Hartford Archives and Special Collections.)

THE HIGH SCHOOL YEARS

Bagwell brings the ball up for Xavier with South Catholic booters in pursuit. Jeff recorded a record 35 goals for the Falcons in his senior season. (Photo from The Don, *1986. Courtesy of Xavier High School.)*

All District, All State and Undrafted: Bagwell at Xavier High School

By George Pawlush

Xavier is an all-male high school in Middletown, Connecticut, a city of nearly 50,000 residents on the Connecticut River. Middletown, as the name implies, is situated near the center of the state and surrounded by many small towns and villages. Xavier was founded in 1963 by the Roman Catholic Diocese of Norwich and the Xaverian Brothers.

The school is highly regarded for its academics. During its first 55 years of existence, the 882-pupil[1] school has had a storied athletic presence, having won many state titles. Xavier competes in Class LL in the Connecticut Interscholastic Athletic Conference's (CIAC) highest classification.

Jeff Bagwell, a Killingworth resident, arrived at Xavier as a freshman in the fall of 1982, transferring from the smaller Haddam-Killingworth school system. Very few student-athletes find their way onto varsity teams at Xavier as freshmen, and Bagwell was no exception. A three-sport athlete, he arrived at the school with very good, but not outstanding, soccer and baseball skills, and was competitive in basketball.

Bagwell's first taste of varsity action came in the fall of 1983 as a sophomore on Coach Marty Ryczek's soccer team. Injuries and inexperience plagued the team, which finished the season with a 4-9-3 record.

With the loss of three key players through graduation, there were many question marks regarding the status of Xavier's 1984 baseball team. However, Coach Terry Garstka was encouraged by a bevy of skilled underclassmen battling for starting spots, especially in the skill positions.

Garstka, who also taught English at Xavier, joined the school as head baseball coach in 1972. He held the position for 23 years before retiring in 1994. Among his accomplishments was winning the 1980 CIAC Class L championship, the lone baseball title in the Falcons' history.

Garstka remembers Bagwell as an athlete who was very eager to succeed. "He was always the one who wanted more groundballs after practice and five more swings in the cage. He was a team player," said Garstka, "who would take people aside and give them a pep talk. He wasn't 'gung ho,' but quiet, and that worked."[2]

Rich Magner is Xavier's director of guidance and was for a longtime the baseball assistant coach. He inherited the head-coaching reins from Garstka and was the Falcons' baseball coach for 20 seasons, 1994 to 2013. Magner recalls that "Bagwell was more mature than other kids physically. Mentally, he was more confident than the other kids. But he didn't walk around with an air of arrogance."[3]

"Baseball is a game where you have to be ready to catch a groundball. When it comes time to hit or pitch, you've got to do it," Magner said. "Jeff was always ready to handle the moment."[4]

Batting in the seventh spot and playing second base, Bagwell had three hits in his first varsity game, on April 10, 1984, as Xavier defeated Woodrow Wilson of Middletown, 16-6. After opening the year with three wins, the Falcons dropped six of their next 10 games.

Xavier entered its May 16 contest against St. Thomas Aquinas of New Britain with a 7-6 record. The Falcons turned their season around that day, blasting their Hartford County Conference (HCC) foe, 15-1. Todd Darling and Bagwell combined to hurl a six-hitter. Bagwell relieved Darling in the eighth inning and retired six of the seven players he faced, five by strikeouts. He also had two hits.[5]

The Falcons then went on a tear, winning five of their next six games. Their only defeat during the stretch was a hard-fought 9-8 loss to Notre Dame of West Haven. In that game, Bagwell pitched five solid innings before walks and four errors wiped out a 3-2 Falcon lead. Notre Dame was ahead, 9-3, going into the bottom of ninth. Xavier rallied with a grand slam by Darling and a key hit by Bagwell, but fell one run short of a great comeback.[6]

The late-season victory drive earned the Falcons a share of the HCC title with South Catholic High School of Hartford. Both clubs ended the year with identical 8-2 logs. During the regular season the teams split, with South Catholic winning the first game, 11-3, and Xavier the second, 4-3.

Xavier had momentum going into the Class LL state tournament. The Falcons opened the CIAC playoff with a 9-3 win over Hamden. Their second game was against heavily-favored Fitch High School of Groton, which came into the game 17-4. Xavier stunned Fitch, 5-4,[7] in what Coach Garstka remembered as "one of the biggest Xavier wins ever."[8]

Bagwell had three hits in the game, including an RBI single that put the Falcons up 4-1 in the seventh inning. Fitch tied it, 4-4, in the bottom of the frame. Fellow sophomore Brendan Beckstein was the hero of the game, lashing a two-out eighth-inning single that drove in the winning run. The win advanced Xavier into the quarter-final round.[9]

Xavier's great run came back to earth when the Falcons were overpowered by a 19-hit onslaught from Fairfield Prep, 14-6. The team ended the season with a better-than-expected 15-8 record after being 5-6 at midseason.

After taking their lumps in 1983, the Xavier soccer team was primed to compete as the 1984-85 athletic season opened at Xavier. The Falcons were prepared for a rugged 16-game schedule that included dates with perennial powerhouses St. Paul's of Bristol and Glastonbury High School.

Fortified with a heavy complement of juniors, the Falcons, with only three seniors, were 5-2 at midseason. One of their big victories was a 5-3 nod over St. Bernard's High School. Xavier pushed its record to 7-3 with an epic 3-2 double-overtime triumph against St. Thomas Aquinas High School. Bagwell netted the game-winning goal.

The Xavier booters closed the year by splitting six games to end 10-6 overall, and 8-4 in the HCC, good for third place. The Falcons advanced to the Class LL state tournament. They debuted by defeating Naugatuck, 3-1, and then had the misfortune to draw Glastonbury, the eventual state champion, as their next opponent. Glastonbury, a 5-0 victor over the Falcons during the regular season, beat them again, 6-2, to eliminate the Falcons from further competition

Bagwell enjoyed a breakout junior season. He tallied 16 of his team's 49 goals, and was honored as Xavier's Offensive Player of the Year. He joined teammates Tom Rossini and Art Carbo to earn HCC All-Star honors. Bagwell was chosen as a co-captain to lead the team in his final senior season.

The Falcons approached the 1985 baseball season with guarded optimism. Four key veterans had been lost through graduation. Coach Garstka looked to a veteran core of seniors who included Todd Darling, Tony Franco, Rick Murray, and Rob Russo, and a bunch of talented juniors to propel Xavier to a successful season.

Xavier copped its season opener on April 7, defeating Hand of Madison, 6-0. They then shutout Northwest Catholic and St. Paul of Bristol to up their record to 3-0. Through the first three games the Falcons had outscored opponents, 18-0. The wins elevated them to second place in the *Hartford Courant's* statewide baseball poll.

The Falcons then knocked perennial Class LL powerhouse Notre Dame from the unbeaten ranks with a 7-4 victory on April 16 in West Haven. A three-run homer by catcher Rick Murray in the third inning, with Bagwell aboard, was the key hit of the game. Bagwell had two hits in the win. He now had seven hits, two of which were doubles, in the team's first four games.

The Falcons' winning days were to be short-lived as they went into a tailspin, dropping three straight one-run seven-inning games, to Maloney of Meriden, 4-3; East Catholic of Manchester, 2-1; and South Catholic of Hartford, 7-6.

Against Maloney, the Falcons were up, 3-0, going into the seventh inning. Maloney, aided by a costly Xavier error, rallied for four runs to steal the victory. A seventh-inning miscue, two wild pitches, a walk, and an infield single by South Catholic haunted the Falcons. Bagwell's two hits and two runs had given Xavier a 6-5 lead over South Catholic going into the final frame.

Xavier halted the slide on April 25 by beating Norwich Free Academy, 3-2. Bagwell, in his first pitching start of the year, allowed just one hit, a double in the sixth inning. Both of Norwich's runs were unearned and resulted from miscues. This time errors didn't contribute to a Falcon loss as Xavier raised its record to 5-3.

The Falcons then won their next six games and were victors in nine of their final 11 contests to end the regular season at 14-5. Their only losses came at the hands of Notre Dame (12-6) and South Catholic (7-3). The two setbacks cost Xavier the HCC championship. However, Xavier recorded a memorable 5-3 late-season triumph over St. Joseph of Trumbull, which two weeks later won the CIAC Class M title.

Xavier opened the state tournament by conquering Hall of West Hartford, 7-0, on May 29. Bagwell played a big role in the win, going 3-for-4 with two RBIs. The Falcons got seven hits but scored little the next day, falling to New Britain, 4-1, to conclude the season with a 15-6 record. It was a memorable season for Coach Garstka, who registered his 175th coaching win during the season. Bagwell hit .403 and paced the Falcons with 20 runs scored.

Expectations were sky-high as Xavier's soccer team prepared for the 1985 season. It was an exciting fall as the Falcons produced one of the school's greatest athletic-team performances of all time. The Falcons were undefeated at 15-0-1 and won the All Connecticut Conference (ACC) championship during the regular season.

The only blot on their record was a 5-3 defeat at the hands of Holy Cross of Waterbury in the CIAC Class LL semifinals. Bagwell scored two of his team's goals in a losing cause. Prior to the agonizing setback, Xavier won preliminary games over Simsbury and Newington. The Simsbury match required two regular 40-minute halves, two 10-minute overtimes, and 18 penalty kicks to complete before the Falcons won, 2-1. Xavier won a second-round game, blanking Newington, 1-0, on a goal by Bagwell.

Led by Bagwell, Xavier placed six players on the ACC All-Star team. Bagwell and goalie teammate Dave Sizemore were named to the All-State team. Bagwell established new Xavier individual career records with 58 goals and 24 assists. He also set a one-season record with 36 goals.

Eight of Bagwell's goals were scored on diving headers. He told the *Hartford Courant*, "It's never been hard for me to head the ball. I'm not a great kicker." When asked about his outstanding season, Bagwell told the reporter, "The ball is there for me and the defenses haven't been double-teaming me." Bagwell said he was not surprised with Xavier's great record: "We played on an unbeaten freshman team and we said then that we couldn't wait until we were seniors."[10]

Many coaches and sportswriters felt that Bagwell was more proficient in soccer than in baseball. East Catholic soccer coach Tom Malin was one of those people. In 1999 Malin told *Hartford Courant* sportswriter Tom Yantz that "Bagwell had all the attributes—power, strength, and, most importantly, a good sense for the ball. He had Division I skills, and who knows how far he could have gone beyond that. He was a natural."[11]

Dave Borges, a sportswriter for the *Middletown Press,* talked to Dave Sizemore in early 2017 about Bagwell's contributions to the 1985 team. Sizemore was until recently the academic dean at Xavier High School and was a goalkeeper on the 17-1-1 soccer squad. "Jeff will admit that he wasn't the best soccer player on the team, but his role was to score goals," Sizemore said. "He just had a knack for scoring goals. He was gifted."[12]

Marty Ryczek, who was the head soccer coach during Bagwell's three years on the pitch, told Borges that "Jeff was there to score but he was real humble about it. Xavier played a three-man front line and it was the wings that did most of the work, taking on the defenders and chipping the ball in the middle to Bagwell, who was always there, often heading the ball in for a goal."[13]

Once the soccer season ended, Xavier basketball coach Rich Magner invited Bagwell to join the team. Bagwell played on the freshman team but didn't come out for the team during his sophomore and junior years. As a senior, he became a role player for the Falcons and was usually was one of the first players off the bench.

The Falcons finished the regular ACC basketball season with a 10-10 record and qualified for the CIAC tournament. Xavier played against a pair of Hartford teams in the playoffs, and gained a split. The Falcons edged heavily favored Hartford Bulkeley, 62-59; and then stayed close to Hartford Weaver before succumbing in the final quarter, 64-54.

During his senior year, Bagwell was recruited by both University of Hartford baseball coach Bill Denehy and soccer coach Allan Wilson to play either Division I sport at the university. Since Hartford ran a fall baseball program, Bagwell had to choose between the two sports. He told Yantz why he picked baseball. "I felt it was my first love, and I had a better chance professionally to make it in baseball," he said.[14]

On April 17, 1986, Bagwell officially committed to play baseball at Hartford. Fred Post, sports editor of the *Middletown Press,* announced Bagwell's decision in his column. He quoted Coach Denehy, who said, "Our entire coaching staff considers Jeff the best right-handed hitter in the state. He is definitely an impact player who will be given the opportunity to move into the starting lineup."[15]

With the pressure of life after high-school soccer and baseball off his mind, Bagwell looked forward to a strong senior baseball season. He and his co-captain, junior

Brendan Beckstein, hoped to build upon the late-season drive by the previous year's team.

However, to accomplish this, Coach Garstka needed to retool a pitching staff that had been anchored by HCC All-Star Tony Franco, who posted an 8-1 record with four shutouts and a 1.35 ERA in 1985. Franco also had led the Falcons with 33 hits and a .423 batting average. Xavier started the 1986 campaign with a pitching staff that had logged only 30 innings of varsity experience the previous year. Most of the innings were turned in by Bagwell, who was 2-2 on the mound as a junior.

Another irreplaceable member of the 1985 club was catcher Rick Murray, who hit over .400 for his third straight season. As a senior, Murray batted .404, clouting two home runs and driving in 19 runs. He was an HCC All-Star and an All-State team selection. Bagwell, the team's steady shortstop and number-three pitcher as a junior, was now being asked to step up and become Xavier's pitching ace.

Bagwell was on the hill for the Falcons' season inaugural, April 14 at Notre Dame, which Xavier lost, 5-2. Coach Garstka told *Middletown Press* reporter Mike DiMauro after the game, "Bagwell pitched well despite the homer [a second-inning blast that put Notre Dame up, 2-0]. He maintained good control (one walk, seven strikeouts) and hung in there in the late innings."[16]

Bagwell's second start was an 11-inning, 2-1 masterpiece against Fairfield Prep. Bagwell pitched the entire game and fanned 12 batters, while walking only two. Prep's only run resulted from a seventh-inning balk by Bagwell. The victory evened the Falcons' season record at 2-2.

The Falcons then sprinted to victories in nine of their 11 games, and an improbable season now appeared very probable as Xavier raised its record to 11-5. During the 11-game span, Bagwell had picked up four victories, two in relief. On April 25 he pitched a 7-2 six-hitter against Norwich Free Academy and belted a homer and double, with three RBIs.

Bagwell authored another gem on May 5 when he shut out perennial nemesis South Catholic, 4-0, on four hits. He again supplied much of the offense. Bagwell went 3-for-4, scoring two runs, hitting a triple, and hitting a home run. Four days later, Bagwell had a no-hitter going in the final (seventh) inning before allowing a hit. He held on to beat Notre Dame, 4-2, striking out 12.

He picked up successive relief victories over St. Thomas Aquinas (10-9), and Northwest Catholic (6-1). Against Aquinas, Bagwell drove in the winning run with an infield hit. Coach Garstka told the *Middletown Press*, "I don't know what more can be said about him. He simply is one of the best players we ever had."[17] Through the team's first 16 games, Bagwell owned a 6-2 pitching record with a minuscule ERA. As a batter, he was hitting over .400 with 6 doubles, 5 triples, 2 home runs, and 14 RBIs.

Happiness then turned to misery for Xavier when the Falcons suffered three straight losses, 7-4 to Fairfield Prep and 7-6 losses to St. Joseph's and South Catholic. Bagwell took the loss in the St. Joseph's tilt. Seven errors doomed the Falcons in the South Catholic clash. Xavier concluded the regular season with a 12-8 record, outpacing cross-town rival Middletown, 7-3.

The Falcons again qualified for the CIAC Tournament. They debuted the tourney by edging Shelton, 2-1, in the preliminary round. Bagwell raised his season record to 7-3, outdueling his Shelton opponent. The Gaels had runners on third and first in the final frame before Bagwell choked the rally striking out the final two Shelton batters.

Xavier bowed out of the tournament by losing to New Britain, 14-6. Falcons assistant Coach Rich Magner summed up the defeat, saying, "In baseball more than any other sport, when you have a bad game, all your liabilities show."[18] Head Coach Garstka was pleased with his team's performance. "At the beginning of the season I prayed for a 10-10 record," he told Mike DiMauro of the *Middletown Press*. "We surpassed what I expected. We started with four new players. I'm not disappointed with 13-9 at all."[19]

Bagwell ended the season with a .390 batting average. He earned several postseason honors, including ACC Pitcher and Player of the Year. He was a District Three All-Star and was chosen to the Class LL All-State team. Bagwell joined two other future major-league players, Brad Ausmus of Cheshire and Pete Walker of East Lyme, as All-State honorees.

Coach Garstka praised Bagwell in the *Hartford Courant's* All State article, saying, "Jeff is an outstanding player who will be missed not only for his baseball ability but also for his leadership capabilities."[20]

First base was the position where Bagwell spent most of his playing time as a major leaguer. (He also made a few appearances with the Houston Astros as a designated hitter and outfielder.) But during his three varsity seasons at Xavier, Bagwell played every position on the field except first base.

Bagwell went undrafted by major-league teams after his senior season. *Middletown Press* reporter Jim Bransfield explained: "While Bagwell was a very good high school player, most professional scouts put the most dreaded letters next to his name in their books—NP which stood for 'no prospect.' I remember one scout telling me that he had a plus bat, but couldn't run, didn't have much of a glove, had an ordinary arm and didn't have a position. Lot of kids like him, the scout said."[21]

It was now time for Bagwell to prove all the critics wrong, with an outstanding career at the University of Harford, the lone Division I college baseball team in America to offer him a scholarship.

JEFF BAGWELL IN CONNECTICUT

SOURCES

In addition to the sources cited in the Notes, the author also consulted numerous Xavier game stories in the *Middletown Press*, and the following:

Borges, Dave. "Jeff Bagwell's HOF Path Got Start at Xavier," *Middletown Press,* July 29, 2017.

Borges, Dave. "Xavier Part of Bagwell's Legacy," *Middletown Press,* January 19, 2017.

Anderson, Woody. "The First One? Fairfield Prep," *Hartford Courant,* April 16, 1985.

Smith, George. "He'll Always Be Player from the Old School," *Hartford Courant,* October 28, 1994.

Altavilla, John. "New Hall of Fame Inductee Jeff Bagwell Made Impression in Hartford First", *Hartford Courant,* January 18, 2017.

O'Connell, Jack. "Bagwell Can't Ask for More", *Hartford Courant,* July 14, 2017.

Xavier High School *Don* (yearbook), 1984, 1985, and 1986 editions.

Baseball-Reference.com.

HartfordBusiness.com (March 3, 2014).

NOTES

1. high-schools.com/directory/ct/cities/middletown/xavier-high-school/00232246/.
2. Terry Garstka, personal interview, May 1, 2017.
3. Rich Magner, phone interview, May 16, 2017.
4. Ibid.
5. Michael Massa, "Xavier Sweeps Past St Thomas 9," *Middletown Press,* May 17, 1984.
6. Massa, "Xavier Rally Falls Short by 1 Run," *Middletown Press,* May 21, 1984.
7. Massa, "Beckstein's Hit Gives Falcs Win," *Middletown Press,* June 6, 1984.
8. 1984 Xavier High School *Don* yearbook.
9. Massa, "Beckstein's Hit."
10. Bohdan Kolinsky, "Bagwell Boasts a Special Knack," *Hartford Courant,* November 5, 1985.
11. Tom Yantz, "Best of the Century, No. 6," *Hartford Courant,* December 28, 1999.
12. Dave Borges, "Xavier Part of Bagwell's Legacy," *Middletown Press,* January 19, 2017.
13. Ibid.
14. Fred J. Post, "keeping POSTed," *Middletown Press,* April 17, 1986.
15. Ibid.
16. Mike DiMauro, "ND Tops Xavier, 5-2," *Middletown Press,* April 15, 1986.
17. Mike DiMauro, "Jeff Bagwell Again Leads Xavier, 6-1," *Middletown Press,* May 19, 1986.
18. Mike DiMauro, "Xavier Bows Out of State Tourney," *Middletown Press,* June 5, 1986.
19. Ibid.
20. "1986 All State Teams," *Hartford Courant,* June 26, 1986.
21. Jim Bransfield, personal interview, May 11, 2017.

The 1983 Xavier High School Freshman Baseball Team. Bagwell is in first row, fourth from the right. (Courtesy Middletown Sports Hall of Fame.)

SUMMARY OF GAMES / 1984 Season Highlights

#	Opponent	Result	Notes
1.	Wilson	Won 16-6	Russo winner; Bagwell 3 hits
2.	Northwest	Won 5-1	Barone winner - 15 K's; Murray & Long H.R.'s and 5 R.B.I.'s
3.	Notre Dame	Won 8-1	Franco winner; Barone & Gollareny 3 hits apiece
4.	NFA	Lost 3-1	We outhit them 9-7; Franco, Murray, Gollareny, Darling 2 hits apiece
5.	Maloney	Lost 6-0	Too many mistakes and too much wind
6.	NFA	Lost 6-2	Barone 12 K's; Murray 2 hits; no errors
7.	Aquinas	Won 7-3	13 hits; Murray 3 hits; No errors
8.	South	Lost 11-3	They outhit us 12-6; Bagwell 2 hits; Triples by Murray, Bagwell and Rosen
9.	St. Paul	Won 8-2	Barone Tough - 9 K's; Murray 2 homeruns - one of them a tremendous shot to left
10.	Aquinas	Tie 8-8	Lucky we did not lose this one - behind 6-0 at one time; called after 5 innings - Rain
11.	Wilson	Won 15-2	Darling 5 hits, 5 R.B.I.'s; Rosen 3 hits, 1 R.B.I.'s; Bagwell 3 hits
12.	East	Lost 6-5	Tough loss in last of 9th inning; Barone 3 hits, 2 doubles + H.R.; Bagwell 3 hits, double + H.R.
13.	St. Paul	Won 6-3	Franco - 9 K's, 3 hits, 2 R.B.I.'s; Gollareny 3 hits
14.	St. Bernard	Lost 4-1	No offense; called after 7½ innings-Rain
15.	Aquinas	Won 15-1	No contest; Darling winner, 6 K's + Bagwell 5 K's; Bagwell + Franco 2 hits; Gollareny 2 hits, 3 R.B.I.'s
16.	South	Won 4-3	Franco all the way + 2 hits
17.	East	Won 10-6	Russo winner with relief help from Barone; Murray, Darling 3 hits; Slomkowski 3 R.B.I.'s
18.	Notre Dame	Lost 9-8	Too many errors (5); Barone 4 hits; Darling Grandslam; almost pulled it out
19.	Northwest	Won 12-1	Barone 4 hitter; Barone 3 R.B.I.'s; Bagwell, Franco, Rosen 2 hits apiece
20.	St. Bernard	Won 11-5	Franco 12 K's; Barone 4 hits, 5 R.B.I.'s; Murray, Rosen 3 hits apiece
21.	Hand	Won 8-2	Russo winner; Darling 4 for 4, 2 R.B.I.'s; Rosen, Slomkowski 2 hits apiece
	TOURNAMENT		
22.	(Playdowns - 1st Round) Hamden	Won 9-3	Barone 16 K's; Murray 3 hits, 4 R.B.I.'s, H.R.; Rosen 3 hits; Slomkowski 2 doubles
23.	(Playdowns - 2nd Round) Fitch	Won 5-4	Franco - superb; GREAT WIN; Bagwell, Murray 3 hits; Beckstein 2 hits, 2 R.B.I.'s including game-winner; Slomkowski, Long, Long Double
24.	(Quarter finals) Fairfield Prep	Lost 14-6	Very Tough Team (19 hits); Darling, Bagwell 2 hits; Barone 2 run H.R.

The 1984 Xavier coach's game highlights for Jeff's sophomore year reveal seven multi-hit games as a batter and a six strikeout relief pitching appearance. (Courtesy Middletown Sports Hall of Fame.)

Jeff brings the ball up against South Catholic. (The Don, 1986, courtesy of Xavier High School.)

1985 Xavier High School Soccer Captains (L-R): Head Coach Marty Ryczek, Pat McHugh, Jeff Bagwell, David Sizemore, Sebby Fazzino, Assistant Coach Jack King. (The Don, 1986, courtesy of Xavier High School.)

VARSITY SOCCER TEAM - Row 1: Mike DiMauro, B.J. Farrell, Scott Herrmann, Jeff Alexander, Dave Sizemore, Pat McHugh, Seb Fazzino. Row 2: Coach Marty Ryczek, Jerry Sofocli, Mike Neisser, Chris Herrmann, Jim Foley, Korey Lee, Chris Blanchard, Coach King. Row 3: Wayne Carlson, Steve Fabian, Art Carbo, Al Golia, Ed Sheiffele, Jeff Bagwell, Chuck Violissi. (The Don, 1986, courtesy of Xavier High School.)

Jeff playing shortstop for Xavier, a position that Bill Denehy later ruled out for college. (The Don, 1986, courtesy of Xavier High School.)

Reaching for one. (The Don, 1986, courtesy of Xavier High School.)

(The Don, *1986, courtesy of Xavier High School.*)

(The Don, *1986, courtesy of Xavier High School.*)

The 1985-86 Xavier Varsity Basketball team. L-R Bottom Row (L-R) Sean Russell '88, Derek Poulin '86, David Sizemore '86, Brenden Beckstein '86, Jeff Bagwell '86, Chris Fritz '88. Back Row (L-R) Craig Salamone '87, Jim Brown '87, Dana Wilson '86, Keane Chapman '87, Kevin Coolican '87, Eric Stearns '88, Mike DiMauro, team manager. (The Don, 1986, courtesy of Xavier High School.)

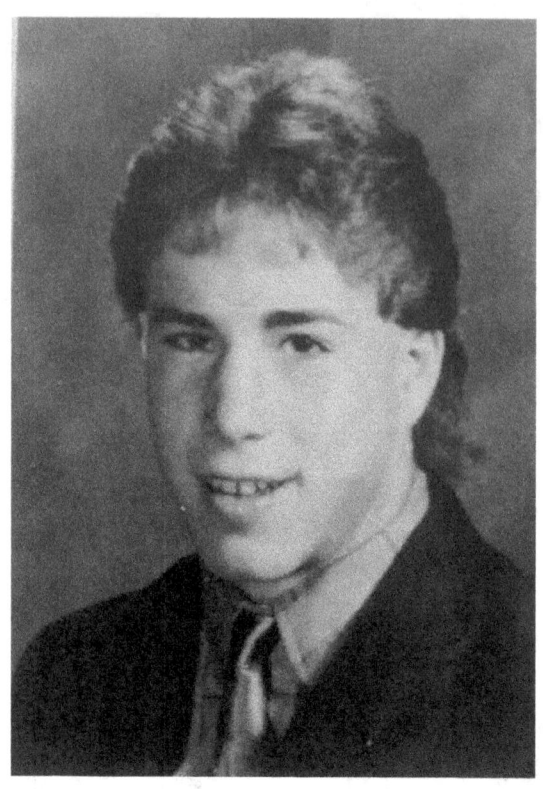

(The Don, *1986, courtesy of Xavier High School.*)

Tony Jaskot, Xavier Athletic Director and Bagwell's freshman coach with the jerseys of four athletes that attended Xavier including Phil Murphy (L.A. Rams), Jeff Bagwell (Houston Astros), Amari Spievey (Detroit Lions) and Will Tye (N.Y. Giants and Jets). Photo Karl Cicitto.

Terry Garstka
Head Baseball Coach
Xavier High School
1973–1993

By William J. Ryczek

Life often brings people together in strange ways. Major Henry Rathbone and his fiancée were in the presidential box at Ford's Theater when Abraham Lincoln was assassinated only because General Ulysses Grant and his wife begged off. Lore has it that Babe Ruth came to the Yankees partly because Boston owner Harry Frazee needed capital to produce *No, No, Nanette*. Terry Garstka became Jeff Bagwell's baseball coach because of a high-school romance.

Garstka was born in Springfield, Massachusetts, on July 13, 1944, but soon moved to Enfield, Connecticut, and attended school there. As a youngster, he was a Cleveland Indians fan—because his brother was a Cleveland fan—and his favorite player was Indians outfielder Rocky Colavito. In 1960, when Colavito was traded to the Tigers, the Indians lost a fan in Enfield. Garstka shifted his allegiance to Boston, and has been a Red Sox fan ever since.

When he was 12, Terry met a girl named Sylvia, and by the time he and Sylvia reached high school, they were dating. Terry was very active in sports and played football and baseball at Enfield High before graduating in 1962. A first baseman, he had good power and played well defensively, but never seriously considered the prospect of a professional career. "I knew I wasn't a star," he said. "Playing baseball and football was just a way to have fun."[1]

In the fall of 1962, Garstka matriculated to the University of Hartford, located in West Hartford, Connecticut. After one year, during which he played freshman baseball, he transferred to Central Connecticut State College (now Central Connecticut State University) in New Britain, Connecticut. Terry didn't play baseball at Central, focusing solely on his goal of becoming an English teacher and high-school coach.

By the time Garstka graduated in the spring of 1967, Sylvia was teaching English at Mercy High School, an all-girls Catholic institution in Middletown, Connecticut. Mercy was the sister school of Xavier High School, an all-boys institution located at the opposite end of Randolph Road. Sylvia heard that there was an opening in the English Department at Xavier and urged Terry to apply. He did and got the job.

That fall, Garstka joined the Xavier English Department and coached junior-varsity soccer. "At that point," he said, "I'd never seen nor touched a soccer ball. But the plan was that I would coach football the next season, so I was happy." Another reason for his happiness was that he and Sylvia were married in November 1967.

In 1968 Garstka, as promised, became the freshman football coach under legendary head coach Larry McHugh. McHugh, Xavier's first football coach, had a fabulous 20-year run that earned him a place in the National High School Coaches Association Hall of Fame. "Larry was a wonderful guy," Garstka said. "From him I learned the basics of coaching. Work hard, know what you're doing, and relate to the kids." In the spring, Garstka served as junior-varsity baseball coach under Peter Sipples, whom he'd assisted on the soccer field the previous fall.

In 1973, when Sipples left Xavier to pursue a career as an attorney, Garstka took over as head coach. His teams hovered around the .500 mark his first couple of seasons, but by the late '70s the Falcons were among the best teams in Connecticut. In 1978, the Falcons were 16-4 during the regular season and beat Newtown in the first round of the Class-L playoffs. In the quarterfinals, they faced Waterford High School's star left-handed pitcher Mark Winters, who'd knocked the Falcons out of the playoffs in the semifinals two years earlier, striking out 18. He was 11-0 thus far in 1978, but Xavier beat him, 3-2. Although they lost in the next round, Garstka said that 1978 was the best season in Xavier history.

After a 19-2 record in 1979, Garstka once again said it was Xavier's best season. But the truly best season was a year away. The 1980 Falcons started slowly, winning just three of their first five games, and their coach was upset. He thought it was probably the most talented team he'd ever had, and should be playing better. But they were erratic, blowing a couple of leads against teams Garstka thought they should beat. Garstka is a very even-tempered man, but after one frustrating defeat he lost his temper. There is a steep hill behind the baseball field at Xavier, and after that loss the 1980 Falcons ran up and down the hill until they realized it would be a good idea to play a little harder. "I think they knew I was mad and meant business," Garstka said. On May 18, Garstka got his 100th win as Xavier beat cross-town rival Woodrow Wilson High School.

For the remainder of the season, the Falcons played the way their coach knew they could, and finished the regular season with a 15-5 record. After they won their first-round game, 11-0, Garstka reminded everyone that they'd won big in the first round the previous year and were eliminated in the next game. This time, two comeback wins followed in the second and third rounds, one from a 6-0 deficit, which sent the Falcons into the Connecticut Class L championship final against Cheshire High School. Xavier rallied from a 3-1 deficit and won, 6-3, giving the school the first baseball championship in its history.

During his 21 years at Xavier, Garstka had over 250 wins and finished his career more than 80 games over .500.

	Season Record
1973	8-8-1 (Co-champion of the Hartford County Conference)
1974	7-11
1975	11-9
1976	15-6 (HCC Champions)
1977	8-11
1978	18-5 (3rd best Class L team in Connecticut)
1979	19-2
1980	19-5 (Class L State Champions)
1981	12-9-1
1982	14-6 (HCC Champions)
1983	13-7
1984	15-8
1985	15-6
1986	13-9
1987	8-12
1988	11-11
1989	13-9
1990	7-12
1991	10-10
1992	14-5 (All Connecticut Conference Champion)
1993	9-13
Total	259-174-2[2]

JEFF BAGWELL IN CONNECTICUT

From 1973 through 1993, Xavier missed the playoffs only three times. The prize player from Garstka's tenure, of course, was Jeff Bagwell, who was co-captain of the 1986 team. Mike Fiala, star of the 1980 championship game who finished his Xavier career with an 11-0 pitching record, also signed a professional contract and was a relief pitcher in the Los Angeles Dodgers' minor-league system in 1985 and 1986.

Garstka retired from coaching after the 1993 season, turning the reins over to Xavier grad and former minor-league catcher Rich Magner, who'd been his assistant since 1980. "My daughter was getting ready for college," he said, "and I needed to spend more time with my family." Coaching had also changed since he'd begun his career in 1967. Parents were more involved than ever, and while most were supportive, it made the coach's job more difficult. "It wasn't as bad as it gets in Little League," he said, "but it sometimes became a negative. And I didn't like that."

Garstka continued teaching English until 2001, spending his final three years at East Granby (Connecticut) High School. After he left teaching, he and his wife operated an antique business for a few years, but he is now completely retired. He spends a lot of time working around the house and, like many baseball fans, is a collector of memorabilia. Unlike most old coaches, he does not play golf. Terry and Sylvia have one daughter, Alexis, who lives in Terryville, Connecticut, and is a recruiter at a major insurance company.

"I really had a great experience at Xavier," Garstka said. "There was a lot of support and a lot of energy." He thought the fact that Xavier was an all-boys institution led to an increased emphasis on sports, and he liked that. "The energy was so much better," he said. While there was always pressure to win, Garstka, unlike some coaches at private high schools, never "recruited" junior high school players. "Whatever came in, came in," he said. One of those who "came in" during the fall of 1982 was Jeff Bagwell, who became Terry Garstka's connection to the Baseball Hall of Fame.

SOURCES

In addition to the sources cited in the Notes, the author also consulted *Middletown Press*, April-June 1980.

NOTES

1. William J. Ryczek, interview with Terry Garstka, September 6, 2017. All quotations from Coach Garstka are from this interview.
2. All records taken from Xavier High School Yearbooks, 1973-1993.

The 1985 Xavier baseball team. Bagwell is in the front row, second from left. Coach Garstka is in the back row on the extreme left. (The Don, 1986, courtesy of Xavier High School.)

Coach Garstka watches his Falcons. (Courtesy of Xavier High School.)

American Legion 1984-1986, Emerging Excellence

By George Pawlush

"Pitching is why we've been in the race all summer. Jeff is in control. He might make a mistake but he won't make the same one twice."

—*Coach Dave Darling,* Middletown Press, *July 29, 1986*

Middletown American Legion Post 75 has a rich and storied baseball history. The post hosted the 1988 and 1999 American Legion Baseball World Series at Palmer Field.

In its glory years, between 1964 and 1984, Middletown won 14 zone titles in 21 years.[1] They captured four state crowns[2] during this period: in 1965 and 1968, under the leadership of Bill Pomfret; and the 1979 and 1982 teams that were guided by Ted Lombardo. Prior to Jeff Bagwell's 1991 debut with the Houston Astros, three other Middletown Legion alumni, Joey Jay, Mark DeJohn, and Bill Denehy, reached the major leagues.

Jim Bransfield, longtime sportswriter for the *Middletown Press*, wrote about Bagwell's first tryout with Post 75. Bagwell was just 15 years old and had recently completed his freshman year at Xavier High School.

Bransfield recalled, "The Legion coach was Ted Lombardo, a guy who turned out one powerhouse Legion team after another. When Bagwell came out, Middletown was loaded. I remember Lombardo saying that he thought the Bagwell kid was going to be a good one someday. But not that day."[3]

Lombardo, who went on to be athletic director and baseball coach at Coginchaug Regional High School in Durham, Connecticut, cut him from the team. "Not many coaches in America can lay claim to cutting a future Hall of Famer," Bransfield said.[4]

Fred Tremalgia, a player with the 75ers in the early 1970s, succeeded Ted Lombardo as coach. Lombardo had resigned to join the University of Hartford baseball staff, piloted by Post 75 alumnus Bill Denehy.

Tremalgia came to the team with an extensive baseball résumé. After high school at Xavier, he played collegiate baseball at Stetson University. He joined Xavier High School as an assistant baseball coach to Terry Garstka for two years after graduation. Tremalgia later became the baseball coach at Ledyard (Connecticut) High School.[5]

During the summer of 1979, Tremalgia was an assistant coach with the Hyannis Mets in the Cape Cod League. Hyannis was Cape League champion that year, going 38-8. Tremalgia took a leave of absence from Ledyard during the 1982-83 school year to become pitching coach and earn his master's degree at Western Kentucky University.[6]

Before the 1984 season, Palmer Stadium was hit with a spring flood that damaged the field and concession stands.[7] Area high-school teams, which normally used the stadium, were forced to find alternate playing sites. Post 75 didn't access Palmer until June 23.[8]

There were some major changes in the Connecticut American Legion Baseball structure for 1984 after a few teams dropped out in Zones 1 and 3. State Legion officials decided to have the two zones play an interlocking schedule with all games counting to determine a final champion for each zone. "It promised to be a very tough year," Tremalgia said. "Everybody guns for Middletown. We knew that teams would be saving their best for us."[9]

Middletown had many new faces on the club. It was a team with a bright future with only four of the 18 players on the squad scheduled to graduate from the squad at the end of the season. After a productive sophomore high-school season, Bagwell made the Post 75 team with ease.

By the time Palmer Field was finally ready for play, the Post 75 road warriors had accumulated a 6-1 record, including 4-0 in zone play. One of those victories was a 4-3 triumph over defending state champion Bristol at Muzzy Field.

However, archrival Meriden got off to a better start. Post 45 was undefeated at 9-0 in zone play while the 75ers were 7-4 when the teams first played on July 19. Middletown stopped Meriden's unbeaten string, beating them 5-3 in a crucial battle that brought Post 75 back in the race.

Middletown then reeled off three straight victories while Meriden dropped three in a row. Bagwell was a key force in two of the 75er wins. He stroked a triple and single in a 14-7 victory over Southington, and then had three hits and four RBIs in a 10-3 triumph against West Hartford on July 23.

In just four days Middletown and Meriden had reversed their positions in the Zone 3 race. The 75ers were now atop the standings at 12-4 after defeating Simsbury, 10-8. Bagwell paced Middletown with a triple, single, and two runs scored. Middletown was two games ahead in the win column, and Meriden, loser in four of its last six games, was 10-4 in zone play.

Just when Middletown thought momentum was going its way, the team suffered consecutive loses to Berlin and Meriden. On July 31, Middletown's zone record stood at 12-7 while arch-rival Post 45 was 14-5.

With five games left on the zone schedule, Middletown was faced with the inevitable task of having to win all its remaining games while Meriden had to lose two of its last five for the teams to tie at 17-7. Middletown, 16-7, won four straight during the final week while Post 45 vanquished three foes, to raise its zone log to 15-5, 1½ games ahead of the 75ers.

All Meriden needed to do was to beat Middletown on Saturday, August 4; or Portland on August 5, to win the zone crown. Fortune proved to be on Middletown's side when Post 75 downed Meriden, 7-3, in the Saturday encounter. Joe Barone scored what proved to be the winning run in the fourth inning when he reached home on Bagwell's fielder's choice. Meriden then did the improbable by falling to Portland, 13-12, on Sunday. Host Portland won the game with a walk-off two-out, two-run homer by Steve Morrison. Middletown and Meriden were now knotted at 17-7 and headed for a best-of-three playoff series to determine the Zone 3 champion.[10]

Middletown rode the pitching arm of Barone to win the playoff opener, 8-1, at Palmer Field. The 75ers jumped off to an early 4-1 advantage and played magnificent defense. In the next game, Meriden evened the series when it scored two runs in the bottom of the ninth to nip Middletown, 3-2.

Post 75 prevailed in the rubber game, outlasting Meriden, 12-10, to win the crown. Both teams came into the game with tired pitching arms. For Meriden, it was the fifth game in five days. "I knew that this was going to be a high-scoring game," Coach Tremalgia told a *Middletown Press* reporter after the game, "because we were both short on pitching."[11]

Middletown spurted off to a 12-7 lead after the sixth inning, scoring three runs on a bases-loaded triple by Darren Fleck. The 75ers were up, 12-8, with two outs in the ninth when Post 45 narrowed the lead to two on a two-run homer. Tony Franco then came on in relief and induced a popup to give Middletown a 12-10 victory and the title.

It was Middletown's third straight zone title and its fifth in six years. Meriden Coach Pete Waldron summed up his team's loss in a postgame interview with the *Middletown Press*. "It was a season when no team really took charge. We had a chance to take charge as did Middletown, but neither of us did."[12]

Middletown's magnificent 7-1 late-season drive appeared to take its toll on the 75ers in the Legion state tournament. After an opening 3-1 triumph over Zone 9 champion Putnam, Middletown bats fell silent in losses to Bristol, 4-0; and New London, 3-1. The 75ers ended their season at 22-11.

"I believe having to play that zone playoff series really took a lot out of us," Tremalgia said. "We reached (our limit) in the final game and it was tough for us to get up for the state tournament."[13]

Tremalgia noticed a big change in Bagwell's baseball development coming into the 1985 season. "Jeff had really matured at the plate. He had become a more disciplined hitter. He loved the challenge. From watching him you could tell that he had good hand and eye coordination and had very strong hands and wrists. Jeff was a good gap hitter especially with power to right-centerfield."[14]

Bagwell got off to a great start in the 1985 Legion campaign. After the first seven games he was batting .475, 19-for-40. But the 75ers won only three of their first seven starts and on June 30 were 2-3 in Zone 3 play.[15] Bagwell continued his hot hitting and had seven consecutive safeties before being stopped in the seventh inning by Wethersfield in a game that the 75ers won on July 1.

Middletown's zone record fell to 6-6 when it lost to first-place Meriden, 5-3, on July 10. Post 45 was now 11-0 and held a comfortable 5½-game lead over the 75ers. Post 75's fortunes began to rise four days later when it dealt Meriden a 4-3 loss, to knock Post 45 out of the unbeaten ranks. Bagwell had a big day in the triumph, slamming a triple down the right-field line in the top of the sixth. He then scored on a squeeze play that put Middletown ahead, 2-0. Bagwell singled in the seventh to drive in the 75ers' third run. Middletown was now 8-6.[16]

75er faithful began to wonder if their team might be able to pull off another miracle finish like 1984. Middletown gave it a valiant try and reeled off seven straight victories to raise its zone log to 15-6. But unlike the previous year, Meriden didn't wilt while the 75ers were streaking.

On July 24, Meriden sealed Middletown's fate, downing the 75ers, 11-9. The victory elevated Meriden's record to 20-1. In the game, Bagwell doubled and scored in the first to give his team a 2-0 advantage. In the seventh, he knotted the game at 8-8 with an RBI single. The 75ers were mathematically eliminated from zone competition the next day, losing to Bristol, 7-5.[17]

Meriden entered the State Legion Tournament with a 26-2 zone and 30-6 overall record and figured to be a strong contender for a state title. Post 45 won three of its first four tourney games before losing to Trumbull in the tournament semifinals.

Middletown launched its 1986 American Legion season with a veteran team and a new head coach. Dave Darling was named skipper of the 75ers, replacing Fred Tremalgia, who wanted to spend more time with his young family. During his two years at the Middletown helm, Tremalgia's teams posted a pair of 20-win seasons—22-11 and 21-12—that included the 1984 zone championship.

After accepting the position, Darling told *Middletown Press* sportswriter Jim Bransfield that "the coaching position is something that I have always been interested in. This is a good time to get involved now that my sons are through with the program."[18]

In 1986, Zone 3 returned to its old scheduling format. Middletown was slated to face Meriden, Portland, Cromwell, Berlin, New Britain, and Wallingford five times during the season, with only zone games counting in the standings. In addition to its zone schedule, the 75ers scheduled exhibitions with defending state champion New London; Manchester, New Hampshire; and two games with Waterbury, Watertown, and Windsor Locks.

The season was hyped up to be a fight to the finish. Meriden returned with all but three players from its 1985 zone championship team. Middletown was intent on atoning for its zone title loss to Post 45. It looked to be an exciting zone race and it was.

Middletown was determined not to repeat its poor 1985 season start, which had proved too much to overcome. The 75ers were undefeated at 9-0-2 during the first third of the season. The only bad marks on their record were a pair of weather-shortened, 6-6 and 7-7 ties with Waterbury Post 1. Bagwell contributed greatly to his team's early success, and was batting at a .560 clip, 14-for-25, after the 75ers' first seven games.[19]

On June 22, Bagwell gave fans a preview of what was to come during his professional career, when he launched a home-run blast during a 14-4 victory over New Britain at Willow Brook Park. The round-tripper was one of his four hits in the game.

Perennial foe Post 45 posted a 9-5 victory over Middletown on June 26 in their first of five scheduled meetings to deadlock the teams at 5-1 in the zone race. Bagwell's torrid hitting continued into July. Through 11 games he was batting .532, 25-for-47, with 16 RBIs.

Middletown upped its zone log to 8-1 on July 6, outlasting Portland, 11-9, in an 11-inning duel on the road. In the contest, Bagwell brought two runs home in the third with a single that hit the center-field fence. In the eighth inning, Bagwell and teammate Rich Murray hit back-to-back homers to knot the game, 5-5. Bagwell hit another round-tripper in the ninth to put the 75ers up 7-5.

Bagwell moved from shortstop to relieve starter Avery Askew in the bottom of the ninth. It was his first Legion mound appearance of the year after being named the All Connecticut Conference (ACC) Pitcher of the Year during the spring at Xavier. Bagwell blew the save opportunity, allowing the tying runs to score in the ninth inning. He hurled scoreless 10th and 11th innings to earn the win. It was Bagwell's best offensive production of the summer as he smacked three hits, two of which were homeruns, and had five RBIs.

Meriden again downed Middletown, 4-2, on July 9 in their second faceoff of the year. Post 45 was now 8-1 with the 75ers close behind at 9-2.

Bagwell made his first pitching start of the season on July 16 and beat Portland, 6-1. He allowed just three hits and struck out 11 batters. Bagwell helped his own cause with two hits and an RBI.

Post 45's hex over Middletown continued on July 18 when Meriden gave the 75ers a 20-5 whipping. Despite Middletown's three straight losses to Meriden, the teams were still close in the race. When Meriden dropped a 16-15 slugfest to Portland on July 20, Middletown, 13-3, was actually a half-game ahead of Post 45.

Meriden vanquished Middletown, 10-3, for the fourth straight time on July 23 to again take command in the zone standings, one game ahead of the 75ers. Both teams then picked up two victories.

Middletown made in three in a row, besting Portland, 3-1, on July 28 to raise its zone record to 19-4. Bagwell picked up the victory, fanning 10 batters and limiting the visitors to five hits. "Pitching is why we've been in the race all summer," Coach Darling told Jim Bransfield. "Jeff is in control. He might make a mistake but he won't make the same one twice."[20]

Two days later, Portland did Middletown a big favor, upsetting Meriden, 5-1. Post 45 and the 75ers were now tied with 19-4 records. Middletown extended its season log to 20-4, with a 9-7 win over New Britain on July 30. Post 45 was now faced with having to defeat New Britain and Middletown to avoid a zone playoff.

Rain washed out Meriden's scheduled meetings with New Britain and Middletown during that final week. Post 45 held on for a 2-1 victory over New Britain in a makeup game on August 3. The stage was now set for a winner-take-all Zone 3 finale between Middletown and Meriden the next night. Not since 1974 had the zone championship gone down to the final game of the regular season.[21]

Bagwell, the most effective pitcher for Middletown during its final stretch, started the game. He was relieved by Tony Franco after allowing two singles in the fifth with the 75ers behind, 2-0. Both runners, charged to Bagwell, scored, increasing Meriden's lead to 4-0.

Joe Busca got the 75ers back into game in the bottom of the fifth with a two-run double. He was driven home by Bagwell's sharp single to center. Middletown tied the game, 4-4, in the sixth inning on a sacrifice bunt and a hard-hit single by Bill McKenna.

The teams remained scoreless until the 12th inning, when Meriden scored on an error with two outs to win, 5-4. The 75ers were unable to answer in the bottom of the frame, giving Meriden the zone crown for the second year in a row.

Coach Darling was proud of his team in defeat. He told *Middletown Press* sportswriter Jim Bransfield, "I don't think two teams can play any better than this. I know we can't. We played as well as we can and you have to hand it to Meriden. That's a great team—they had to beat us five times."[22]

Middletown finished the season 23-8-2 overall and 20-5 in Zone 3. The 75ers were 20-0 against all other Zone 3 teams but 0-5 versus Meriden. The team's inability to handle Meriden was the difference in the race.

Bagwell finished the season with a .439 batting average. He had 47 hits in 107 at-bats, scored 36 runs, and had 30 RBIs. He and teammate Rich Murray each had four home runs. Murray, who batted .406 and accumulated 41 RBIs, provided Middletown with a powerful tandem, hitting third and fourth in the 75ers batting order. On the hill, Bagwell was 3-2 and recorded a 3.05 ERA. He struck out 53 batters in $38\frac{1}{3}$ innings pitched.[23]

Bagwell's Legion participation was cemented in the national organization's baseball history when he was honored as Legion's 2003 Graduate of the Year at Minute Maid Park in Houston on July 14. The American Legion recognizes a major-league player each year who best represents the ideals and goals of the Legion baseball program. The award is based upon leadership, citizenship, community service, sportsmanship, good conduct, playing ability, and integrity.

Previous Graduates of the Year include Greg Maddux (1994), Ryne Sandberg (1984), George Brett (1980), Carl Yastrzemski (1967), Ted Williams (1960), and 13 others. All 18 of those honored were Legion baseball alumni, like Bagwell, who were later inducted into the Baseball Hall of Fame at Cooperstown, New York.

SOURCES

In addition to the sources cited in the Notes, the author also consulted:

Bransfield, Jim. "Legion Alum Is New Coach," *Middletown Press*, March 13, 2003.

Bransfield. "The Face of Legion Baseball Marks Milestone," *Middletown Press*, June 1, 2007.

Bransfield. "Monday Musings: Post 75 State Champs Honored," *Middletown Press*, January 29, 2017.

Bransfield. "Some Tough Times for American Legion Baseball," *Middletown Press*, July 30, 2017.

Canfield, Owen. "When It Comes to Baseball, Moe Knows," *Hartford Courant*, July 7, 1992.

Kolinsky, Bo. "People, Places & Things. Bagwell Is American Legion's Graduate of the Year," *Hartford Courant*, July 6, 2003.

McHugh, Larry. "Larry McHugh: August Starts Right With American Legion's Baseball Tournament," *Middletown Press*, August 1, 2010.

Serra, Thomas J. "Letter: Middletown Hall of Fame's Newest Inductees to Be Honored," *Middletown Press*, January 4, 2017.

legion.org/baseball.

NOTES

1   "Middletown Opens Bids for States," *Middletown Press*, August 10, 1984.

2. Ibid
3. Jim Bransfield, "Bagwell Announces Retirement," *Middletown Press*, December 16, 2006.
4. Ibid.
5. 1983 W. Kentucky Baseball Media Guide, 6.
6. Ibid.
7. "Post 75'ers Hitting Road to Wallingford for Game," *Middletown Press*, June 17, 1984.
8. "Is Middletown A.L. Really as Strong as Results Indicate?" *Middletown Press*, June 25, 1984.
9. Fred Tremalgia, telephone interview, August 16, 2017.
10. "Middletown and Meriden Tied, Playoff Starts Tonight," *Middletown, Press*, August 6, 1984.
11. Jim Bransfield, "Post 75ers Win Zone 3 Title," *Middletown Press*, August 9, 1984.
12. Ibid.
13. Tremalgia telephone interview.
14. Ibid.
15. "Franco Paces 75'ers' Win Over Cromwell," *Middletown Press*, July 1, 1985.
16. "Post 75'ers Top Previously Unbeaten Meriden Team, 4-3," *Middletown Press*, July 15, 1985.
17. "Post 75'ers Lose to Bristol," *Middletown Press*, July 26, 1985.
18. Jim Bransfield, "Middletown's Post 75ers Get a Darling of a Coach," *Middletown Press*, April 3, 1986.
19. "75'ers Take Wins," *Middletown Press*, June 23, 1986.
20. Jim Bransfield, "Bagwell Pitches Post 75ers to a 3-1 Win Over Portland," *Middletown Press*, July 29, 1986.
21. "It's a One-Game Season for Post 75'ers Tonight," *Middletown Press*, August 2, 1086.
22. Jim Bransfield, "Meriden Edges Post 75ers for Zone 3 Championship," *Middletown Press*, August 5, 1986.
23. Jim Bransfield, "In Retrospect, the 75'ers Had an Impressive Year," *Middletown Press*, August 6, 1986.

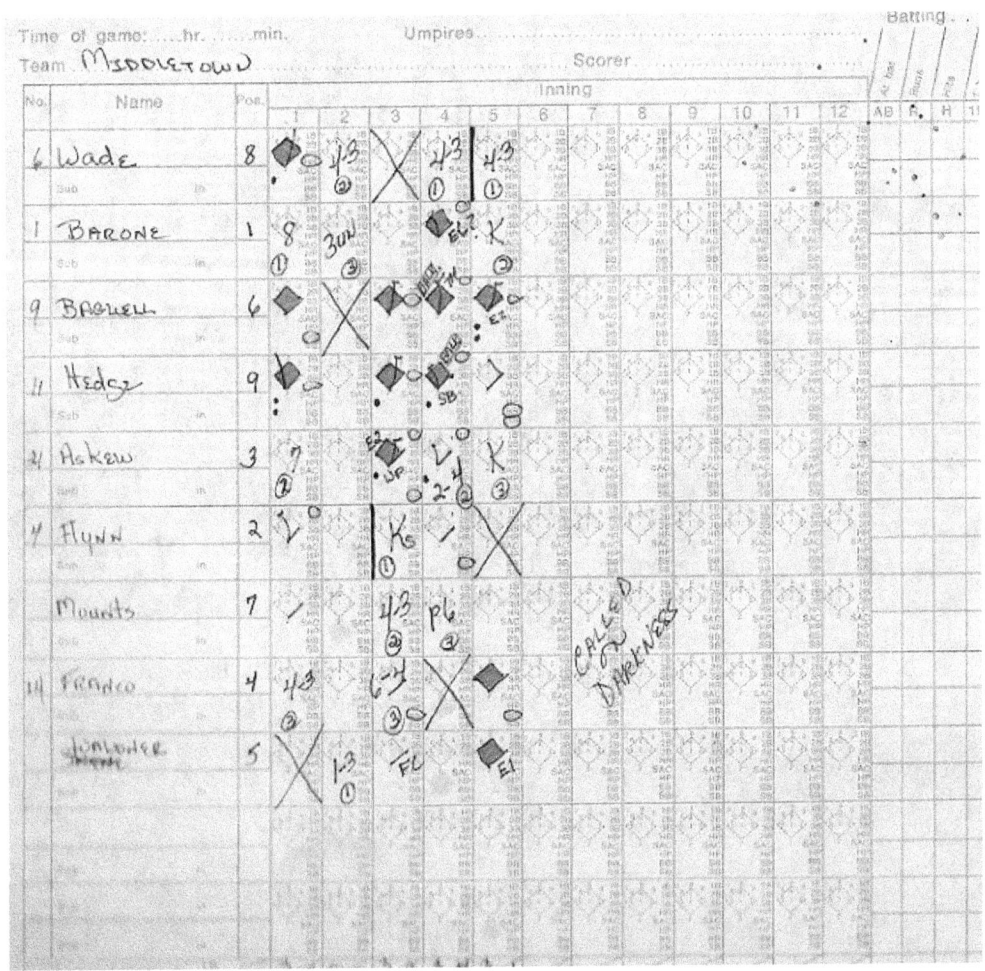

Scorecard from the June 25, 1985 American Legion game between Middletown and Cromwell. Bagwell scored 4 times in 4 at-bats with two triples, a single and a walk. Batting cleanup behind Jeff is his future Hartford Hawk teammate, Pat Hedge. Mr. Hedge also reached base 4 times that day, with a home run, single, triple and a walk. (Collection of Dave Darling.)

The 1984 Middletown American Legion Post 75 team. Bagwell is in the row that is kneeling, extreme right. (Courtesy Middletown Sports Hall of Fame)

Bagwell accepts the 2003 American Legion Graduate of the Year Award with Middletown's (Larry McHugh third from left), Bill Pomfret (fifth from left) and Dave Darling (next to Bagwell) at Minute Maid Park. McHugh, Pomfret and Darling are Middletown American Legion, coaching and community leaders. The annual award is given to a Legion alumnus that exemplifies citizenship, leadership, sportsmanship, good conduct, integrity and playing ability. (Courtesy Middletown Sports Hall of Fame.)

Dave Darling, one of Bagwell's American Legion coaches, holds Jeff's Middletown Sports Hall of Fame induction plaque. (Photo Karl Cicitto.)

Philip Cacciola (left) and Dave Darling (right), officers of the Middletown Sports Hall of Fame, hold a banner made in honor of both of Bagwell's Hall of Fame inductions in 2017. (Photo Karl Cicitto)

Palmer Field

By Jim Bransfield

For generations, Palmer Field has been at the center of Middletown amateur sports. It's primarily a baseball field, but over time it morphed into a multi-sport facility hosting not only youth, high-school, American Legion, and collegiate baseball, but also soccer and high-school football.

It's also been used as the site for the city's annual Fourth of July fireworks show and, indeed, for a rock concert.

If you live in Middletown and can't find your way to Palmer Field, we revoke your citizenship.

What makes the park unique is its urban setting. Donated to the city ages ago, it sits hard by busy Route 66 in a stretch lined with gas stations, fast-food restaurants, an auto-body shop, a car wash, and once upon a time the Palmer Mills factory that later became a discount clothing store, a poor man's version of the box stores so common today.

And therein lays a story.

On July 5, 1975, the Palmer Mills factory and long-since closed store burned to the ground in a spectacular fire that broke out during an American Legion game at the nearby ballpark. As flames roared out of control in the building some 1,000 feet away, the game went on. If someone had taken a photo of the crowd on the third-base line watching the game while flames devoured the building behind them that might have been Pulitzer Prize stuff.

The game ended when the south wall of the four-story building that lined what used to be called Factory Street—now Bernie O'Rourke Drive (named in memory of the city's beloved late director of recreation)—collapsed, taking with it the power lines, plunging the park into darkness.

Prior to all of that, Palmer Field was essentially an old country ball yard with no fences and no lights. Everything was day baseball. The prime tenant was the Ahern-Whalen Intermediate League for 13- to 15-year-olds. Each August it would hold an invitational tournament of twilight and weekend games and crowds in the hundreds would turn out.

Those were simpler, and maybe better, times.

In 1965, everything changed. The city's American Legion team, long just a summer pastime, won a state championship and went to the final game of the Northeast Regional tournament in Manchester, New Hampshire, before losing 8-5 to Berlin, New Hampshire, a team it defeated 9-1 in the opening round.

But the success of the team transformed interest in baseball, and the city administration—in those days when Democrats and Republicans actually worked together for the common good –approved money to put lights and fences in the ballpark. Interest in local Legion baseball exploded.

Through the years, the Post 75ers, as they came to be known, won zone title after zone title and won three more state championships, in 1968, 1979, and 1982. Governor John Dempsey threw out the first ball for Middletown's opening-night game in the 1968 regional.

The park hosted numerous state and regional Legion tournaments, and crowds of 1,500 for tourney games were commonplace.

Middletown received a bid to hold the Legion World Series in 1988, so in 1987 the park was closed for extensive renovations. Not only were new lights, new stands, and a new press box installed, the field itself was moved 100 feet toward the northeast.

In the World Series, former major-league stars like Brooks Robinson and Mel Stottlemyre showed up to throw out first pitches. The winning team was Budde Post of Cincinnati, and the shortstop on that team was Pete Rose Jr.

During the tourney, Pete Rose called the press box often to ask, "How's my kid doing?"[1]

A total of 19,423 fans attended the event and the 3,759 who saw the final game made up the largest crowd ever to see an amateur game in Connecticut. A second World Series was held in 1999 with 17,000 paying their way in.

The field also became Xavier High's home football field and it was on this field that Xavier fashioned a 34-game winning streak which stood as a state record for a long time. It was common for 2,000 to 3,000 to show up for a Xavier game, clogging neighborhood streets and business parking lots. In 1975, Xavier won its first state championship, then won four more, packing the fans into the ballpark.

Middletown High also played its football games there and the annual Middletown vs. Woodrow Wilson game for the city public-school championship routinely put crowds of 4,000-plus into the park on Thanksgiving.

Some of the baseball stars who played at Palmer were Bobby Valentine, whose Legion team played in a tournament, and Bill Almon of Warwick, Rhode Island. Almon played for many years in the major leagues for the Mets, Athletics, White Sox, and predominantly for the Padres.

Baseball Hall of Famer Jeff Bagwell, who played for Middletown Post 75 in the 1980s (and was not regarded as a prospect out of high school); Mark DeJohn, who played in the Tigers' system for years and spent many years as a major-league coach, mainly for the St. Louis Cardinals; and Mike Flanagan, a Cy Young Award winner for the Baltimore Orioles, also played at Palmer.

It was Flanagan who pitched in one of the greatest amateur games ever played in Middletown. It was for the New England Regional Championship in August of 1970 and more than 1,600 paid their way in to see the showdown between Middletown and Manchester (New Hampshire).

Flanagan pitched nine innings. He faced only 27 batters. He gave up one hit, to Ed Mann, who singled, and was out trying to stretch it into a double. (Mann went on to become Sen. Christopher Dodd's main aide.) Flanagan struck out 13.

Opposing pitcher Tom Morrison struck out three times on nine pitches. "I never saw the ball; I just didn't want him to hit me," he said.[2]

With Flanagan's dominance helping to shape the day, the game was 0-0 after nine as Morrison threw a little bit of this and a little bit of that for eight-plus innings, keeping Manchester off-balance.

Flanagan came out after nine and Middletown got a run in the top of the 10th. But Manchester got two in the bottom of the inning to win.

Palmer Field still hosts high-school football, but not as many games as it once did. It remains the site of baseball and is busy virtually every day from late April through late August. The Middletown Legion, Xavier High, and Middletown High play on the diamond along with the youth 13-15-year-old league.

State and regional Legion tournaments are routinely played there, as is the CIAC state high-school baseball tourney. The four high-school games pack 4,000 to 5,000 in every June.

More renovations are underway. A newly designed entranceway for both baseball on the west side and football on the east side are being built. The infield dirt is being replaced with Fenway Park-like red stone dust, and new grandstand seats are in the offing.

But for all the newness, the charm remains. The Coginchaug River runs past the trees behind the left-field fence and the field sometimes floods when the Connecticut River backs up in the spring. In 1984, the park was buried under 8 to 10 feet of water and Department of Environmental Protection crews were hand collecting fish that had been trapped by the fences and tossing them back into the receding river.

An occasional freight train still passes by over the Route 66 bridge to the southeast and the neon lights of businesses flash near Palmer. The din of cars, trucks, and emergency sirens still echo across the park. But locals don't notice. It's what makes there there.

The outfield fence is lined with signs. Each high school in town has a sign extolling its virtues, local businesses have signs. There's no mistaking that you're in an American cityscape here.

It is an island of green in the middle of the city, in the middle of the state, and is a rarity: a solely amateur park for kids. There is a kind of innocence at Palmer Field, it's yesterday, today.

May it ever be so.

SOURCES

Middletown Press

NOTES

1 Telephone conversation in press box with Pete Rose, August 27, 1988.
2 Postgame interview by the author with Tom Morrison, August 30, 1970.

Action at Palmer before the 1975 fire that destroyed Palmer Mills, visible in the background. (Courtesy Xavier High School.)

Palmer's centerfield bleachers, often filled for football games, and press box are visible in the background. (Courtesy Xavier High School.)

Palmer Field photographed after the 1988 renovation when the diamond was moved 100 feet closer to the center field fence. (Courtesy Middletown Sports Hall of Fame.)

THE COLLEGE YEARS

The 1988 University of Hartford Baseball team. (Collection of Brian Crowley.)

1987 To 1989: Soaring Like A Hawk

Bagwell at the University of Hartford

By Pete Zanardi

Four balls wound up in the screen atop Fenway Park's Green Monster. Two of Jeff Bagwell's batting-practice shots bounced off the left-center-field wall, one with such force that it nearly bounced all the way back to the infield. The University of Hartford's Bagwell, the ECAC New England Collegiate Player of the Year for the second straight season, was tuning up for the 1989 New England College All-Star game. The date was June 6, 1989.

Later that day, Bagwell's third-inning RBI double gave the University Division first blood in a 4-2 win over its College Division counterparts.[1] Still later that day, the Boston Red Sox drafted third baseman Bagwell in the fourth round of the free-agent draft.

Scout Erwin Bryant told the *Hartford Courant*'s George Smith that the Red Sox liked Bagwell's "power potential" that was "just now scratching the surface."[2] In retrospect, it is classic understatement, one of many uttered about Bags in his three seasons at the University of Hartford.

Bagwell's final effort as a collegian is rivaled by his first official game on March 19, 1987, as a University of Hartford Hawk when he hit for the cycle in an 18-17 loss at St. Leo College in Florida. The evening of the same day, the Hawks lost again, 11-10 to the University of South Florida, but Bagwell was 8-for-10 for the day with a pair of doubles. He scored six runs and drove in six.

He rarely stopped hitting. In three seasons (1987-89) at U. of H., "Bags" set many school career records for home runs (31), RBIs (126), batting average (.413), and slugging percentage (.733),[3] in 400 at-bats. Three times All-New England, he was twice the region's player of the year and once a third-team ABCA All-American. Bagwell delivered offensively for three different coaches—former major-league pitcher Bill Denehy, Don Cook, and Dan Gooley—taking what each offered.

"Coach Denehy is the only one who ever recruited me so I owe him a lot," Bagwell told the *Middletown Press*'s Jim Bransfield.[4] Considering Bagwell's impressive statistics as a hitter and pitcher with both Xavier High and the Middletown Legion Post, it is counterintuitive that only one college wanted him. His soccer statistics (58 career goals, including 36 as a senior in 1985) at Xavier were equal to if not superior to his baseball prowess.

"I saw him as a junior for the first time and the thing that impressed me the most was that he had an awful lot of power to the opposite field," Denehy told Smith in 1994.[5] Twenty years later in his autobiography, *Rage*, Denehy, who "once saw [Bagwell] hit a home run 380 feet to right-center field," explained that he "always liked hitters who could hit to the opposite field. They were tougher to pitch to than dead pull hitters."[6]

There was a strong Middletown flavor at U. of H. Denehy, hired in August 1984 to bring the school into Division I, was a star at Woodrow Wilson High and the Middletown Legion before signing with the New York Mets. Assistant Ted Lombardo was the American Legion coach in Middletown from 1975 through 1983, averaging 21 wins a year, grabbing seven zone and two state titles.[7] He was inducted into the Middletown Hall of Fame in 2017. Ted Lombardo cut a 15-year-old Bagwell in 1982.[8] Don Lombardo, Ted's brother, handled the hitters for Ted with the Middletown Legion while Paul Labella had been the third-base coach. Since both Lombardos and LaBella coached Bagwell in American Legion, Hartford had a leg up in recruiting him.[9]

Two Xavier products, pitcher Tony Franco and catcher Rick Murray, were already at Hartford. They were part of Denehy's 1985 recruiting effort, which remains a major factor in the university's baseball history and a vital part of Bagwell's college career as well.

The *Hartford Courant* on April 23, 1985, reported that Brian Crowley, a second-team schoolboy All-American[10] from Newington and a Team USA member, had decided to attend U. of H. Also headed to the Hawks was Chris Petersen, a one-time high-school and Legion standout from Manchester who was transferring from Sacred Heart University, where he had gone to play soccer.[11] The next day Denehy told the *Courant*'s Bohdan Kolinsky, "This is just the first wave of recruits...These signings indicate the caliber of players we are interested in having attend U of Hartford the type of players who are willing to build a program."[12]

Pat Hedge, who hit 18 homers in his final two seasons[13] at Morgan High of Clinton and was Bagwell's Middletown Legion teammate, committed in August. The quartet became known as the Crunch Bunch at Hartford and in their best year, 1988, combined for 245 hits (40 of which were home runs), 188 runs scored, and 184 runs driven in.[14]

Pitchers Mark Czarkowski, a Newington High product, and Keith Wiley, out of Nauset Regional on Cape Cod, were also part of the class that had a season of college baseball behind them when Bagwell arrived in the fall of 1986. "The soccer coach (Allan Wilson) wanted [Bagwell] too," Denehy details in *Rage*. He wanted us to share a scholarship so Bagwell could play soccer and baseball. This was ... not what you did in Division I. I told him Bagwell would play soccer over my dead body."[15]

Denehy, hardly an academic, didn't specialize in making friends at the university. And he wasn't always right baseball-wise. While stating the obvious about Bagwell in the 1987 *U. of H. Media Guide*—"...Tremendous prospect. ...Hits with power. ...Able to go to opposite field"—Denehy was way off by predicting Bagwell "could develop into one of the finest shortstops in New England. ..."[16] In actuality, Denehy's moving of Bagwell from shortstop to third base is a story that has near-folklore status.

1987

Jeff displayed definite defensive liabilities at shortstop early in 1987 and Denehy decided he was better suited to third base. For the third game of the season, Denehy moved Petersen to first and put Pablo Melendez, a freshman from Wilbur Cross in New Haven, at short. When Bagwell did not buy what was a "hedge...a bullshit excuse," Denehy writes in *Rage*, he got a dose of honesty: "you're too f.....g slow at short," he was told.[17]

Offensively, Denehy was right on. Heading into the 1987 home opener against Dartmouth on April 1, Bagwell was 22-for-46, a laudable .478. That included 4-for-7 in a doubleheader at Yale Field on March 28. He was 3-for-4 with two homers, a double, and three RBIs against Dartmouth, bringing his average to a statistical .500 (25-for-50). His batting average became part of every game story in the *Courant*.

After a horrible start, the Hawks were becoming more competitive. Coming off a doubleheader split with UMass on April 9, Hartford (4-13) headed for a three-game weekend series at perennial power University of Maine. On April 11 Hartford beat the Black Bears, 3-0, on a Crowley blast in the first game of a doubleheader and then lost the second game. They won the next day, April 12, by a score of 12-10, in what is one of the biggest games in U. of H. baseball history. Bagwell's single up the middle started the four-run seventh-inning rally that helped make Hartford the first school in 16 years to win a best-of-three series in Orono against an iconic New England team.[18]

On April 16 Denehy was fired, the results of an ill-timed quote following a messy affair at the University of Connecticut. The UConn-Hartford game was marred by fistfights and the game was declared no contest, angering Denehy. The *Norwich Bulletin* quoted Denehy as saying UConn Assistant Coach Mitch Pietras "had no class" and suggesting that when Pietras came to Hartford as a soccer official he hoped "somebody bombs his car." Denehy claims he didn't believe his comments were for publication,[19] but Don Cook, in his first year as AD, said they were a "broad embarrassment to University of Hartford,"[20] and fired Denehy along with assistants Labella and the Lombardos.[21]

Don Cook was the Fairfield University baseball coach for many years before taking the Hartford AD position and replacing Denehy as the manager. In Cook's debut as head coach, Hartford was no-hit by Central Connecticut's Al Donovan.

Although Denehy's departure had to distract the Hawks, Bagwell continued to hit. He helped salvage a split with Boston University, collecting a pair of hits including a three-run first-inning dinger on April 23. On April 26 he had three hits and drove in three runs in an 11-5 win over Northeastern, that effort coming the day after he had the only hit in a 4-0 blanking by the same team. Bags hit his sixth homer of the season, a fourth-inning grand slam, in an 11-9 home loss to Fairfield on April 29. The next day he homered for a school record-tying seventh time in a 10-inning, 6-5 conquest of Providence College.

The Hawks ended the 1987 season with an 11-27 record but Bagwell's stats were impressive—a .402 batting average with 7 homers, 32 RBIs, and 86 total bases.[22] He arrived as a bona-fide star at the New England Collegiate All-Star game at Fenway Park.

Cook was notably understated in praising Bagwell's freshman performance, declaring, "He's a line-drive hitter who, when he gets his pitch, can drive it. He always hits the ball hard and he has good bat control."[23]

In the summer of 1987, Bagwell played with Middletown-based Mallove's in the Greater Hartford Twilight League before and after he stayed on Cape Cod (June 12 to August 8)[24] playing for the Chatham A's in the Cape Cod League. When he wasn't washing dishes at a local Friendly's to make a dollar, Bagwell batted .206 for Chatham manager John Mayotte.

Despite the low average, Bagwell insisted that playing for Chatham was instrumental in his development. "I got my chance in the Cape Cod League. …A lot of players from the best programs came to play there in the summer. … Albert Belle was playing there. Frank Thomas. I [only] hit about .205 … but I looked at those guys and decided I could play with them," he told *Sports Illustrated*'s Leigh Montville six years later.[25]

1988

Dan Gooley loves telling the story of his first encounter with Jeff Bagwell. "I thought I was shaking hands with a blacksmith," he told the *New Haven Register*'s Chip Malafronte. "He was so strong, he crushed my hand. I told him, 'I can't even spell your last name yet, will you take it easy on me?'"[26]

A CONSISTENT LAD IN THE LAND OF STEADY HABITS

One of 78 applicants, Gooley was named U. of H. baseball coach on June 18, 1987. He had spent 11 seasons as head coach at Quinnipiac University, compiling a 203-126 record including a trip to the 1983 Division II World Series. Among his Quinnipiac players was major-league pitcher Turk Wendell. He quickly hired assistants Randy LaVigne, already an assistant AD at Hartford, and Moe Morhardt, who ended a very successful run as coach at the Gilbert School in Winsted to join Gooley. Both LaVigne and Morhardt were former multisport standouts at UConn. Both had pro experience. Morhardt played briefly for the Chicago Cubs and LaVigne played for five years in the Cubs organization, reaching Triple A with Iowa.

"Each day before practice [Bagwell] spent 30 minutes working on a different aspect of the game. One day it might be extra hitting or defense or working with a pitcher to better understand left-handed pickoff moves," Gooley told Malafronte.[27] There is, however, no end to his praise for the work of his assistants, notably Morhardt, in the development of the entire team, especially the "Crunch Bunch."

Rick Murray and Pete Daniels, a New England All-Star in '87, were among those who left after the '87 season, but Gooley's squad went 13-3 in the fall and started big in the spring of 1988. Going into the home opener vs. Dartmouth on April 2, Bagwell was hitting .362 with seven homers for the 9-3 Hawks, part of an offense that included Chris Petersen's .388, Al Tolomeo at .355, and Brian Crowley's .353. Bagwell batted fourth, behind either Petersen or Crowley, who were slotted at third and fifth in the order. Pat Hedge was a fixture batting sixth.

Bagwell's first home run came in the season opener, against Cleveland State on March 18 in Greensboro, North Carolina; his fifth-inning blast was the difference in a 3-2 win. He had three consecutive bombs as part of a four-hit day in a 20-11 win at the University of Richmond on March 23. He soon homered against James Madison and Delaware. Back up north, he cleared the fences at spacious Yale Field in each game of a doubleheader split with Yale. After walking three times at Fairfield University (two were intentional) Bagwell tuned up for the home opener with a three-hit, four-RBI effort in a 20-0 crushing of Holy Cross at Fitton Field on March 31.[28]

Bagwell had a double and a single in a 5-3 win over C.W. Post[29] on April 6 and had two more hits the next day in a 6-5 loss at UMass, ending a six-game Hartford winning streak.[30] He then collected eight hits in a three-game set at New Hampshire on April 9 and 10, including his eighth homer in a 19-11 victory. In the only win in a three-game series with Central Connecticut, Bagwell was 3-for-4 with two RBIs on April 16.

His 10th homer has become legend, due no doubt, to the frequency with which Dan Gooley tells the story. It's April 19, the bottom of the 11th. U. of H. and UConn are tied, 4-4. Bagwell is in the on-deck circle watching a UConn reliever take his warm-up tosses. He turned and said to Gooley, "Skip, it's over," and then launched the first offering high above the light tower at McKenna Field.[31] The blast was one of three hits for Jeff in the game.[32] The victory evened the season series with UConn, which had beaten Hartford 7-6 on April 14 despite another three-hit effort by Bagwell.

Bags hit a three-run blast in a 22-1 crushing of Fairfield on April 26 and the next day got his 12th home run (he also had a sacrifice fly and single) in beating Maine 12-7, earning a split at home.[33] With victories now vital for tournament consideration, Hartford took three straight from Northeastern. In the second game (April 30), Hartford was being no-hit before Bagwell's single in the seventh broke up the bid and Hartford soon took the game, 2-1.

Two days after the announcement that Bagwell was the 1988 ECAC New England Player of the Year, Hartford (26-10) joined Fordham (32-11), C.W. Post (26-14), Fairleigh Dickinson (24-11), LeMoyne (26-9-1), and Maine (32-22) in the ECAC tournament at New Britain's Beehive Field. Bagwell headed into the tournament hitting .399 with 12 homers, 43 runs, and 50 RBIs. Petersen was at .380, Hedge at .374 with eight homers and Crowley .308 with nine homers. All were greatly improved over 1987 and each acknowledged Morhardt as the reason.

In a tribute to Morhardt in the *Courant*, George Smith detailed the Crunch Bunch contribution prior to the tournament. "[T]he Hawks are hitting .338, three points away from making the nation's top 10 list in Division I, according to 'Collegiate Baseball,'" Smith wrote. "Everybody is hitting. Senior second baseman Todd Reynolds of Norfolk, who hit .222 as a reserve last season, is batting .394 in the No. 2 spot with four homers, five doubles, two triples and 33 RBIs. Freshman designated hitter Mike Scrapchansky of Killingly leads off with a .365 batting average, and junior left fielder Brian Bushwell ... the only lefty in the line-up, hits eighth with a .345 mark."[34]

"When you get guys around you hitting, it rubs off on everybody," Bagwell told Smith.[35] Two decades later Hedge acknowledged the role Bagwell played: "You knew you could count on him to hit every day and we all fed off how competitive he was. If one player had three hits in a game, he wanted four. He made us all better."[36]

Sophomores Mark Czarkowski (6-1), Tony Franco, Michael Garbeck, and the workhorse Wiley (9-2), all Denehy recruits, formed a reliable staff of starting pitchers. Hawk hitting was also talented and deep but when it came to stick work, Smith concluded, "[I]t's the Crunch Bunch that has done the most damage."[37]

Along with Petersen, Bags was a "Hogger," a competitor who, Hedge explained, "would spit, swear and chew." A "no-nonsense...let-it-hit-you-in-the-teeth ballplayer," offered Crowley. "He wasn't flamboyant, but he always shined."[38]

Bagwell shined in the tournament, hitting .478 with 11 hits including two homers.[39] After losing the opener, 7-2 to Fordham, the Hawks came back to win three straight in the losers' bracket. Bagwell had three hits in an 8-2 win to give Maine its first loss;

was 4-for-5 with two doubles and 4 RBIs in a 10-6 win over C.W. Post, and collected his 13th homer in a 24-2 assault on Fairleigh Dickinson, the latter setting up a return game with Fordham the same day.

The Hawks went ahead 8-4 on Bagwell's 14th home run, a two-run shot in the seventh, but the Rams rallied with six in the bottom of the frame, aided by three Hartford errors, and went on to win, 10-8. The game ended with Bagwell striking out, stranding a runner at third. Hawks hitters actually outhit the Rams. Hawk pitchers issued 10 walks. Hartford ended with a 29-12 record, their best ever.

Bagwell, who finished with a .410 average, scored 49 runs, and drove in 58, participated in his second straight New England Collegiate All-Star game. Hedge hit .389 with 12 homers; Crowley finished at .310 with 10 round-trippers.[40]

Hartford ranked 10th nationally in hitting among Division I teams with a .344 mark. (*Baseball America, 1989 Almanac*) Teammates Petersen (1b) and Bagwell (3b) were All New England First Team. Todd Reynolds (2b), Hedge (cf), and pitcher Keith Wiley were All New England Second Team, and Gooley was Coach of the Year.[41]

1989

Hartford and Bagwell got plenty of preseason attention in 1989. After a strong performance with Chatham in the Cape Cod League in the summer of 1988, Bagwell was a legitimate high-round prospect. Although his red-hot hitting cooled off in the second half of the Cape League season, Jeff registered .318 with 6 homers, 26 runs, and 22 RBIs for Dartmouth coach Bob Whalen at Chatham. He had four hits and homered in the All-Star game and was part of the Cape team that prevailed in a special College Leagues Tournament in Florida in late summer.[42]

On February 16 the *Courant* reported that *Baseball America* rated Bagwell the second-best college third baseman in the country behind Southern Cal's Rodney Peete. With Crowley, Hedge, Czarkowski, and Wiley rated prospects as well, *Baseball America* predicted that the Hawks would be New England's premier team. Departing seniors Chris Petersen and Todd Reynolds were the only real losses.[43] Reynolds died in a tragic accident on Jan. 17, 1989. Petersen took an assistant coach role for 1989.

The scouts were around from the start. Tom Mooney, a scout for more than three decades, worked for the Houston Astros when he filed a report about Bags on March 28, 1989. On a scale from two (poor) to eight (outstanding), Bagwell's "overall potential" averaged 45.1. Defensively, Mooney was not impressed and prophetically suggested "...may have to move to first base." Mooney wrote that Bagwell was "low waisted" and had a "fleshy body." These were hardly compliments. But the seven after "power evaluation" was extraordinary.[44]

"The interesting thing was the power potential," Mooney told the *Boston Globe*'s Alex Speier almost 30 years later "... I don't throw 70's around a lot. He must have been really, really dramatic with the power. ... [A] 70 grade represents the ability to get the ball out of any ballpark. He generated that kind of bat speed, that kind of explosiveness when he squared the ball up. This was going to be impact-type power. It wasn't going to be (batting) six, seven, eighth in the lineup. It was going to be middle of the order. ...Nobody gets eight(y)s. I don't think I ever gave Ken Griffey Jr. an eight(y) in anything. Seven(ty) was about as high as I'd go. That meant that I thought he'd be an elite power guy."[45]

Bagwell was worth watching. After getting two hits in a season-opening 6-5 loss at Duke on March 17, he homered in the 9-5 second-game triumph. He had three hits and two RBIs in a 15-6 loss to George Washington on March 18 and followed that the next day with a two-hit, four-RBI effort in a 17-6 win at the University of Virginia.

Bagwell's hitting underscored what Gooley said before the Mid-Atlantic swing when he called Bagwell "the best third baseman I've ever had. I haven't had anybody in my 18 years of coaching that has hit and hit with power like him."[46]

Bagwell was "the best everyday player in New England," Padres scout Leo Labossiere reported on April 21. Saying, "I've liked this kid since he was a freshman," Labossiere added, "His bat is what everyone likes because he can hit for [average] and power. He also stands in good and can hit a [curveball] which many people can't do."[47]

On the day of Labossiere's report, Bagwell hit his sixth homer of the season in a 19-2 assault on Vermont in Brookline, Massachusetts, a makeup game. Over the next two days he unloaded on Central Connecticut. Bagwell was 7-for-10 with four homers as the Hawks took two of three. In the third game, on April 23, a 13-11 win, Bagwell was 4-for-4 with two homers including a three-run shot in the 10th. He also walked twice and scored four times with six RBIs.[48] He was hitting .433 and slugging .822 with a .564 on-base percentage. The team, however, was 11-15-1 despite a .299 batting mark. Hedge was hitting .311 and Crowley .308 with 10 homers. But the team's ERA was 5.70.

Bagwell's single was a key part of a five-run ninth that resulted in a 10-9 win over Fairfield on April 25. The Hawks won their last seven, ending the season with a 3-1 win over Northeastern on May 1, Bagwell's ninth-inning double the vital blow. His .429 with 10 homers and 36 RBIs earned Bagwell a second straight New England Player of the Year prize but the Hawks' 17-15-1 final record was not good enough for a return to the postseason. Three losses each to Maine and UConn, despite five home runs by Crowley in those six losses, all but removed the Hawks from playoff contention.[49]

As a sophomore and junior, Bagwell hit safely in 60 of 79 games, half of them multiple-hit performances.

A month before the draft, Angels scout Jon Niederer was to the point: "This fellow is the best-looking hitter on the East Coast and I think he's got a chance to hit .300 with power in any league, right up to the majors. Reminds me of Al Oliver. Everything he hits is hard. His defense would bother me more if we were an Astroturf club, but

A CONSISTENT LAD IN THE LAND OF STEADY HABITS

I don't think he's hopeless at third. Has no fear and his work habits are good. Would like to see us get him."[50]

The question was, *who would get him?*

After the University Division's 4-2 win at Fenway in which Pat Hedge's run-scoring single in the seventh proved to be the gamer, the Red Sox selected Bagwell. It happened about 7 P.M. although Bagwell didn't know until 9:45. "I called [home] about 5 P.M. and nobody knew. I was a little nervous. When I returned home, I asked my dad if he had heard. 'You'll never guess,' he said and then he threw me a [Red Sox] shirt. ... I was surprised because I hadn't talked to the Red Sox all season."[51]

Ironically, Bagwell had taken no chances. He was on Mallove's roster for the 1989 Greater Hartford Twilight League as a backup in case he was not drafted and assigned to a minor-league team.

The Bagwell family are longtime Red Sox fans and they were elated about the draft result.[52] Among the disappointed was Ed Buckie, a greater Hartford baseball mainstay and a veteran bird dog/scout then in the employ of the Astros. "We always thought very highly of him. We contacted Boston and asked them if they were interested and they said 'mildly' so we put him in the sixth round. Wouldn't you know it, they decided to take him in the fourth."[53]

On June 13, the *Hartford Courant* reported that Bagwell, who as of 2018 still held the U. of H. career records for batting (.413) and slugging percentage (.733), was "on his way to the Red Sox' Class A team in Winter Haven, Florida.[54] Picked by the Orioles in the 22th round, Hedge, who hit 26 homers and drove in 107 runs in four years at Hartford, was headed to Erie, Pennsylvania. Crowley, who had 29 homers and 115 RBIs as a Hawk, was the Texas Rangers' 33rd-round pick and bound for Butte, Montana. Bellingham, Washington was the destination for Czarkowski, the Seattle Mariners' 51st-round pick. Czarkowski made 52 appearances in four years at the U. of H.[55]

"The greatest tribute to Jeff is how his teammates feel about him," Petersen said in a Hartfordhawks.com release. "Every person he has ever played with, whether it be in high school, college, or the pros, loved him."[56]

Classic understatement? Sure, but incredibly apt.

SOURCES

In addition to the sources cited in the Notes, the author also consulted:

University of Hartford media guides for 1985, 1988, 1989, 1990, 2006.

Baseball America Almanac, 1988, 1989, 1990.

Price, Christopher. *Baseball by the Beach* (Hyannis, Mass.: Parnassus Imprints, 1998).

The *Hartford Courant* and *Middletown Press* were used as daily primary sources.

NOTES

1. Fred J. Post, "Keeping Posted," *Middletown Press*, June 8, 1989: 21.
2. George Smith, "Bagwell: Right Spot, Right Time," *Hartford Courant*, June 7, 1989: F8.
3. hartfordhawks.com/news/2017/1/18/bagwell-elected-to-baseball-hall-of-fame.aspx, accessed May 12, 2018.
4. Jim Bransfield, *Middletown Press*, June 7, 1989: 17.
5. George Smith, "He'll Always Be Player From the Old School," *Hartford Courant*, October 28, 1994: C1.
6. Bill Denehy with Peter Golenbock, *Rage, the Legend of "Baseball Bill" Denehy* (Las Vegas: Central Recovery Press, 2014), 223.
7. 1987 U. of Hartford Media Guide, 11.
8. Jim Bransfield, *Middletown Press*, June 7, 1989: 17.
9. Denehy with Golenbock, *Rage*, 223.
10. 1987 University of Hartford Media Guide, 15.
11. 1987 University of Hartford Media Guide, 16.
12. Bohdan Kolinsky, "U of H Gains Crowley," *Hartford Courant*, April 23, 1985: D6.
13. 1987 University of Hartford Media Guide, 15.
14. 1989 University of Hartford Media Guide, 10.
15. Denehy with Golenbock, *Rage*, 224. Xavier soccer coach Marty Ryczek agreed with Denehy. "I told [Bagwell] I was getting calls from a lot of colleges about him as a soccer player. I said it would be my suggestion that if you have a chance to go play baseball you should go play baseball because I'm pretty certain you're never going to make a living playing soccer professionally." (Jimmy Zanor, "Xavier Part of Bagwell's Legacy," *Middletown Press*, January 20, 2017: B1).
16. 1987 University of Hartford Media Guide, 22.
17. Denehy with Golenbock, *Rage*, 229.
18. 1988 University of Hartford Media Guide, 5.
19. Denehy with Golenbock, *Rage*, 233.
20. George Smith, "Hawks Ax Falls; School Fires Baseball Coach, Staff," *Hartford Courant*, April 17, 1987: E1.
21. Denehy's role in Bagwell's development is well documented. In a 1992 interview with this writer, Dan Gooley called Denehy "the right man at the right time for the University of Hartford baseball-wise." On the eve of the Hawks' 1988 appearance in postseason play, the *Courant*'s Owen Canfield wrote, "Denehy recruited top players with extraordinary success and got Hartford's Division I baseball program off on the right foot. Any coach or manager ... will tell you that in the long haul, a team will go only as far as its talent takes it." (Owen Canfield, *Hartford Courant*, April 28, 1988: G1, G6). The *Middletown Press*'s Jim Bransfield summed it up perfectly: "What Denehy did—which made all the difference for Bagwell—was to take Hartford into the big time. He wanted big-time baseball at Hartford. He made a good effort and made it a nice place to play." (Jim Bransfield, *Middletown Press*, June 7, 1989: 17). Denehy told the *Courant*'s George Smith "I feel very fortunate I didn't screw him up. Jeff always had a tremendous work ethic. You never had to get on his case. I never had to tell him twice. When other kids might have doubted your methods, he never did." (George Smith, "He'll Always Be Player From the Old School," *Hartford Courant*, October 28, 1994: C4).
22. 1988 University of Hartford Media Guide, 6.

A CONSISTENT LAD IN THE LAND OF STEADY HABITS

23 Roy Hasty, "Bagwell Playing Like a Veteran," *Hartford Courant*, April 30, 198:, D2.

24 1987 Chatham A's Media Guide, 7-8.

25 Leigh Montville, "Trade Deficit Proved—By Trading Him to Astros the Red Sox Made a Ruthian Blunder," *Sports Illustrated*, July 26, 1993, retrieved February 6, 2018.

26 Chip Malafronte, *Middletown Press*, January 19, 2017: 3.

27 Ibid.

28 "Hartford Dumps Holy Cross, 20-0," *Hartford Courant*, April 1, 1988 (U of H Clip File).

29 "Hartford Wins 13th, beats C.W. Post," *Hartford Courant*, April 7, 1988 (U of H Clip File).

30 "UMass Ends Hawks Winning Streak at 6," *Hartford Courant*, April 8, 1988: E4, E12.

31 "Jeff Bagwell built his baseball resume at Xavier in Middletown, University of Hartford," *New Haven Register*, January 18, 2017. nhregister.com/sports/article/Jeff-Bagwell-built-his-baseball-resume-at-Xavier-11315630.php, retrieved February 6, 2018.

32 "Hartford Downs UConn," *Bridgeport Post*, April 20, 1988.

33 "Hartford Raps Maine 12-7, Salvages Split," *Hartford Courant*, April 28, 1988: G6.

34 George Smith, "Hartford's Crunch Bunch," *Hartford Courant*, May 4, 1988: F1.

35 George Smith, "Hartford's Crunch Bunch," *Hartford Courant*, May 4, 1988: F2.

36 Hartfordhawks.com, "Bagwell Elected to Baseball Hall of Fame," January 18, 2017, retrieved February 6, 2018.

37 George Smith "Hartford's Crunch Bunch": F1.

38 George Smith, "He'll Always Be Player From the Old School," *Hartford Courant*, October 28, 1994: C4.

39 George Smith, "Fordham Takes ECAC Tournament Title," *Hartford Courant*, May 24, 1988: E3.

40 1989 University of Hartford Media Guide, 10.

41 George Smith, "Fordham Takes ECAC Tournament Title." 3

42 Whalen, who coached against Bagwell while at Dartmouth, recalled that coaching him was a "distinct privilege." "I realized two things about him right away," said Whalen in the web release that celebrated Bagwell's Hall of Fame selection. "First, he did not want to be good, he wanted to be great, in every aspect of the game. Second, he made the commitment to becoming a major-league player every day. Many kids enjoy the competition and status of being in the Cape League but Jeff showed up for early workouts every day to work at getting better. Jeff is one of the most loyal and hardest working players I've ever coached. He put the numbers up. ...." Sean Gonsalves, Cape Cod Baseball League, "Bagwell's Road to Cooperstown: Swung Through Cape Cod Baseball League," January 19, 2017. capecodbaseball.org/news/league/?article_id=2343, retrieved February 6, 2018. Christopher Price (*Baseball By the Beach*: A History of America's National Pastime on Cape Cod (Orleans, Massachusetts: Parnassus Imprints, 1998, page 99, calls 1988 one of the greatest seasons in terms of future major leaguers in Cape Cod League history.

In addition to two other Connecticut products—Mo Vaughn at Wareham and Kevin Morton at Hyannis—the league also had batting champ and MVP Chuck Knoblauch at Wareham, Tim Salmon at Cotuit, Mike Myers at Brewster, Eric Wedge and Denny Nagle at Yarmouth-Dennis, Jeromy Burnitz and John Valentin at Hyannis, and Frank Thomas and J.T. Snow at Orleans. The list of those who reached the majors extends to over 80, including Bagwell's Chatham teammates Rick Horton and Mark Sweeney.

43 George Smith, "Outbreak of Measles Put Blotch on Siena's Basketball Season," *Hartford Courant*, February 16, 1989: D4.

44 Alex Speier, "Scout Saw Jeff Bagwell's Potential Back in College," *Boston Globe,* December 16, 2016.

45 Ibid.

46 George Smith, "Change of Pace: Hawks Go From 'Hunter' to 'Hunted,'" *Hartford Courant,* March 19, 1989: E9.

47 collection.baseballhall.org/PASTIME/jeff-bagwell-scouting-report-1989-april-21, retrieved February 6, 2018.

48 "Hawks Win in 10th on Bagwell Homerun," *Hartford Courant*, April 24, 1989: B2.

49 Crowley, who hit .320 with 10 homers as a senior, joined Bagwell on the All-New England team. Hedge, .323 with 7 homers, was a second-team pick. As a team, Hartford hit .309 with six players above .300. The team ERA was 5.19. "Division 1 All New England baseball," *Hartford Courant,* May 27, 1989: E20.

50 Rob Neyer, "Eight Scouting Reports That Really Nailed It," *SB Nation*, May 15, 2013. sbnation.com/2013/5/15/4311000/baseball-scouting-reports-accurate-nailed-it, retrieved February 6, 2018.

51 George Smith, "Bagwell: Right Spot, Right Time."

52 Christopher Cosenza, "Who Knew Bagwell Was Going to Be This Good?" *Middletown Press*, October 28, 1994: C5.

53 Ibid.

54 Earl Snyder, who played four years (1995-98), broke most of Bagwell's Hartford career records, including the single-season (18) and career home-run standards. Snyder had a limited major-league career of 19 games but had 220 minor-league homers (plus one major-league home run), seven times hitting 20 or more in the minors.

55 1988 University of Hartford Media Guide, 6; thebaseballcube.com/players/profile.asp?ID=76105, accessed May 12, 2018.

56 Hartfordhawks.com, "Bagwell Elected to Baseball Hall of Fame," January 18, 2017, retrieved February 6, 2018.

NAME Jeff Bagwell
POSITION(S) Shortstop/pitcher
HIGH SCHOOL, PREP SCHOOL, AND/OR JC Xavier High School
HEIGHT 6'0" WEIGHT 190
BIRTHDATE 5/27/68 BATS Right THROWS Right
HIGH SCHOOL, PREP SCHOOL, COACH(ES) Toby Terrance Gartska
COLLEGE ENROLLED IN (i.e., Engineering) Barney
MAJOR finance

BELOW AND ON THE BACK OF THIS SHEET, PLEASE LIST ALL AWARDS, HONORS, TEAM ACCOMPLISHMENTS, AND STATISTICS THAT YOU HAVE HAD IN HIGH SCHOOL, PREP SCHOOL, LEGION TEAMS, JUNIOR COLLEGE, ETC. IT IS IMPORTANT I KNOW AS MANY FACTS ABOUT YOUR PLAYING CAREER AS POSSIBLE. PLEASE BE SPECIFIC AS TO WHEN AND WHERE THESE ITEMS OCCURED. I'VE ATTACHED AN EXAMPLE SHEET FOR YOU TO FOLLOW.

Baseball
3 yr starter for Xavier High School
Batted .403 Jr. year.
Batted .396 Sr. year
Jr year All ACC second team
Sr year All ACC first team
voted MVP of ACC Sr. year
Sr year voted class LL All state
named to the CIAC senior All star game
Earned 3 letters under coach Terrance Gartska
Captain Sr year of Xavier High School Baseball
Played for Middletown American Legion.
named to all-star team Conn. vs Mass

(over)

Soccer
3 year starter at Xavier High School
scored school record 56 career goals.
scored 35 goals in one season (school record)
Jr. year voted first team ACC
Sr. year voted first team ACC
Sr year voted All state LL Hartford Courant Coaches Association
Sr year voted All New England
All Middlesex County Jr & Sr. year
can't spell coaches name? Martin Ryzeck

Bagwell's student athlete questionnaire, freshmen year. Jeff used a lot of space to write in the experience and honors he tallied at Xavier High School. (Courtesy of University of Hartford Archives and Special Collections.)

(Courtesy of University of Hartford Archives and Special Collections.)

(Courtesy of University of Hartford Archives and Special Collections.)

(Courtesy of University of Hartford Archives and Special Collections.)

(Courtesy of University of Hartford Archives and Special Collections.)

(Courtesy of University of Hartford Archives and Special Collections.)

(Courtesy of University of Hartford Archives and Special Collections.)

(Courtesy of University of Hartford Archives and Special Collections.)

Beyond Expectations
The 1988 University of Hartford Team

By Karl Cicitto

Brian Crowley's father, James Crowley, shot VHS tapes to chronicle his son's baseball life, from American Legion to the pros.

The first tape is labeled "Legion Ball, Bristol, Simsbury, Middletown, 1985-86."

The last is labeled "Butte Montana 1989 Copper Kings, Texas Rangers, Brian's Rookie Year."

They show the journey of an All-Stater from Newington, Connecticut, to A ball in the Pioneer League.

Some of these home videos show the University of Hartford baseball team playing on peaceful college diamonds. Some have cityscapes in the background. Others are bordered by forests and parking lots. All games are played before small crowds between 1987 and 1989.

Jeff Bagwell is seen batting in Crowley's video of the ECAC Tournament championship game on May 23, 1988. Hartford played Fordham at Beehive Stadium in New Britain that day. The weather is now a warm 72 degrees. It's dry.

Bagwell, who stands 6 feet and weighs 190 pounds, is in his dark red Hartford Hawks jersey and gray pants. He has number 27 on his back.

He wears a different number, 26, on his home whites. This is because someone has stolen his 27 white jersey.[1]

When he relaxes, hands at his side, Bagwell's forearms don't droop to his sides; his arms remain half-cocked. He is young but there is tension in his upper body that suggests he just chopped a cord of wood. Strong-looking kid.

He is a sophomore, from Killingworth, Connecticut, and a graduate of Xavier High School, where he excelled on the soccer pitch as well as the diamond.[2] The Hawks media guide says Bagwell has unlimited potential. He is on *Baseball America*'s Watch List. In his freshman year he led the ECAC New England in hitting and set three team records. No one drafted him coming out of high school. Only one Division I baseball coach had the vision to recruit him: Bill Denehy, then at the University of Hartford.[3]

In the video, Bags stands in the box against the Rams' Paul LoGiudice and his batting crouch is not nearly as pronounced as it would be in the big leagues. He waggles his bat end in a tight orbit, the picture of pre-swing tenseness.

Bagwell, the Hawks' starting third baseman, looks every pitch back to register where it thuds into the catcher's mitt. He does this on every pitch that he does not attack. He is capturing data, systematically. Over and over. The other players do the same thing but only on occasion. Bagwell doesn't fail to do it. He is locked in.

Bagwell smacks a pitch through the hole near shortstop for a single.

Brian Crowley also appears in the video, standing in the box, sans waggling, relaxed and focused, facing LoGiudice. He takes a lot of pitches, fouling several off, each time returning to a poised, motionless stance.

Crowley stands 6-feet-1, weighs 195 pounds, and hails from Newington, where he starred for Newington High and toured Europe with a team of high-school all-stars.

Now in his junior year, he was a schoolboy All-Stater, a second-team high-school All American and one of Denehy's recruiting prizes of 1985. He is not the only dangerous hitter in the Hawk lineup but he is the only one who will smack four home runs in a game as he did against the Black Bears of Maine on April 15, 1989.[4] The rightfielder has an outstanding arm and is typically flawless in the field. In 1987 he batted .272 with 3 home runs and 15 RBIs. Under the professional hitting approach of new Hawks coach Moe Morhardt, his 1988 line rose to .310, 10, 42.

Coach Morhardt was as important as anyone associated with the team. His retooling of the Hartford hitters reached up and down the Hawks lineup and improved individual batting averages by as much as 209 points over 1987.

Crowley gets under one of LoGiudice's pills and pops a fly to short centerfield for an out.

Soon we see number 22, Chris Petersen, step up. He is listed at 6-feet-2, 190. The Hawk first baseman looks loose and relaxed during his at-bat. There is no crouch in his stance. He's a patient hitter. He seems to be evaluating the umpire's calls, alternately looking back at and nodding to the man in blue.

Petersen is batting .380 and leading the team in hits and doubles. The senior from Manchester (Connecticut) High has been Hartford's most consistent performer since transferring from Sacred Heart in 1985. When the 1988 season commenced, Peterson owned the team records for career hits and doubles. Another blue-chipper. His offensive gain with Coach Morhardt was from .276, 3, 26 in 1987 to .370, 4, 35 in 1988.

> *Petersen strokes a grounder to the left of second base for a single.*
>
> *Centerfielder Pat Hedge, number 14, has a distinct look in the batter's box. Both of his knees are bent while he bounces up and down in his stance, waggling the bat all the while.*

The former football player stands an even 6 feet and weighs 190 pounds. One sportswriter referred to him as a "human bulldozer,"[5] encapsulating his effectiveness as a high-school running back at the Morgan School in Clinton. Hartford Coach Dan Gooley called him a daring and fearless competitor. His vicious swing would earn him the highest honors available in this ECAC tourney.

Morhardt's coaching did not just help Hedge's plate effectiveness; it ignited it. Hedge went from .165, 0 HR, 7 RBIs in 1987 to .374, 12, and 49.

> *Hedge attacks a pitch, stinging a liner right at the left fielder, a hard-hit out.*

These four players were Coach Gooley's magnificent warriors in 1988. Their cumulative potency did not go unnoticed by the press.

The cover of the *Hartford Courant*'s sports section on May 4, 1988, carried a photo of Bagwell, Hedge, Crowley, and Petersen at the top of the section's front page. "Hartford's Crunch Bunch," the headline announced. A stat box titled "Smash Hits in Hartford" spelled out the slash lines for the completed regular 1988 season.[6]

Bagwell: .399 BA/12 HR/50 RBIs.
Petersen: .380 BA/4 HR/33 RBIs.
Hedge: .374 BA/8 HR/38 RBIs.
Crowley: .308 BA/9 HR/38 RBIs.

Forty percent of their hits were for extra bases. The composite line for 573 at-bats was .365 BA, 40 doubles, 10 triples, and 159 RBIs. Potent indeed.

The 1988 Hartford Hawks were much more than the Crunch Bunch. There were 13 other players who provided dependable pitching and hitting-in-bunches. The result was a team that won at a .707 clip. They were so offensively strong that the winning was frequently gaudy to behold.

Indeed, Hartford's other players were talented in their own right.

The shortstop was Steve Scialabba, a diminutive sophomore and contact hitter who struck out only eight times as a freshman. Like Crowley, he starred at Newington High School, where he was All-County and a District All-Star. Scialabba got into only 22 games as a freshman but he led the team in walks and recorded a .419 OBP. With Morhardt's magic, Scialabba's line rose from .179, 0, 1 to .271, 0, 15.

Senior Todd Reynolds from Norfolk, Connecticut, was a rough-hewn second baseman, a throwback from an earlier time. Gooley described him as "an old piece of scrap iron." The good-fielding, dependable Reynolds moved from spot starting to the regular second-baseman role in 1988. Reynolds' offense rose from .222 BA, 0 HR, 0 RBIs to .384, 4, and 45.

Big Al Tolomeo, a 6-foot-3, 205-pound junior from Stratford, Connecticut, was the starting catcher. He was an intelligent, good receiver with a quality arm. His smart play aided in the turnaround of the Hawks pitching staff. Tolomeo was a consistent hitter before and after Morhardt.

Freshman Joe Bellino hailed from Waterbury, where he was All-City, All-Conference, and All-State for Holy Cross. His role in his first year at Hartford was as the backup infielder and the DH against right-handed starters.

Dashing Brian Bushwell came by way of Livingston (New Jersey) High and North Carolina State, from which he transferred to Hartford. His father, Ron, was All-Conference in basketball at UConn in 1953-1956. For Brian, 1988 was the first year of eligibility. The speedy lead-off hitter flourished under Morhardt as well, improving from .231/0/4 at NC State to .355/0/29 in 1988 for Hartford.

Freshman Mike Scrapchansky from Killingly, Connecticut, was All-Conference and All-State twice. His role in 1988 was as Hartford's backup outfielder and the DH against left-handed starters. Morhardt's tutelage helped Scrap to a .364/2/15 line in 1988.

David Greene, a junior catcher out of Fairfield Prep in Shelton, Connecticut, was a light-hitting, great-fielding utility man in 1987, making only one error in 38 chances at three different positions.

The Hawk pitching staff was a question mark going into the 1988 season. None of the Hartford hurlers had emerged as consistent and dependable performers in the previous season of 1987.

Additionally, the pitching staff was small. Although they would compete against teams that had up to 11 pitchers, there were only six moundsmen on the Hawks roster—and one of them, Bob Teachman, was injured and was unable to pitch until after the 30th game of the 1988 season.[7]

Mark Czarkowski, was a 6-foot-3, 190-pound junior, a lefty who started the '88 season designated for several roles: spot starter, long reliever, and closer. Czar played with Crowley at Newington High and was All Conference. His 0-8, 10.96 ERA with 15 hits per 9 innings average in 1987 didn't portend great things.

Gary Gallagher, a right-handed sophomore from East Walpole, Massachusetts, headed into 1988 as co-owner of the team record for wins (five in a season) and was the established ace of the staff with a 5-3 won-lost record and 3.76 ERA in 1987. His 1.21 WHIP stood out.

Tony Franco, a righty pitcher from Durham who played with Bagwell at Xavier, projected to be a spot starter and reliever in '88, following a year in which he did both and went 1-2 with an 8.72 ERA.

Mickey Garbeck, a lefty out of East Catholic High School in Manchester, Connecticut, was a junior. Recruited heavily by Big East teams before picking Hartford, Garbeck began to live up to expectations in 1987, shutting out Pace and winning the ECAC New England Pitcher of the Week. He projected to start in 1988.

Bob Teachman, a righty junior from Windsor (Connecticut) with an 0-4 WL and 15.68 ERA in 1987, projected to be a starter or a closer.

Keith Wiley, a junior righty from Orleans, Massachusetts, went 0-6 in 1987 despite throwing five complete games. Although his 6.21 ERA was unattractive, he allowed just 16 walks in 42 innings. He was projected to start.

Dan Gooley preached optimism before the start of the 1988 Hartford baseball season. He said his team's efforts would eventually result in a national championship but would first begin with the Hawks' first winning season since 1974.

Gooley looked to be correct about 1988 when the Hawks won six of their first eight games to start the season, all on a Southern road trip. The junket covered 1,500 miles from Hartford to North Carolina, Virginia, and Delaware as the Gooley Men faced Duke, Richmond, James Madison, and four other teams.

On March 18 in Greensboro, Bagwell and Steve Scialabba had two hits each as the Hawks won a close one over Cleveland State, 3-2. Gary Gallagher got the win. Bagwell's fifth-inning homerun was the difference-maker.[8]

Two days later, Hartford swept a pair from Duke in Durham. The Hawks took the opener, 8-1, on Al Tolomeo's three-run homer and Keith Wiley's five-hitter. (Bagwell tripled.) Hartford won the second game, 2-1, as southpaws Mickey Garbeck and Mark Czarkowski combined for 13 K's.[9]

On March 21, Hartford hammered William and Mary, 13-2, in Williamsburg. Hedge had three hits. Bushwell, Peterson, Crowley, and Tolomeo had eight of the Hawks' 15 hits. Hedge homered. Tony Franco scattered seven hits over nine innings for Hartford.[10]

It was apparent something special was happening. The Hawks earned their fourth win in only their fourth game. The prior year it had taken 16 games to record four wins.

On the 22nd, Hartford took its first loss while in Richmond, losing 8-3 to Virginia Commonwealth even though the Hawks outhit the Rams 12 to 9. Hartford stranded 13 runners. Gary Gallagher took the loss.[11]

It would be an understatement to say that the Hawks bounced back from their first loss. In the next two games, they outscored their opponents 40-11.

On March 23, Hartford spanked Richmond 20-11 in Richmond and the headline in the *Courant* said, "Bagwell hits three consecutive homers." Bagwell started the day with a single. He drove his next three hits out of Pitt Field. Peterson and Hedge also homered as part of Hartford's 23-hit attack. The Hawks scored in all nine innings.[12]

The very next day Hartford's Keith Wiley, the ace-to-be on his way to a 9-2/2.88 season, tossed a three-hit shutout at the James Madison Dukes in Harrisonburg. Hartford won, 20-0. Bagwell hit his fifth homer of the season, tying the single-season team record. Home runs were also hit by Mike Scrapchansky, Crowley, backup catcher David Greene, and Hedge. Hedge's came with the bases full of Hawks. It was a merciless pounding. Seventeen Hartfords batted in the third inning, 11 of them scoring.[13]

Coming off those two heady wins, Hartford had one last game on the trip. It was against Delaware in Newark, Delaware, on March 25. Hawks starter Tony Franco was quickly solved by the Fighting Blue Hens. Despite Todd Reynolds' three hits and dingers from Crowley and Tolomeo, Delaware crushed Hartford, 12-3.[14]

The junket had ended on a losing note but Gooley's optimism proved to be well-founded. In eight games Hartford scored 70 runs. They won by an average of eight runs per game. Hedge already had three home runs. Bagwell tied the season team record with five. The offensive contributions came from up and down the lineup.

The pitching showed promise. Keith Wiley had pitched two complete games, allowing just one run in 18 innings. Mark Czarkowski had been effective and at times unhittable in 12 innings of relief. Franco fired a seven-hitter. Gallagher gave the Hawks a chance to win in both of his starts, losing only when the Hawks bats sputtered. Mickey Garbeck had given them four solid innings in the first game, another win.

Next, they played a doubleheader against the Elis at historic Yale Field on March 27. The road-tested Hawks split the twin bill, winning the first game, 8-7, and losing the second, 7-3. Bagwell homered in both games.[15]

There were still two more games to be played before the 7-3 Hawks would play at home at Ray McKenna Field in East Hartford.

On March 29 Hartford defeated Fairfield, 9-4, at Alumni Field. Brian Bushwell starred with three hits and two walks. Peterson homered. Crowley tripled and had two RBIs. Wiley lasted into the eighth.[16]

On March 31 the Hawks embarrassed Holy Cross, 20-0, in Worcester. Czarkowski yielded two hits in six shutout innings. Bagwell, Crowley, and Peterson each had three hits. Bagwell had four RBIs and four other Hawks knocked in two runs each. Hartford base runners were abundant. They got 16 hits. They drew 16 walks.[17]

With a 9-3 record and the best start in Hartford history, the Hawks cracked the seal on their home schedule by sweeping Dartmouth, 4-3 (in 12 innings) and 3-0, on April 2. Lefty Mickey Gerbeck hurled a complete-game four-hit shutout in the first game, and Crowley hit a dinger. Freshman DH Joe Bellino hit a walk-off homer in the 12th inning to win the second game.[18]

A CONSISTENT LAD IN THE LAND OF STEADY HABITS

On April 5 the Hawks set the school record for victories in a season, earning their 12th with a 7-1 win over URI in Kingston, Rhode Island. Wiley got his fourth win (4-0), a six-hit complete game. Crowley homered and Reynolds had two hits including a dinger. Best of all, Hartford made the New England Coaches Poll for the first time ever that week, landing in third place, behind only UMass and UConn.[19]

On April 6 Brian Crowley hit in his 15th consecutive game, getting two hits including a home run to lead the Hawks to a 5-3 win over C.W. Post at McKenna Field. Hartford scored two unearned runs on an error by Post's shortstop. Franco (3-1) got the win with four scoreless innings in relief.[20]

Hartford's six-game winning streak ended on April 7 against New England top-ranked UMass and its star shortstop, Gary DiSarcina. Hartford was down 5-0 after five innings but clawed its way back to a 5-5 tie. DiSarcina had a career day, getting five hits in six at-bats, with a double, home run, and four RBIs. The Minutemen shortstop won it with a walk-off double in the bottom of the 11th inning at Lorden Field in Amherst. The final score was 6-5.[21]

The Hawks lost consecutive games just twice in 1988. The loss to UMass on April 7 started one losing skein. The next game, the first of a doubleheader versus the University of New Hampshire in Durham on April 9, completed it. The double dip started with a 6-2 defeat as Wildcats starter Joe Teixeira tossed a seven-hit complete game and hit a home run to boot.[22]

The second game was another pummeling of opposing moundsmen by Hartford batters, a 19-11 victory. This time Hedge homered twice and tripled. Four of his teammates also went yard: Bagwell, Peterson, Crowley, and Scrapchansky. Bagwell's dinger was his eighth of the year, another new record.[23]

The hit parade continued the very next day, April 10, in the third consecutive game against New Hampshire. Hedge, Reynolds, and Bushwell homered in a 17-1 win in their final game in Durham. Hedge and Bagwell each had four hits in four at-bats. Reynolds and Scialabba had three RBIs each and Scialabba tripled. Wiley threw a seven-hit complete game and went to 5-0.[24]

Hartford's dream season continued two days later in Providence against Brown when Pat Hedge's three-run home run keyed a four-run rally. Crowley tripled. Bagwell doubled. Gallagher notched a complete-game victory. Hawks 8, Bruins 3.[25]

On April 14, Hartford lost to the number-2 UConn Huskies by a score of 7-6 in Storrs. Down 7-1 after five innings, Bagwell's three hits helped the Hawks close the gap to one run but UConn's Craig Gaudio shut Hartford down in the eighth and ninth innings. By losing this game, third-ranked Hartford had lost one-run games to both number-1 UMass and number-2 UConn.[26]

On April 16, Hartford split a doubleheader with Central Connecticut State at Beehive. They lost 3-1 with Al Donovan on the mound for Central. There were no extra-base hits for Hartford against Donovan. It is fair to say that Donovan excelled against Hartford, having no-hit the Hawks in 1987.[27]

Bagwell led Hartford to an 8-1 win in the second game with three hits and two doubles. Brian Crowley homered. The next day Central freshman Ed Malley beat Hartford, 3-2, limiting them to five hits and going the distance.[28]

And then Bagwell and the Hawks took down UConn.

UConn beat Hartford all three times they had ever played before their meeting on April 19. But the headline in the next day's *Manchester Journal Inquirer* said, "Bagwell's Homer Stuns UConn." Hartford won a nail biter, 5-4, on a Bagwell walk-off home run in the bottom of the 11th inning. Czarkowski won in relief after Franco was superb for 6⅓ innings, allowing just one run.[29]

Through the first 26 games of 1988, the Hawks won 18. They scored 17 runs or more five times. They blew out their opponents by 10 or more runs six times. They outscored their opponents 204-97. The U Hartford single-season record for wins by a pitcher and home runs by a player, and the team record for wins in a season had all been broken with 10 games left in the regular season.

The Crunch Bunch rollicked on.

On April 20 the Hawks banged out 15 hits, defeating Providence on the road, 11-8. Wiley recorded his sixth win, a new team record. Crowley and Reynolds homered and Hedge tripled.[30]

The team journeyed to Burlington, Vermont, for a doubleheader on April 23, splitting the pair. In a 14-4 opening win, Hartford got 14 hits. Tolomeo had a three-RBI triple. Bagwell and Hedge each singled and doubled and had two RBIs. Crowley tripled, Reynolds stroked three singles, and Wiley raised his record win total to seven.[31]

The next day was getaway day for the Hawks. Before heading home they fell behind 5-0 but scored five in the eighth inning and won 7-6. Todd Reynolds went 2-for-4. Czarkowski won in relief, raising his record to 5-0.[32]

The Hawks crushed another opponent, this time Fairfield, on April 26 as Bagwell hit his 11th home run. Reynolds and Crowley led the team with four hits each, Reynolds blasting two home runs and Crowley three doubles. Peterson and Hedge had three hits each, one of Hedge's a circuit blast with the bases loaded. When the thrashing was over at Ray McKenna Field in East Hartford, the Hawks had defeated Fairfield 22-1, with Teachman and Czarkowski pitching a combined four-hitter.[33]

The competition for the next two games, which were played on April 27 at McKenna, was the Maine Black Bears. Maine is a traditional baseball powerhouse in New England. Hartford dearly wanted to beat Maine and extend the impression the team made by winning two of three from them in 1987. By taking the series in Orono in 1987, the Hawks became the first team to defeat Maine in a home series since 1971.[34]

A CONSISTENT LAD IN THE LAND OF STEADY HABITS

In the first game, Hartford blew a 6-1 lead as Mark Sweeney homered to drive in the winning runs in an 8-7 Maine win. Sweeney, drafted and signed in 1991 by the Angels, subsequently got 175 pinch-hits, the second-highest pinch-hit total in major-league history.[35]

The loss to Maine was the last time the Hawks were defeated in the 1988 regular season.

In the second game of the doubleheader Peterson and Bagwell homered and helped to build a 10-1 lead by the third inning. Maine hit five home runs off Gary Gallagher, who threw a complete game, but in the end Hartford earned a split, 12-7.[36]

Just three games were left before the postseason and Hartford ran the table. They swept Northeastern at McKenna, 10-6 and 2-1. Reynolds got three hits and Hedge hit another grand slam in the first game. Bagwell ended Jim Walker's run at a no-hitter with a single in the seventh inning of the second game and the Hawks earned the sweep on two runs via a Brian Crowley home run and a sacrifice fly by Al Tolomeo.[37]

The final game of the 1988 Hartford regular season was not a nail biter. On May 1 at McKenna, the Hawks beat Northeastern 14-3, with Hartford scoring seven runs in the fourth inning and Wiley hurling a complete-game victory to end the season at nine wins against one loss.[38]

Regular season record: 26-10.

"Baseball Hawks Win ECAC Tourney Berth," said the headline in the *Hartford Courant* on May 7, 1988.[39]

The Cinderella Hawks left behind their 11-27 record of 1987, not to mention their 8-34, 2-24, and 0-15 records of 1986, 1985, and 1984, respectively.

Dan Gooley was gracious and gratified. "I'm thrilled to death. ...When I came on, things were a little disjointed. ... Nobody really knew me. Nobody knew my assistants (Randy LaVigne and Moe Morhardt). But things came around because of a mutual respect and loyalty to each other. ... I have really come to love this team."[40]

The 1988 ECAC Division I Baseball Tournament was set for May 19 to 22 at Beehive Field in New Britain and the winner would earn an automatic entry into the Northeast Regional of the NCAA Division I Tournament.[41]

Five of the six teams in the ECAC Tournament earned their berth by capturing their conference regular-season championship. Hartford was the only at-large selection. The seeding for this double-elimination tournament was as follows: Number 1, Maine (32-22); 2, Fairleigh Dickinson (24-11); 3, Hartford (26-10); 4, Fordham (32-11), 5, C.W. Post (26-14); 6, LeMoyne (26-9-1).[42]

The field was loaded with talent. Farleigh Dickinson hit .342 and stole 96 bases in 120 attempts. Maine featured Sweeney (.394, 10 HRs) and an outstanding reliever in Mike LeBlanc. LeMoyne had four players batting over .390 and righty pitcher Peter Hoy (6-2, 1.68), who would reach the majors with Boston four years later. C.W. Post had .400 hitters in Mark Imbasciani and Julio Morales and a stingy righty starter in Jim McCauley, 8-3, 2.10. The Fordham Rams, the defending ECAC champions, had speed and hitting to go with starters Paul Darrigo (8-1) and Paul LoGuidice (9-1).[43]

Like Fordham, the Hartford Hawks now brought well-established pitching to the competition, too.

Hartford's pitching was not expected to be their strength in 1988. But their hurlers had improved greatly under the guidance of Gooley, LaVigne, and Morhardt. The team ERA dropped from 6.32 in 1987 to 4.02 in 1988.

Wiley and Czarkowski were cases in point. Wiley improved from 0-6/6.21 in 1987 to 8-1/2.87 in 1988. He pitched twice as many innings (42 vs. 81) while reducing his walks (16 vs. 13) and doubling his strikeouts (21 vs. 45) in 1988.

Czarkowski had been persuaded by Athletic Director Don Cook not to transfer to Trinity after the firing of Coach Bill Denehy in April 1987.[44] Czar flourished under his new Hartford coaches. He headed into 1988 with a 0-8/8.85 record at Hartford. He turned in a 6-0/2.25 season, his confidence surging as he threw from three different arm angles to baffle batters.[45]

Despite the fact that Hawks pitching was much improved, it had a striking limitation. Hartford still had only six pitchers. In the ECAC Tournament field, only Fairleigh Dickinson had that small a staff. C.W. Post had 10 hurlers. Fordham had 11. LeMoyne had 9, and Maine had 11.[46]

Pitching was indeed the determining factor when Hartford took on Fordham in the first ECAC Tournament game on May 20, 1988, at Beehive. Wiley yielded two runs in the first innings on two walks, an error, and a passed ball. The Rams hit Wiley for three more scores in the fourth as they sent 10 men to the plate. At the end of four innings, Fordham led 7-0.

Czarkowski relieved Wiley and limited further damage but Fordham's Paul Darrigo scattered six hits over nine innings, containing Bagwell, Hedge, Cowley, and Petersen. The only Hartford offense came as Tolomeo, Bellino, and Bushwell scratched out two runs on just one hit in the fifth. The final was Fordham 7, Hartford 2.[47]

It took just one Ram to silence the Crunch Bunch. Darrigo had throttled the Hawks and Fordham showed it would be tough. They were the reigning champion and had brought back many players from the 1987 title team, Darrigo included.[48]

Ironically, Darrigo felt he started poorly. "I didn't have my good fastball," said the righty from Miller Place, New York. It took me two or three innings to find the curve, my best pitch. But we got the victory. That's really important, especially in double elimination."[49]

After the game, Hartford stood 0-1 along with LeMoyne and C.W. Post, the other first-round losers. Losing another game meant going home. Gooley was plain about the situation: "This is a tough way to start out, in the loser's bracket. It's vicious the rest of the way out. We'll find out what we're made of now."[50]

On May 21, the Hawks faced the Black Bears of Maine, who had nipped LeMoyne, 2-1. The results were completely opposite to the loss to Fordham. Hartford jumped out to a 7-0 lead and Hawks pitching dominated the Bears.[51]

The Hawks' Gary Gallagher entered the game with a career 8.24 ERA against Maine but this day he went the distance, striking out four, allowing no bases on balls, and throwing 77 strikes out of his 102 pitches.[52]

With all that said, Gallagher was actually hittable. He allowed 13 hits over nine innings. But Tolomeo thought Gallagher showed "the best pop he's had on his fastball all season." Gallagher agreed, saying his heater "tailed away nicely from the lefties and the Bears swung early on his split-finger."[53] Helped by error-free fielding and a successful hidden-ball trick executed by Scialabba, the righty from East Walpole carried a shutout into the ninth before finally yielding two runs.[54]

Meanwhile the Hawks offense pelted Maine pitching with 15 hits. Home runs by Pat Hedge and Brian Crowley were respectively described by Gooley as a "blast" and "titanic." Bagwell and Hedge had three hits each.[55]

At the end of tournament play through two games, Farleigh Dickinson sat atop the pile with a 2-0 record, having beaten Fordham 6-5 in 14 innings in the second round. Fordham was now in the same position as Hartford, C.W. Post, and Maine: holding a 1-1 record and one loss away from elimination. Le Moyne lost the first two games and was out.

The rest of the road to an ECAC championship for Hartford was challenging. The Hawks would have to defeat C.W. Post on May 22, and then win a morning-afternoon doubleheader on May 23.[56] But winning four games in a row was plausible. They had done it three times in the regular season.

Mark Czarkowski started the game against Post. Czar was on one day of rest, having relieved in the opening loss to Fordham. He pitched the first three innings, allowing four runs and four hits. In the end, the Hawks defeated Post, 10-6, and the win went to reliever Tony Franco, who did better, yielding two runs over the last six innings. Still, Czarkowski was the hurler who made the most memorable play in the game when in the third inning he fielded a sharp grounder, was unable to free the ball from his glove, and recorded the assist by tossing the glove and ball to first baseman Peterson ahead of the runner.[57]

Against Post, the Hawks offense maintained the form it found against Maine, banging out 13 hits. Crowley had three singles and scored three times. Pat Hedge hit his 10th home run of the year. Bagwell was 4-for-5 with two doubles and four RBIs. "I know we can win this thing because we can hit with anybody," he said. "As long as pitchers throw strikes and we play defense, we're going to score runs. We all have confidence, the pitchers and the hitters."[58]

The table was set for a historic doubleheader on May 23. Hartford spirits were high. Bagwell and company had dropped the opening game, 7-2, and roared back in winning the next two games by a combined 18-8. Now they would start Wiley (8-2/3.12) against Farleigh Dickinson at 10:30 A.M. and, assuming a win, would have lefty Mickey Garbeck (2-2/6.77) on the mound for the ECAC championship against Fordham at 1:30 P.M.[59]

Hartford embarrassed Farleigh Dickinson in the morning game, 24-2. Old Scrap Iron, Todd Reynolds, had nine RBIs in the game. The Hawks second baseman had two doubles, a single, and two sacrifice flies. His double-play partner, Steve Scialabba, went 5-for-5 at the plate, including a double.[60] Hedge homered twice and Bagwell hit a dinger. Hartford had 26 hits in the game. Wiley, the ace, went the distance, allowing two runs on nine hits with eight strikeouts and no bases on balls.[61]

The afternoon championship game against Fordham was a gut-wrencher. After Garbeck allowed the Rams a run in the first inning, the Hawks pounded Paul LoGiudice for six runs of their own.[62] Todd Reynolds stroked an RBI single. Hedge also singled and drove in two more. Al Tolomeo clocked a two-RBI double. After 2½ innings, Hartford had a nice lead, 6-1, and the path to a title was clearer than ever.[63]

But Mickey Garbeck faltered for the Hawks in the fourth inning when he walked four consecutive Rams, then allowed a single by Kevin Condon. Three Fordham runs scored. Hartford led 6-4 at the end of four.[64]

Yet, things were still looking good for Hartford. If their pitching could hold together for five more innings, it could end well.

But things did not end well. James Crowley's home video tells the story with clarity, as follows:

> *In the top half of the seventh, the Hawks took an 8-4 lead after Crowley slammed a two-out double and Bagwell followed with a homerun over the center-field wall. Crowley high-fived Petersen after touching the plate.*

No one could blame them for this modest celebration.

Gary Gallagher took the mound to face Fordham in the bottom of the seventh with a four-run Hartford lead.

> *Gallagher quickly got Tom McManus on a ball to Bagwell at third. The next batter, Ray Montgomery, hit the first pitch for a single to left. Chris Faicco then drilled a 1-0 offering from Gallagher to left for a double. Next, in a critical play, Matt Brown popped one up behind the plate and the Hawk catcher Tolomeo set up under it for what should have been out number two.*

A CONSISTENT LAD IN THE LAND OF STEADY HABITS

Tolomeo's mitt wasn't quite open on impact and the ball bounced safely off the top of the glove. Five pitches later Brown walked to load the bases. Tom Levy promptly lined a Gallagher pitch off the Brass Lion Cafe sign on the left-field wall for a three-RBI double. The score was now 8-7, with one out and a Ram runner at the keystone.

Dan Gooley decided to not test Gallagher further. He brought in Czarkowski, who had pitched the day before against Post. The next batter, Jack Allen, knocked a single into centerfield, scoring Levy and the score was tied, 8-8.

Czar got the second out of the inning when Mike Anquillare grounded out to Reynolds at second base.

Then the Hartford defense and Lady Luck gave Fordham two go-ahead runs.

Reynolds misplayed a groundball for an error, Kevin Condon reaching base. Then Brad Howland hit a routine grounder to Scrap at shortstop for the potential inning-ending out. The ball high-hopped sharply just as it reached Scrap's glove, sailing into centerfield.

Allen scored easily. Condon slid home safely ahead of Hedge's throw from center. Czar got the last out on a grounder to Reynolds, 4-3.

Both teams failed to score in the eighth.

Fordham 10, Hartford 8. Hartford needed a ninth-inning rally to continue the dream.

Mike Scrapchansky led off the ninth for the Hawks. He beat a grounder to the Fordham second baseman who mishandled it and declined to throw. A noisy U Hartford crowd called for a rally.

Todd Reynolds lifted a fly that had a very good chance to fall in for a safe hit but the Ram right fielder sprinted and dove under it, turning a hit into out #1.

Brian Crowley stepped in. The first pitch danced past his toes on its way to the backstop. Scrap advanced to second base. Crow hit a chopper to second, out 4 to 3, and Scrap stood at third base with two outs. Now it was Bagwell's turn.

The young third baseman from Killingworth, relaxed and focused, stepped into the box. Seconds later Fordham coach Mike Bruehart halted the proceedings, visiting the mound and spoke with Fordham's lefty hurler, Bob Aylmer. Bruehart went back to the dugout and Aylmer went to work, his first pitch skidding in the dirt under Bagwell's feet. Ball One. The next pitch sailed inside and low but caught the plate. Strike One. The third offering was outside and the count stood 2-and-1. Bags then fouled off the fourth pitch, swinging viciously, his momentum carried him across the plate and toward first. 2 and 2, now. Alymer looked in and took a beat before the fifth pitch. The next toss came in high and hard with a slight drop at the end. Bagwell swung and missed. It was a beautiful and explosive swing that just missed, a millisecond slow.

It was Bagwell's 10th strikeout in 187 plate appearances that year.

Bob Aylmer raised both arms and turned to his dugout. The Fordham Rams charged the field, forming a scrum in front of the mound. The Hartford Hawks quickly reached their dugout, silent.

There would be no ECAC crown for the University of Hartford and the young prince of Connecticut baseball.

As Fordham celebrated, Czarkowski, who finished the game for the Hawks, stood at the back of the line with his face lowered, covering his eyes and holding his head in hands. He took a moment, wiped his tears and got behind the sturdy Hedge at the back of the line.

Maybe the tears flowed because the Hawks had come so close to a crown. Or maybe because the tying and go-ahead runs had scored with him on the mound. Maybe it was just because this wild ride of a baseball season was over. Or maybe it was for all those reasons.

After the cordial hand-shaking, both teams retreated from the field and presentations began. Fordham's Dan Gallagher accepted the tournament championship plaque. Four members of the Hartford Hawks were All-Tournament: shortstop Steve Scialabba, third baseman Jeff Bagwell, centerfielder Pat Hedge, and leftfielder Brian Bushwell. Hedge, who had four homeruns and 11 RBIs in five tournament games, was also the Tournament MVP.

The awards put a bittersweet ending on a day in which the Hartford Hawks had played twice, scoring 34 runs and allowing 10 while losing the ECAC tournament and an invitation to the NCAA dance.

The 10-8 loss to Fordham was disappointing, yet 1988 had been a smashing success for the Hartford Hawks.

According to the *Hartford Courant* (May 24, 1988), Gooley was named Coach of the Year by the New England Baseball Coaches Association and Peterson and Bagwell were named to the All-New England first team. Hedge and Wiley made the second team.

The 1988 season was a blend of new coaches and a talented, previously underestimated, pool of players. Gooley, Lavigne and Morhardt taught and led with elevated insights and a new spirit. The team responded with stunning results all season long.

In the words of Jim Keener, sports information director for the 1988 Hawks, "You could not have put together that collection of people and personalities intentionally.

A CONSISTENT LAD IN THE LAND OF STEADY HABITS

It was as much about the people as it was about the talent. Take away one of those people, take away Todd Reynolds, for instance, and it's not the same team."[65]

SOURCES

Unless otherwise indicated, all baseball data comes from the 1987, 1988, and 1989 University of Hartford Baseball Media Guides.

NOTES

1. Karl Cicitto interview with Brian Crowley, November 18, 2017.
2. Dave Borges, "Xavier Part of Bagwell's Legacy," *Middletown Press*, January 19, 2017: 22.
3. Jim Bransfield, *Middletown Press*, June 7, 1989: 17.
4. "Hawks' Crowley Hits 4 Straight HRs," *Hartford Courant*, April 16, 1989: E16.
5. "Scholastic Football Preview," under Shoreline/Morgan, *Hartford Courant*, Sept. 9, 1984: D12.
6. George Smith, "Hartford's Crunch Bunch," *Hartford Courant*, May 4, 1988: F1.
7. Owen Canfield, "Give Gooley Letter S for Success," *Hartford Courant*, April 28, 1988: G6.
8. "In the News," *Hartford Courant*, March 19, 1988: E2.
9. "In the News," *Hartford Courant*, March 21, 1988: C5.
10. "Hartford Remains Undefeated," *Hartford Courant*, March 22, 1988: D2.
11. "VCU Hands Hartford 1st Loss," *Hartford Courant*, March 23, 1988: F8.
12. "Bagwell Hits Three Consecutive Homers," *Hartford Courant*, March 23, 1988: F8.
13. "Hartford Blows Out Madison," *Hartford Courant*, March 25, 1988: E8.
14. "Colleges," *Hartford Courant*, March 26, 1988: C9.
15. "UConn Sweeps…Hartford Splits Two with Yale," *Hartford Courant*, March 28, 1988: C5.
16. "Hartford Downs Fairfield 9-4," *Bridgeport Telegram*, March 30, 1988: 20.
17. "Hartford Dumps Holy Cross, 20-0," *Hartford Courant*, April 1, 1988: D4.
18. "Colleges," *Hartford Courant*, April 3, 1988: D7.
19. "Wiley Wins Fourth for 12-3 Hartford," *Hartford Courant*, April 6, 1988: D11.
20. "Hartford Wins 13th, Beats C.W. Post," *Hartford Courant*, April 7, 1988: D2.
21. "UMass Ends Hawks' Winning Streak at 6," *Hartford Courant*, April 8, 1988: E4.
22. "Wildcats Split," *Portsmouth* (New Hampshire) *Herald*, April 10, 1988: 19.
23. Ibid.
24. "Wiley Wins Fifth as Hartford Romps, 17-1," *Hartford Courant*, April 11, 1988: B6.
25. U of H Clip files: "Hedge and Crowley Star as Hartford Whips Brown," 8-3.
26. "UConn Defeats Hartford, 7-6," *Hartford Courant*, April 15, 1988: E4.
27. "Central, Hartford Split Doubleheader," *Hartford Courant*, April 7, 1988: E14.

28 "Central Defeats Hartford," *Hartford Courant,* April 18, 1988: B3.

29 "Bagwell's Homer Stuns UConn," *Journal Inquirer,* April 2, 1988: 44.

30 "Hartford Offense Too Strong for Providence," *Journal Inquirer,* April 21, 1988: 38.

31 "Hartford Splits with Vermont," *Hartford Courant,* April 24, 1988:E4.

32 "Hawks Overcome 5-Run Deficit," *Hartford Courant,* April 26, 1988: D2.

33 "Hawks Get 22 Hits, Rip Fairfield, 22-1," *Hartford Courant,* April 27, 1988: D4.

34 "Hartford Raps Maine 12-7, Salvages Split," *Hartford Courant,* April 28, 1988: G6.

35 Ibid.

36 Ibid.

37 Colleges, "Nagy Strikes Out 17...," *Hartford Courant.* May 1, 1988: E4.

38 Colleges, "Central Rallies…," *Hartford Courant,* May 2, 1988: D2.

39 Michael Arace, "Baseball Hawks Win ECAC Tourney Berth," *Hartford Courant,* May 7, 1988: C3.

40 Ibid.

41 Ibid.

42 "Hawks Seeded Third in ECAC Tourney," *New Britain Herald,* May 10, 1988: 12.

43 George Smith, "ECAC Division I" Capsules, *Hartford Courant,* May 19, 1988: C3.

44 George Smith, "U of H's Small Pitching Corps Handed a Large Assignment," *Hartford Courant,* May 19, 1988: 53.

45 Ibid.

46 1988 ECAC Tournament Program.

47 Smith, "Fordham Takes Command Early to Stop Hartford 7-2 in Tourney," *Hartford Courant,* May 21, 1988: E3.

48 Owen Canfield, "Plenty of Stars at Muzzy….," *Hartford Courant,* May 21, 1988: E3.

49 Ibid.

50 Smith, "Fordham Takes Command Early to Stop Hartford 7-2 in Tourney."

51 Smith, "Hartford Beats Maine 8-2," *Hartford Courant,* May 22, 1988: D17.

52 Larry Mahoney, "Hartford Whips Punchless Bears," *Bangor Daily News,* May 22, 1988: 9.

53 Ibid.

54 Ibid.

55 Chris Elsberry, "Hartford Remains Alive in ECAC Baseball Tourney," *Bridgeport Post,* May 22, 1988: 22.

56 Smith, "Hartford Beats Maine 8-2," *Hartford Courant,* May 22, 1988: D17.

57 Robert P. Mayer, "Hawks Corral C.W. Post in ECAC Tourney Play," *New Britain Herald,* May 23, 1988: 15.

58 Smith, "Hartford Keeps NCAA Hopes Alive," *Hartford Courant,* May 23, 1988: D3.

59 Smith, "Fordham Walks Over Hartford, 10-8," *Hartford Courant,* May 24, 2018: E1.

60 Ibid.

61 "Colleges," *Hartford Courant,* May 24, 1988: E7.

62 Ibid.
63 Dave Solomon, "Hartford Edged in ECAC final," *New Haven Register*, May 24, 2018: 51.
64 Ibid.
65 Karl Cicitto interview with Jim Keener, January 2, 2018.

The Crunch Bunch. L-R, Jeff Bagwell, Pat Hedge, Brian Crowley and Chris Petersen. (Courtesy of University of Hartford Archives and Special Collections.)

Todd Reynolds: An Unassuming Soul

By Jim Keener

It was a cold, blustery November day when I visited the final resting place of Todd Reynolds in his hometown of Norfolk, Connecticut. The arrival of the new year in January 2018 marked 29 years since Todd lost his life in a car accident. He continues to be in the thoughts of many, including myself, especially during 2017, during which we celebrated the induction of Todd's former teammate Jeff Bagwell into the National Baseball Hall of Fame.

The 1988 University of Hartford baseball team, with Bagwell and Reynolds among an extraordinary cast of characters, is the most successful in the program's history (29-12). Conversations about the team were threaded throughout the Bagwell narrative throughout the summer of '17. I know Todd would have been pleased that his teammates' accomplishments were being remembered and applauded.

Todd was many things—reserved, hard-working, and talented, to name a few. He was an unassuming soul whose approach to playing the game set the tone for the team. Todd was revered by his teammates. So much that first baseman Chris Petersen named his first son after him.

"Todd was the epitome of a team player," said Petersen. "His play almost went unnoticed, but that anonymity was undeserving. Todd was a prolific hitter and should have been included as a member of the 'Crunch Bunch' (the nickname for the team's group of prolific hitters). However, it didn't bother him because he was happy to be part of something bigger."[1]

Petersen continued, "Todd appreciated everyone for who they were and got along with everyone. He had an innocence to him but was also mature in his own way. His work ethic and unselfishness were contagious."[2]

As the interim head baseball coach in 1984, I recruited Todd Reynolds. I did not realize at the time how important and personally gratifying the decision would be. When I took over the job, I was told to recruit one player. It was suggested by Associate Athletics Director Roger Wickman that I take a look at a shortstop at Wilbraham Munson Academy in Wilbraham, Massachusetts, Todd Reynolds. Coach

Wickman, who was the University of Hartford's head coach for many years, had a son-in-law as the athletics director at Wilbraham.

Todd was prepping at Wilbraham Munson after attending Wamogo High School in Litchfield, Connecticut, where he played both basketball and baseball. A first team All-Berkshire League selection, Todd was a two-time baseball captain and hit .446 with 31 stolen bases as a junior. He did not strike out in 150 league plate appearances the last two years. He excelled on the basketball court as the starting point guard. At 5-feet-10 and 175 pounds, Todd was physically as solid as a rock.

It was a cool, damp day in Wilbraham when I sat in the cab of my blue truck and evaluated Todd. As I recall, he had a couple of hits and fielded a few balls without incident at shortstop. He seemed like someone who could help the team. I met with him after the game and eventually offered him a scholarship to the University. His family was grateful. The Reynolds were a blue-collar family from the northwest hills of Connecticut. Todd's father, Hubie, was a sheet-metal worker and his mother, Maureen, worked for the Hartford Insurance Company.

Todd's first three years at Hartford were met with mixed results in the classroom and on the diamond. He started with an undeclared major in the College of Arts and Sciences, then enrolled in Ward Technical College hoping to become a civil engineer. It was challenging, especially with baseball in play.

"I remember sitting with Todd at the kitchen table talking about his future," said Hubie. "I asked him if he wanted to put in the time necessary to be an engineer, or did he want to play baseball. Baseball was the answer."[3]

Todd eventually landed in the Barney School of Business, majoring in accounting.

On the diamond, he played in 26 games at shortstop as a freshman in 1985. Todd hit .258, but led the team in hits (25), runs (11), and total bases (31). He sat out his sophomore year in 1986 to focus on academics.

Todd returned in 1987, appearing in 15 games and starting 10 as a second baseman. He was limited to 36 at-bats that year and hit .222 after losing a starting job early in the season. It was deflating.

"The previous coaching staff (in 1987) didn't give me any confidence," said Todd back then. "I made an error and I felt like I was in the doghouse. I never got a chance to prove myself."[4]

Under first-year head coach Dan Gooley in 1988, the second-base job was Todd's to win or lose. With a strong fall season, and Gooley's display of confidence, Todd won the job.

In the spring, Reynolds started all of the Hawks' 41 games at second base and finished with a .384 BA and 45 RBIs. Named ECAC All-New England, Todd hit .451 over the final 16 games of the season and helped Hartford to a program-best 29-12 (.707) record and a trip to the championship game of the ECAC tournament. In one of the most memorable highlights of his career, Todd drove in an ECAC playoff record nine runs in a 24-2 victory over Fairleigh Dickinson University. That victory put the Hawks in the championship game.

"Todd was my roommate when I was a junior," said right-handed pitcher Keith Wiley. "His soft demeanor was contrasted by the way he played the game. Todd had a great love for baseball and its old school ways—chewing tobacco, beer, and a dirty uniform. His positive attitude spread throughout his team and he quickly won a place in our hearts."[5]

Wiley gave Todd his nickname, "Nitter." As the story goes, Todd was asked by someone what number he wore. He stumbled in answering, and said, "I…ni…ni…nine." Wiley caught wind of it and came up with Nitter. It stuck.

Todd capped his collegiate career playing in the New England College Baseball All-Star game on May 31, 1988, at Fenway Park. The University Division squad (Division I) faced the College Division team (Divisions II and III) that day and head coach Dan Gooley brought him to the game as a reserve.

Todd replaced Boston College's Mike Nyhan in the sixth. He banged out an RBI triple that inning and had a key double in the University Division's four-run eighth to lead his team to a 7-4 victory. He was declared the game's unofficial MVP by Gooley.

"This was the highlight of my collegiate career," said Todd at the time. "It was like reaching the top of the pyramid."[6] The magnitude of the moment playing in such a historic venue was not lost on him. "It was a dream come true to play in Fenway," he said. "It was a great way to end my career in front of my family."[7] From bench-warmer to All-Star game MVP in a year's time.

Tuesday, January 17, 1989, was the day Todd died of injuries suffered in a car accident. He had attended a Greater Hartford Twilight League Awards Banquet at Willie's Steak House in Manchester, Connecticut, on Saturday night where he was named the League's Rookie-of-the-Year, Most Versatile and batting champion. Todd had led Moriarity Brothers to the league championship the summer before, hitting .493. After dropping off a friend in Manchester, he was driving home in his 1981 Toyota heading west on Route 44 in Barkhamsted when, at about 4:45 A.M., his car slid on a slick spot on the road and rammed a utility pole. He died of multiple traumas at Hartford Hospital two days later.

The Twilight League batting championship trophy has since been named in his honor.

Todd had taken classes in the fall of 1988 and was ready to take classes in the spring to finish his degree. He finished with 114 credits and was awarded a business degree, posthumously, by the University of Hartford. His mother accepted his diploma at the spring commencement.

As I said goodbye to Todd at St. Mary's Cemetery in Norfolk, I focused on the photo medallion on his crossed gravestone. It is one of his UHart media guide headshots. He is wearing his Hartford jersey and hat (with a thin interlocking UH). Todd's head was tilted and his pointed chin stood out. The most prominent parts of his facial features, however, were his warm eyes and self-deprecating smirk. In a Hartford uniform being Todd. I am sure it is how he would have liked to be remembered.

SOURCES

University of Hartford registrar's office.

University of Hartford, 1987 Baseball Media Guide.

Smith, George. "U of H Baseball Star 'Critical' After Car Crash," *Hartford Courant*, January 17, 1989.

Todd Reynolds obituary, *Hartford Courant*, January 19, 1989.

NOTES

1. Chris Petersen, email exchange, December 7, 2017.
2. Ibid.
3. Hubie Reynolds, phone conversation, December 6, 2017.
4. Gerry deSimas, "'Scrap Iron' Reynolds Loves the Game of Baseball," Spring 1988, *New Haven Register*, from the University of Hartford SID clip files.
5. Keith Wiley, email conversation, November 21, 2017.
6. Marvin Pave, "Reynolds Leads University Division Stars, 7-4," *Boston Globe*, June 1, 1988.
7. Ibid.

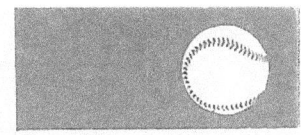

9
Todd Reynolds
2B Junior
Norfolk, CT

Height: 5-10   Bats: Right
Weight: 175   Throws: Right
High School: Wamogo

The
UNIVERSITY OF HARTFORD

Upon recommendation
of the Faculty of the Barney School of Business and Public Administration
and by the authority of the Board of Regents
the degree of

Bachelor of Science in Business Administration

is hereby conferred upon

Todd Michael Reynolds

in recognition
of the successful completion of the requirements for this degree,
together with all the associated honors, rights, and privileges.
Given under the seal of the University of Hartford,
Connecticut, May 19, 1991

_____
Chairman of the Board of Regents

_____      _____
President   Dean

_____   _____
Senior Vice President for Academic Affairs   Chair, Faculty Senate
and Dean of the Faculty

The University of Hartford posthumously conferred Todd's degree in 1991.

Todd's mother, Maureen, accepts Todd's degree. (Permission of the Reynolds family.)

Jeff Bagwell and the Cape Cod Baseball League

By Andrew Blume

The summers of 1987 and 1988 served as important landmark periods in the professional development of Jeff Bagwell. During that time, he would compete with and against the most talented class of future major-league players the Cape Cod Baseball League had ever seen at a time when the league's conversion from aluminum bats to wood bats served as the ultimate separator of the "pingers" from the "thwackers."

Bagwell had already proved his ability to hit with the aluminum at the college level as a University of Hartford Hawk. On the university's team he was a member of the "Crunch Bunch," a name given to a quartet of Hawks sluggers—Bagwell and teammates Pat Hedge, Brian Crowley, and Chris Peterson—during his time there from 1987 to 1989. The heart of the Hawks lineup combined for 209 hits and 159 RBIs in 36 games in 1988, leading Hartford to the ECAC tournament.[1] Bagwell's number 27 was retired by the school in 2004 after a college career in which he was both the school's all-time batting average leader (.413, with 165 hits in 400 at-bats) and its all-time slugging leader (.733, 31 homers, 126 RBIs). According to hartfordhawks.com, Bagwell commenced his college career as a shortstop, following up a 4-for-5 cycle-hitting, 4-run, 4-RBI performance with another 4-for-5 in his second game. However, his performance with the glove was not quite so stellar. Four errors in three games at shortstop moved Bagwell to third base, where he remained until he was traded by the Boston Red Sox to the Houston Astros organization.

After his freshman year at Hartford, Bagwell joined the Chatham Athletics, also known as the abbreviated "A's," of the Cape Cod Baseball League. After being an aluminum-bat league from 1974 to 1984, the Cape League returned to wood bats in 1985. Baseball writer Peter Gammons explained the significance for professional prospects of the move back to wood in Christopher Price's book *Baseball By the Beach*: "The move to wood back in '85 was huge. It took it to a place where guys could really prove they could really play. It also made things much easier for scouts, to gauge a hitter's ability."[2] The changeover to wood bats, noted baseball executive Dan Duquette in the book, "was probably the best step [the league] could have made at the time to assert themselves as the preeminent league in the country. The kids became serious about developing their skills for a pro career, and the teams that are scouting the league for talent became serious, and those two things came together."[3] The transition to wood was a difficult one for Bagwell in 1987; he hit just .208 in 32 games under manager John Mayotte, the team finishing sixth in the eight-team Cape League with a 17-25 record. While struggling to adapt to hitting with wood, Bagwell was saddled with the additional Cape League obligation to work to earn money for living expenses outside of the room and board traditionally covered by host families. Under NCAA rules, athletes with amateur eligibility remaining playing in a certified summer league that received a grant of $10,000 or greater "must be offered the opportunity to be gainfully employed in a real and necessary job. Compensation paid to such athletes for work performed must be commensurate with the going rate of that locale for service of like character, and shall be given for services actually performed."[4] Sham jobs were clearly not a fact of life in the Cape League, and Bagwell was put to work in the unglamorous position of washing dishes at the Chatham Friendly's Restaurant in 1987. It is subject to speculation whether dishpan hands contributed to his difficulties at the plate.

Whatever the reason, Bagwell's first summer's struggles at the plate could not be attributed to the lack of a professional work ethic. "Something my father instilled in me when I was a kid was to never quit," Bagwell said in his National Baseball Hall of Fame induction speech. "Don't quit at anything you ever try. I've pretty much stuck to that. There are certain situations that I wish I had quit, a couple of jobs that I had. I was a dishwasher at Friendly's in Cape Cod. I should've quit that. Sometimes I probably should've quit baseball, too, but deep inside of me I just never gave up."[5] College summers in the Cape Cod League marked the first time Bagwell thought he could play professionally. His work ethic made it happen. Twenty-nine-year (as of 2017) Dartmouth College baseball coach Robert Whalen took over as Chatham's manager in 1988 and knew Bagwell from his previous employment as an associate head coach at the University of Maine.

Whalen raved about that work ethic in interviews with this writer and the Cape Cod league public-relations office. "I had the pleasure of watching Jeff play in high school and at Hartford University and I had the distinct privilege of coaching him in Chatham in the summer 1988. He was a terrific player that had a great presence about him wherever he went. I realized two things about him right away: First, he did not want to be good, he wanted to be great, in every aspect of the game. Second, he made the commitment to becoming a major-league player every day. Many kids enjoy the competition and status of being in the Cape League but Jeff showed up for early workouts every day to work at getting better. Jeff is one of the most loyal and hardest working players I've ever coached. He put the numbers up and earned this (Hall of Fame) distinction on his own," Whalen told the Cape League public-relations office.[6]

"He played the game hard," Whalen told this writer, echoing his previous sentiments. "He showed up every day, wanted groundballs at third and to hit. He recognized the importance to set a daily schedule in a way he could get better all the time. Wherever he was in the lineup was fine to him."[7]

Bagwell's willingness to play wherever the team needed him was demonstrated by a memory of an A's catcher who sustained a concussion in a game, whereupon Bagwell went to the manager with an offer to catch despite his lack of experience with the position. Whalen opined that Bagwell made himself a really good third baseman, and had "no doubt" he could have excelled at that position in the professional ranks.[8]

Bagwell's work ethic combined with a high baseball IQ during his college years. His college coach, Dan Gooley, told John Altavilla of the *Hartford Courant* that his initial impression upon meeting Bagwell in 1988 and shaking his hand was that his hand "was that of a blacksmith. That was my first impression and it foreshadowed the high work ethic and commitment Jeff represented throughout my time with him. I knew he was going to be something special."[9] Brian Crowley, Bagwell's fellow "Crunch Bunch"-er and the Hawks rightfielder during Bagwell's college tenure, noted his instincts and feel for hitting: "Jeff Bagwell could slow the game down like no other — 95 mph, 70 mph, overhand, underhand or side-arm — if the ball crossed the plate he hammered it…to all fields. The best hitter I have ever seen, hands down."[10]

Bagwell returned to the Cape in 1988 to a league that expanded by two teams to two five-team divisions and with talent that it had probably never before witnessed. Forty Cape Leaguers from the 1988 season would advance to play major-league baseball. Chatham had Bagwell along with Andy Cook, P.J. Forbes, Dave Swartzbaugh, and Sweeney. Cape League champion Wareham fielded Mo Vaughn, batting champion Chuck Knoblauch, Darron Cox, Kevin King, and Matt Ruebel. League finalist Orleans featured Frank Thomas, Brian Barnes, Jesse Levis, and J.T. Snow. Brewster was led by first baseman and league MVP Dave Staton, who narrowly missed the Cape League Triple Crown, Erik Bennett, Mike Myers, Craig Paquette, F.P. Santangelo. Brian Turang played for Harwich. Cotuit was led by Jeff Kent, J.T. Bruett, and Tim Salmon. Hyannis's roster included Jeromy Burnitz, Kirk Dressendorfer, Kevin Morton, and John Valentin. Bourne's lone representative was Mark Johnson. Yarmouth-Dennis had Mike Mordecai, Denny Neagle, Steve Parris, and Eric Wedge. Harwich included Mike Lansing, Rafael Novoa, Ross Powell, and Alan Zinter. Falmouth had Gary Scott, Mike Trombley, and George Tsamis.

Robert Whalen took over in 1988 as Chatham manager and the A's came in fourth in the newly realigned Cape League East Division, advancing to the playoffs with an overall 19-24 record. Bagwell's offensive numbers soared under Whalen's tutelage. He batted .315 with six homers in 44 games. Jeff was the starting third baseman for the East Division All-Stars against their West Division counterparts in a newly revamped Cape League All-Star game. (From 1970 to 1987 the Cape League had sent an all-star team to take on the Atlantic Collegiate Baseball League.) The game, held at Orleans' Eldredge Park, was won by the West All-Stars, 4-3. The game was preceded by a home-run-hitting contest. Bagwell, Frank Thomas, Dave Staton, Eric Wedge, and Steve O'Donnell represented the East while the West had Mo Vaughn, Chuck Knoblauch, Mark Johnson, Jody Hurst, and John Farrell. The "Big Hurt" won the contest with a bat reportedly provided by fellow Auburn athlete Bo Jackson. Bagwell saved his heroics for the main event, slugging a home run and notching a 4-for-4 game.

The 1988 season featured the only year the league marketed a printing of a 30-card baseball card set produced by Ballpark Cards, which included Bagwell. According to Andrew Wirtanen of codball.com, a single print run of 6,000 sets was produced and sold by the company for $5 a set or given to players and league officials and volunteers. Another company, P&L Promotions, produced a 186-card set that also included Bagwell. The P&L set drew the wrath of the NCAA with its alleged unauthorized use of the NCAA name on the cards.

After the 1988 season, a Cape League All-Star team including Bagwell traveled with their wood bats to the Boardwalk and Baseball complex in Florida to take on the best of the other college summer baseball leagues, including the Shenandoah Valley League, the Great Lakes League, and the Central Illinois League. Playing out of the loser's bracket and trying to stave off elimination, the Cape Leaguers trailed the Great Lakes Leaguers, 4-3, in the eighth inning. A double by Bagwell tied the game and Bagwell was singled home by Tim Salmon to force a winner-take-all final against the Great Lakes that the Cape Leaguers won, 8-7. They returned to Cape Cod to the reported headline in the *Cape Codder* newspaper, "Wood Still Makes the Biggest Noise As Cape League Stars Take Title."[11]

Bagwell returned to Hartford for his junior year and capped his collegiate career with a .429 batting average and a 1.311 on-base-plus slugging percentage (OPS) in 33 games en route to recognition as North Atlantic Conference Player of the Year. It was time for the next level; Bagwell was a fourth-round selection of the Boston Red Sox in the 1989 major-league draft. He was on his way on a journey that would ultimately land him in Cooperstown.

Cape Cod Baseball League Commissioner Paul Galop opined to Jake Eisenberg of chathamanglers.com that 1988 "was probably one of the best years of Cape Cod Baseball League talent. And Bagwell was part of it."[12] Upon Bagwell's being elected to the Baseball Hall of Fame, Galop and the Cape Cod Baseball League celebrated:

"It's a big deal; it's very exciting for anyone involved in the Cape League at all. It's why we do it. We love to watch the kids grow from when they leave here, watch them get drafted, and make it (to) the majors. To have someone reach the Hall of Fame—that's the pinnacle of the sport."[13]

SOURCES

Kaplan, Jake. "Before Life as Killer B, Jeff Bagwell Part of Hartford's Crunch Bunch," houstonchronicle.com/sports/astros/article/Before-Killer-B-Jeff-Bagwell-Hartford-Crunch-Bunch-11525561.php.

"Bagwell Becomes First Hawk in Baseball Hall of Fame," hartfordhawks.com., July 29, 2017.hartfordhawks.com/news/2017/7/28/bagwell-becomes-first-hawk-in-baseball-hall-of-fame.aspx?path=baseball.

Doyle, Paul. "Bagwell Still Pals with Hartford Teammates, Who Remain in Awe of Him, courant.com, July 28, 2017.courant.com/sports/baseball/hc-jeff-bagwell-hartford-0729-20170728-story.html.

National Alliance of College Summer Baseball,nacsb.pointstreaksites.com/view/nacsb/.

"Bagwell's Road to Cooperstown Swung Through Cape Cod Baseball League," CCBL Public Relations Office, capecodbaseball.org, January 19, 2017.capecodbaseball.org/news/season/index.html?article_id=2343.

Eisenberg, Jake. "Former Chatham A Jeff Bagwell Elected to Baseball Hall of Fame," chathamanglers.com, January 18, 2017. chathamanglers.com/index.cfm?base=33&articleID=1218

Kaplan, Jake. "Jeff Bagwell Thanks Shapers of Career in Hall Induction Speech," houstonchronicle.com/sports/astros/article/Jeff-Bagwell-thanks-shapers-of-career-in-Hall-11719360.php.

Altavilla, John."New Hall of Fame Inductee Jeff Bagwell Made Impression in Hartford First," courant.com, January 18, 2017.courant.com/sports/baseball/hc-bagwell-hall-of-fame-0119-20170118-story.html.

"1988 Was a Very Special Year. Twenty Years Ago This Season, 40 Eventual Major Leaguers Starred on Cape Cod Baseball League Diamonds," capecodbaseball.org, June 16, 2008.capecodbaseball.org/news/season/index.html?article_id=1072.

"Cape Cod Baseball League All-Star Game Results," wickedlocal.com, July 23, 2008.capecodbaseball.org/archives/allstar/previous/2008allstar/.

Wirtanen, Andrew. "The 1988 Cape Cod Prospects Set," codball.com, August 14, 2016.codball.com/blog/2016/8/14/the-1988-cape-cod-prospects-set.

NOTES

1 Paul Doyle, "Same Old Bagwell," *Hartford Courant*, July 30, 2017: E1.

2 Christopher Price, *Baseball by the Beach* (Hyannis, Massachusetts: Parnassus, 1998), 95.

3 Ibid.

4 Price, 68.

5 chron.com/sports/astros/article/Jeff-Bagwell-s-Hall-of-Fame-induction-speech-11719257.php. Eighth paragraph. Accessed May 6, 2018.

6 capecodbaseball.org/news/league/?article_id=2343.Accessed May 6, 2018.

7 Andrew Blume, interview with Robert Whalen, December 8, 2017.

8 Ibid.

9   John Altavilla, "Bagwell's In," *Hartford Courant*, January 18, 2017.
10 Paul Doyle, "Same Old Bagwell," *Hartford Courant*, July 30, 2017.
11 Price, 106.
12 chathamanglers.com/index.cfm?base=33&articleID=1218. Accessed May 17, 1918.
13 Ibid.

FRED EBBETT
COMMISSIONER

DAVID MULHOLLAND
PRESIDENT

SCOTT BANKHEAD
Wareham 1983

JOE MAGRANE
Harwich 1984

JEFF REARDON
Cotuit 1976

TERRY STEINBACH
Cotuit 1982

PETE INCAVIGLIA
Wareham 1983

BOBBY WITT
Chatham 1983

1988 ROSTER BOOK

Cover of the 1988 Cape Cod League Record Book. The League would feature 66 future MLB players in 1988, including Bagwell, Frank Thomas and Mo Vaughn. (From the collection of Brian Crowley.)

NO.	NAME	POS	BT	TH	WGT	HGT	BIRTHDATE	CLASS	HOMETOWN	COLLEGE
	CHATHAM ATHLETICS	MGR: Robert D. Whalen, Jr.			ASST MGRS: Dan Callahan		GEN MGR: Everett A. Larson			
							Paul Kostokopolous			
9	Jeff Bagwell	IF	R	R	190	6'0"	05/27/68	1990	Killingworth, CT	U Hartford
1	Grant Brittain	IF	L	R	167	6'0"	12/10/67	1990	Hickory, NC	West Carolina
28	Russell Cormier	P	R	R	205	6'4"	01/21/68	1991	Leominster, MA	Northeastern
15	Brian Dour	P	R	R	200	6'3"	01/08/67	1989	Virginia, IL	Bradley
3	Matt Dunbar	P	L	L	160	6'0"	10/15/68	1990	Crystal Bch, FL	Florida State
10	Clint Fairey	IF	R	L	200	5'10"	12/15/66	1989	Clemson, SC	West Carolina
16	Michael Gardella	P	R	L	195	5'10"	01/18/67	1990	Bronx, NY	Oklahoma State
8	David Hajek	IF	R	R	165	5'10"	10/14/67	1989	Citrus Hgt, PA	Cal Poly-Pomona
13	Curry Harden	P	R	R	165	6'0"	11/02/66	1990	Starkville, MS	Texas
19	Michael Hinde	IF/OF	L	L	180	6'0"	09/17/67	1990	Apopka, FL	Miami
4	Don Hutchinson	OF/IF	L	L	165	5'10"	02/11/66	1989	Natick, MA	U Maine
26	James Jones	P	R	R	185	6'1"	08/31/67	1989	Seekonk, MA	U Conn
21	Michael LeBlanc	P	R	R	225	6'1"	12/02/65	1989	Skowhegan, ME	U Maine
18	Scott Odierno	C	R	R	190	6'0"	07/07/67	1989	Melville, NY	Brown
11	Tim Riginos	OF	R	R	180	6'3"	04/05/68	1990	Sfty Hrbr, FL	Stetson
6	Robert Rivell	IF	R	R	175	5'9"	02/21/68	1990	Glendora, NJ	U Virginia
14	Colin Ryan	C	R	R	192	6'2"	01/21/67	1989	Newtonville, MA	U Maine
12	Scott Shockey	OF/IF	L	L	195	6'1"	07/04/67	1989	El Toro, CA	Pepperdine
20	David Swartzbaugh	P	R	R	190	6'2"	02/11/68	1990	Middletown, OH	Miami-Ohio
17	Mark Sweeney	OF	L	L	195	6'1"	10/26/69	1991	Holliston, MA	U Maine

CHATHAM

Chatham A's roster from the 1988 Cape Cod League Record Book. Joining Bags on the roster is the University of Maine's Mark Sweeney who played 14 MLB seasons and recorded 175 career pinch hits, second most in history. (From the collection of Brian Crowley.)

JIM JONES — Pitcher
Bats Right/Throws Right
Junior — 6'1 185 Lbs.
Hometown: Seekonk, MA

Jim Jones was the number two starter for the University of Connecticut the past two years. As a sophomore he led the team with five wins and racked up an impressive 49 strike-outs. He is a workhorse, having started over twenty games the past two seasons. Jim has a fast ball as his number one pitch and only his wildness needs to be corrected for him to become an outstanding pitcher. He was a three-sport captain at East Providence High School, where he was All Division in Baseball and Football.

JEFF BAGWELL — Third Base
Bats Right/Throws Right
Sophomore — 6'2 195 Lbs.
Hometown: Killingworth, CT

Jeff Bagwell is a veteran of Cape Cod League play, having arrived in Chatham late last year and performed very well at third base. Only a sophomore this year he is looked to to provide leadership and a steady performance at the "hot corner." Jeff has rewritten the record book at the University of Hartford, where he led the team in 13 different statistical categories this past year. For the second year in a row he was named as the team's Most Valuable Player.

CURRY HARDEN — Pitcher
Bats Right/Throws Right
Sophomore — 5"11 160 Lbs.
Hometown: College Station, TX

Curry Harden was drafted out of High School by the Baltimroe Orioles. He was named first team All District for three years while attending A&M Consolidated in College Station, Texas. He was named All State as an outfielder. At the present time he is the ace of the Texas staff, posting an 8-1 record in early May. Has unlimited experience as a starter and reliever. His freshman year at Texas he ended up with an ERA of less than 2.0. Could be the Chatham A's may have the successor to Roger Clemens and Greg Swindell in their midst.

The cover and a page from the 1988 Chatham A's scorecard. (Collection of Karl Cicitto.)

Dan Gooley

By Pete Zanardi

Dan Gooley was the head baseball coach at the University of Hartford for Jeff Bagwell's sophomore and junior seasons. He coached at the U. of H. for five years. The well-seasoned coach had a long stint helming the Quinnipiac University nine, too. In Hartford, Gooley took the program to new heights and aided in Bagwell's development. In his Hall of Fame induction speech, Jeff spoke directly to Gooley: "Coach Gooley, Skip—just a memorable time playing for you, we had such a great team."[1]

Dan Gooley, a fourth-generation Irish-American, was born on March 3, 1947, in a snowstorm in New Haven to Raymond Gooley, a postal worker and restaurant owner, and his wife, Roseanne. His great-grandparents immigrated to the United States from County Cork. The Gooley family ran a restaurant called Danny Gooley's on Kimberly Avenue in New Haven at one time. Dan was a student athlete at Hillhouse High School and Cheshire Academy before attending Quinnipiac University.[2]

While pitching at Cheshire Academy in 1966 for Coach Steve Cook, Gooley had Kent School's Steve Greenberg, the son of Hall of Famer Hank Greenberg, down 0-and-2 in the count. Some 25 years later Gooley, then the head coach at the University of Hartford, recalled the contest.

"I threw a fastball up and he hit it—home run," Gooley said. He recalled Cook coming out to the mound and saying, "Never throw a pitch up to a kid with glasses. He can see it too well. You always throw it down because he has to look through the lens and that can be tough."[3]

Gooley, who also attended Hillhouse High, lost that day in 1966, the only defeat he suffered at Cheshire, a no-hitter against Laurelcrest among the victories.[4] Still, the loss and the advice are part of the Gooley legacy. "Where you've been, where you are, and where you're going is all part of the big picture," Gooley said, "because nothing, nobody, is bigger than the game itself."[5]

Announcing Gooley's appointment as the new University of Hartford baseball coach in June of 1987, Athletic Director Don Cook told the *Hartford Courant*'s George Smith, "[Gooley] is a true baseball person, one that strikes the best balance between educational and athletic values. His reputation and integrity speak for themselves."[6]

After 27 years of coaching, after 1,500 games, Cook's appraisal remains right on. Does it get any better than being mentioned in Hall of Famer Jeff Bagwell's acceptance speech? It was perfect because Gooley's wife, Sue, and daughter, Bree, were in Cooperstown with Dan to share it. But he's more than the guy who coached two major leaguers, including Turk Wendell, at Quinnipiac. He is a baseball man with a list of friends as wide as the game itself.

Coming from Quinnipiac College, where he had a 203-122-5 record including a trip to the 1983 Division II World Series, Gooley beat out 78 applicants for the Hartford job. Then 40 years old, he was the perfect choice to take over a troubled program that had suffered through a devastating campaign in 1987. Cook, the athletic director, had become temporary coach after an incident in a game with UConn forced the firing of Bill Denehy.[7]

While one may immediately think of Quinnipiac at the mention of his name, Gooley played a vital role at the University of Hartford and in the success of Bagwell. His first step at Hartford was hiring Moe Morhardt and Randy Lavigne as assistants. Both had sterling reputations. Success was immediate—a very successful fall program in 1987.[8]

Blessed with great talent including a quartet (Bagwell, Brian Crowley, Chris Petersen, Pat Hedge) grouped together as the Crunch Bunch, and pitching prowess led by Mark Czarkowski and Keith Wiley, UHartford went to the postseason in 1988 for the first time in its baseball history. It lost to Fordham in the ECAC tournament finale, a contest that went to the final pitch.[9]

Gooley never failed to acknowledge that the 1988 success came with a Denehy-recruited team. That same spring, however, a Gooley-gathered group at Quinnipiac, led by Wendell, won the Northeast 10 crown and went to the NCAA Division II Northeast Tournament.[10]

His time at the University of Hartford notwithstanding, Gooley is the face of Quinnipiac athletics. He points to two Quinnipiac stars—the late Burt Kahn and Frank Vieira—as forces in helping him post the résumé that so impressed Cook in 1987. Coach/AD Kahn, of course, was an ally while University of New Haven baseball coach Vieira, a Quinnipiac grad, was a rival. All three are Quinnipiac Hall of Fame members.[11]

It was Kahn who brought Gooley to Quinnipiac as a player. He won a record 20 games over four years in Hamden, setting records for innings pitched (269) and strikeouts (316). His 20th victory came on May 23, 1970, Gooley striking out 11 in a 9-5 decision that eliminated Eastern Connecticut State from the NAIA district tournament.[12]

The list also includes a 15-inning, 4-1 win over Monmouth College in New Jersey on April 28, 1968. Gooley, while fanning 11, battled future major leaguer Ed Halicki for 14 innings, each allowing a run.[13] Four days later, Gooley fanned 12 beating the University of New Haven 7-1 on a five-hitter.[14] His reputation was established in 1968 when, in an NAIA District 32 contest, he struck out 20 in 11 innings in a game Quinnipiac won 1-0 in 15 innings.[15]

It was Kahn who hired Gooley in 1971 as an assistant in three sports (including baseball under Bill Merrill) and as director of sports information. Whether the latter was part of Kahn's genius is debatable, but there can be no doubt about the relationship Gooley enjoyed with the media over the years. It is rivaled only by how the scouts regard him.

And it was Kahn who made Gooley head baseball coach in 1977.[16] College baseball in New Haven was not an easy place. Coaches Joe Benanto at Yale and Joe Bandiera at Southern Connecticut were hardly pushovers and there was nobody tougher than Porky Vieira at the University of New Haven. And nobody was more willing than Kahn to help a young coach's psyche when it was needed. Gooley never fails to acknowledge that.

The 1983 season may be the pinnacle of his first tour at Quinnipiac. After failing to make the tournament in 1982 (despite a 22-7-1 record) the Braves had stellar pitching—Frank Trasacco (7-2), Tom Signore (8-5), John Glenn (6-2), and Tom O'Neil (4-0). The team hit 50 homers, led by the Bruise Brothers—Tim Saller, Andy Riccio, Vin Anasasio, and Dave Palo.

In the 1983 Northeast Tournament in Syracuse, Quinnipiac beat New Haven twice on the final day, 12-9 and 6-4, the latter on tournament MVP Bob Bruzik's three-run homer in the seventh. Quinnipiac had lost earlier to New Haven, 7-6. Victory led to the school's first visit to the College World Series.[17]

Gooley was New England Division II Coach of the Year for the second time in '83. He won it in '79 when Quinnipiac was 23-8. It was New Haven, however, going to the Division II World Series, eliminating Quinnipiac in the Regional final. Quinnipiac returned to the regional in '84, this time losing to New Haven and future major leaguer Mike Raczka, 12-3 in the finale.[18]

Between 1979 and 1987, Quinnipiac never won fewer than 18 games. Gooley saw Tom Signore replace him as Quinnipiac's all-time winning pitcher, recording his 21st win beating the University of Bridgeport 9-0 on April 23, 1985. The 22-7-1 1982 team not earning a postseason berth was disappointing, as was the 20-10 effort in '86.

Gooley was never a believer in excuses. After missing the postseason at Hartford in 1989, he gave the *Courant*'s George Smith a little more of his baseball philosophy: "In no way am I disappointed with the effort of the kids, but I am disappointed with our performance and I include myself in that category. When you don't earn [a bid]—as we should have—we don't deserve it. ... That's what makes the game of baseball great. When you earn it, you get it."[19]

JEFF BAGWELL IN CONNECTICUT

The fact that Bagwell, Crowley, Hedge, and Czarkowski were major-league draft picks in 1989 was cause for some joy. The year before, four Gooley recruits, pitchers Wendell, Dominic Rovasio, and Brian Landy, and first baseman Doug Bond, were drafted out of Quinnipiac. Gooley was the only coach to recruit Wendell, who posted 13 wins, 7 saves, and 169 strikeouts in 180⅓ innings over three seasons in Hamden. He went to Atlanta in the fifth round. Wendell spent 11 years as a major-league reliever, appearing in 552 games.

After losing campaigns in 1990 and '91, Gooley returned to the postseason with UHartford in 1992. The team started 1-6 but won 12 of its last 15 games to earn an at-large ECAC bid. Shortstop Mike Desjardins and pitcher Scott LaRock (a '94 draft pick) were tournament All-Stars. Catcher Mike Lane and first baseman Bob Nenna were NEIBA All-New England, and second baseman Steve Mathews and outfielder Aaron Leonard were second-team All Conference picks. It was Gooley's team.[20]

Then everybody gasped when Gooley took a job with New Haven-based sports-equipment company Starter right after the tournament.[21]

Gooley was back at Quinnipiac as director of athletic development before the dawn of a new century and back as baseball coach in 2002. Now running a Division I program, Gooley suffered through two tough campaigns before running off a streak of four straight winning efforts, topped by an NCAA Division I Tournament appearance in 2005—the first in the school's history. Draft picks Bryan Sabatella, Ari Kafka, and Pat Egan, the latter two pitchers, and MVP Ryan Rizzo, a sophomore, guided Quinnipiac through the Northeast Conference tournament, only to run into eventual champion University of Texas in the first round of the NCAA super-regionals.[22]

The last eight seasons were not winners but Gooley's place in Connecticut baseball remains brilliant.

Steve Greenberg went from Kent to stardom at Yale, to Triple A in professional ball, and, armed with a law degree, to a turn as deputy commissioner of baseball. Dan Gooley went from Cheshire to a lasting place in the state's baseball lore, surrounded by a multitude of friends.

Dan Gooley holds a master's degree from Southern Connecticut State University. Susan, his wife, is a master chef. She was working at a restaurant in New Haven when she and Dan met. They've been married for 30 years and in May 2018 they welcomed a granddaughter into their family, Reilly Rose. Dan is very active in his community and his church and in the Greater New Haven Diamond Club.

SOURCES

University of Hartford Baseball Media Guides, 1990-1995.

Baseball America's Almanacs, 1980-95.

A CONSISTENT LAD IN THE LAND OF STEADY HABITS

Anderson, Woody. "Quinnipiac Picking Up in Baseball," *Hartford Courant*, April 30, 1983.

NOTES

1. youtube.com/watch?v=-OUxX7dMe_M . 7 minutes and 58 seconds into the speech. Accessed May 19, 2018.
2. Telephone interview by the author with Dan Gooley, May 19, 2018.
3. Interview with Dan Gooley by Pete Zanardi at the University of Hartford, February 1, 1992.
4. "Gooley Hurls Cheshire Over Laurelcrest," *Hartford Courant*, May 1, 1966: C3.
5. Interview with Dan Gooleyby Pete Zanardi at the University of Hartford.
6. George Smith, "U of H Baseball Taps Quinnipiac's Gooley," *Hartford Courant*, June 19, 1987: E1.
7. Ibid.
8. *1990 University of Hartford Baseball Media Guide*.
9. Ibid.
10. Chip Malafronte, "Quinnipiac Baseball Coach Built More Than a Legacy," *New Haven Register*, May 11, 2014.
11. Ibid.
12. Bill Newell, "Eastern Bows in NAIA Event as Charters Win Title," *Hartford Courant*, May 24, 1970.
13. Quinnipiac Beats Monmouth 4-1 in 15," *Hartford Courant*, April 29, 1969: 31.
14. "Quinnipiac Stops New Haven 7-1," *Hartford Courant*, May 3, 1969: 27.
15. "Quinnipiac Captures NAIA District 32," *Hartford Courant*, May 19, 1968: C5.
16. "Quinnipiac Baseball Coach."
17. Ibid.
18. *1984 Baseball America's Almanac*.
19. Smith, "Hawks Coach Not Expecting ECAC At-Large Bid," *Hartford Courant*, May 9, 1989: E2.
20. *1994 University of Hartford Baseball Media Guide*.
21. "Gooley Leaves for Promotions Job," *Hartford Courant*, June 5, 1992: E3.
22. Mike Anthony, "Man Who Built Bobcats Up Is Stepping Down, Quinnipiac Baseball Coach Dan Gooley to Retire After 2013-14 Season," *Hartford Courant*, June 28, 2013: C7.

Dan Gooley's Coaching Record, compiled by Pete Zanardi.

YEAR	School	Record	Post Season	Draft Picks
1977	Quinnipiac	8-19-2		P-Bill Martin
1978	Quinnipiac	16-14		
1979#	Quinnipiac	23-6	Northeast Div II Regional	
1980	Quinnipiac	9-15-1		
1981	Quinnipiac	18-8		
1982	Quinnipiac	22-7-1		

Year	Team	Record	Postseason	Honors
1983#	Quinnipiac	25-10	Northeast Div. II Regional, Div. II World Series	SS Bob Bruzik
1984	Quinnipiac	25-8	Northeast Div. II Regional	P-Francesco Trasacco
1985	Quinnipiac	18-12		
1986	Quinnipiac	20-10-1		
1987	Quinnipiac	19-11		
1988#	UHartford	29-12	ECAC Div. I	
1989	UHartford	17-15-1		3B-Jeff Bagwell OF-Brian Crowley OF-Pat Hedge P-Mark Czarkowski
1990	UHartford	15-20		
1991	UHartford	13-22		
1992	UHartford	27-21	ECAC Div. I	
2002	Quinnipiac	12-30		
2003	Quinnipiac	17-24		
2004	Quinnipiac	23-21	Northeast Conference	
2005	Quinnipiac	26-24	Northeast Conference, NCAA Regional	P-Pat Egan P-Ari Kafka 3B-Bryan Sabatella
2006	Quinnipiac	22-24-1	Northeast Conference	P-Pat Egan
2007	Quinnipiac	29-18-1	Northeast Conference	SS-Randy Gress
2008	Quinnipiac	16-36		P-Chris Gloor SS-John Delaney
2009	Quinnipiac	18-34		P-Chris Gloor
2010	Quinnipiac	14-39		
2011	Quinnipiac	15-32		
2012	Quinnipiac	9-38		
2013	Quinnipiac	17-36		
2014	Quinnipiac	16-31		

New England Coach of the Year

Morhardt and LaVigne: True Baseball Men

By Jim Keener

Meredith "Moe" Morhardt and Randy LaVigne joined the University of Hartford baseball coaching staff when Dan Gooley took over the reins of the program in 1988. When deciding who to bring on board as assistants, Dan turned for advice to his coaching colleagues, specifically Connecticut's Andy Baylock and Eastern Connecticut's Bill Holowaty. Moe and Randy were the clear choices.

"I never thought in a million years I could get them," said Gooley. "Moe had been a highly respected high-school coach for 21 years at The Gilbert School. When he came to UHart, he kept his day job at the school and traveled every day from Winsted. Randy came on board in a dual role as an athletics development officer and assistant baseball coach. He was considered a real pro."[1]

Gooley continued, "In the eyes of the players, their presence legitimized what we were doing and trying to accomplish as a program."[2]

Moe and Randy arrived at Hartford with a great deal in common. Each was an All-American outfielder at the University of Connecticut, albeit 20 years apart, and both played in the College World Series. Each was drafted by the Chicago Cubs; Moe enjoyed a brief stay with the Cubs and Randy reached Triple A. Each wanted to play the game the right way, valued character, and used a positive attitude as a motivator.

Morhardt was the team's hitting coach and LaVigne was in charge of outfield defense, but their roles were often interchangeable.

"As a staff we were very serious about the game and it was all business," Randy recalled. "There was a purpose to everything we did. Dan provided the structure and was very organized. He handed out the discipline and Moe and I were the good cops."[3]

Within the first two weeks of their first fall season together, the trio sensed the team's potential. "Randy turned to the two of us one day," Gooley remembered, "and said, 'You know, these guys are pretty good.' Each of us nodded our heads in agreement and didn't say a word."[4] The statement turned out to be prophetic.

The 1988 season was the most successful in the program's history. The Hawks, who set a New England record [since broken] with a .344 team batting average, reached the postseason and were one win away from reaching the NCAA tournament. (The season before, the Hawks were 11-27 and hit .250.)

"This team wanted to play, was receptive, and got along well," said Moe. "They were also very talented."[5]

"The 1988 team was something special," Randy said. "They were committed to improving and being the best baseball players they could be. They lived for the game. As they started seeing the results and how fun it was to win, they wanted even more."[6]

The dynamics of the staff in their two years together was a key part of the team's success.

"Coach LaVigne was a calming influence," said first baseman Chris Petersen. "He was a giant of a man, physically and intellectually. Coach LaVigne was a 'touchstone' for the team and he would often take us aside and ask how we were doing. He never raised his voice and when he spoke it meant something. Coach LaVigne also brought the importance of schoolwork to our attention."[7]

"Physically, Randy was impressive and earned immediate respect," said Moe. "He wasn't a screamer, didn't curse or throw things, or belittle the players."[8]

"If the players don't trust you, you lose them," said Moe. "You can't lie or they will know it."[9]

The pair also had a knack for putting things in perspective, often saying or doing little things that made a big difference.

"I remember giving up 11 runs one day against Davidson," said right-hander Gary Gallagher. "I came off the mound a defeated man and sat at the corner of the dugout with my head in my hands, wondering what just happened. Coach Moe came over to me and I said, 'What the heck just happened.' He smiled at me and said, 'Gary, sometimes the hitters win.' I didn't realize what he meant at the time, but now that I'm coaching my own kids, I do."[10]

The offensive turnaround in 1988 was historic in the annals of New England baseball, and Moe Morhardt was given much of the credit. As a baseball soothsayer and devout student of the game, he combined skills as a baseball mechanic, psychologist, and cheerleader.

His teachings were sometimes textbook.

He preached the importance of hitting the ball to all fields. He said in 1988 that good hitters "hit the ball foul line to foul line. If the ball is hittable on the outside of the plate (to a right-hander), then go to right field. If it's over the plate, go up the middle."[11]

Other times, they were measured and intuitive.

"If a player is feeling good mentally, I don't disturb him," he said. "When a batter asks for assistance, that is when you can help him the most. I also believe if the hitting coach has a hunch, then he should play that hunch and interject the suggestion to the player."[12]

He said that for every mechanical suggestion you offer, you also need to also provide two or three mental tips that may help. And he stressed patience.

"Patience is always on time," he said. "It is never too fast or too slow."[13]

Pat Hedge was one of biggest beneficiaries of Morhardt's wisdom in 1988. His average jumped from .165 in 1987 to .389 in 1988, second on the team to future Hall of Famer Jeff Bagwell.

Hedge commented in 1988, "I've never met anyone who knows as much about baseball. I just do what he says. It's like osmosis being around the guy."[14]

Moe had his players playing mental games before they entered the batter's box. He had them creating a picture in their mind of a time they made good contact and asked them to trigger this image by touching a body part before they entered the batter's box.

Hedge, who began slapping himself on the hip before getting in the batter's box, was a free swinger with a temper to match. Morhardt called it Hedge's "good time touch."[15] He cut his strikeout ratio in half in 1988 from the previous season.

"Pat learned that you can hit the ball hard without swinging hard. The bat does the work," said Moe. "You hit the ball naturally, effortlessly, and in tempo — one tick below trying. That's how you hit."[16]

Moe's teachings were impactful and lasting.

Outfielder Brian Crowley remembered the visual of Moe walking out to the practice field on campus carrying his brown fungo bat. "I felt like Moses was on his way with his brown stick ready to impart baseball wisdom on us all."[17]

Morhardt recorded in spiral notebooks his observations of what was happening on and off the field, a practice he began in 1964 while playing in the Texas League in his final professional season. "All I did was start to write down all that I heard, saw, and thought about the game. I counted (the notebooks) the other day. I have 65 spiral notebooks filled with 'junk' and I'm working on my 66th."[18]

He would share that "junk" with the team on a regular basis and, years later, the players he mentored were using the information in the notebooks to develop their own players.

"Baseball is hard," said Moe. "It is an individual game within a team game. You can't play two second basemen or have two players pitch at the same time. There is no safe space to hide. But just like those guys with the ruffled shirts in 1776 who yelled at each other across the table, you have to hang together. It's America."[19]

Morhardt's and LaVigne's athletics résumés were substantial before they arrived at Hartford.

Moe was signed by the Chicago Cubs as a 22-year-old in the summer of 1959. He spent the next two seasons in the minor leagues before making his major-league debut on September 7, 1961. The Cubs had seven first basemen in 1961, but heading into spring training in 1962, they had none. So Moe and Ernie Banks, who was moving from shortstop to first after dealing with injuries, were in a battle for a starting spot at first base. Morhardt batted .368 that spring, but future Hall of Famer Banks was given the job to start the 1962 campaign.

Moe was primarily a pinch-hitter in the early part of 1962. He was frustrated and asked to be sent back to the minors so he could play every day.

"The Cubs knew what I could do," said Morhardt.[20] It was clear that they wanted to see what else they had as Moe played both in the outfield and at first base. He played the next two years in the minors and, heading into 1964, there was a "50/50 chance" he would retire. Moe finished the season playing in the Texas League and retired, partly because his desire to compete had slipped.

"You just get a feeling. You know," he said. "I didn't want to do it anymore." Moe played in 25 major-league games.[21]

After retiring as a player, Morhardt completed his graduate work in physical education at Southern Connecticut State University. Eventually, he landed at The Gilbert School in Winsted, Connecticut, as baseball coach and physical-education instructor. Moe compiled a 299-134 record in 21 years as baseball coach and guided his teams to three state championships (1973, '76, '79), and eight league championships. He was the Connecticut Interscholastic Athletic Conference Coach of the Year in 1980. He was inducted into the Connecticut High School Coaches Association Hall of Fame in 1993. Moe also coached soccer and basketball at Gilbert.

Morhardt, a native of Manchester, Connecticut, was an All-American soccer goalkeeper at UConn. In fact, he is the only two-sport All-American in the history of UConn. Moe graduated with a physical-education degree in 1960. He is a member of the Manchester Sports Hall of Fame.

Asked how he came to the game, Moe said, "I remember getting a glove from my uncle one Christmas. There was a playground two and a half blocks from my house and I just started playing. I learned it in the sandlots."[22]

Randy LaVigne was a seventh-round draft choice of the Cubs (168th pick overall) in 1979. He played five seasons in the minor leagues, reaching Triple-A Iowa in 1982. His best season was at Double-A Midland in 1980; he hit .300 that year with 17 home runs and 95 RBIs. Overall, as a professional, Randy hit .292 in 507 minor-league games with 54 home runs and 315 RBIs. He hit .300 or better in three of his five minor-league seasons.

Beginning in his third season, LaVigne's shoulder started to weaken. By his fifth season, it was very painful and diagnosed as a rotator-cuff problem. Also, a "lazy eye" issue that he suffered with as a youngster had returned. It affected his depth perception.

"I started to hit the ball at the plate and not in front of the plate as I normally would," he said. "I didn't know why. My power numbers were down. I learned later that my eyesight was being affected."[23]

LaVigne asked to be traded and joined the Milwaukee Brewers for spring training in 1984. It became obvious that his skills were diminished as a result of his ailments and he decided to retire.

Randy was a two-sport athlete at Connecticut. On the baseball diamond, he was a third team All-American as the Huskies posted a 31-13 record and advanced to the College World Series in 1979. He set six Connecticut single-season records that year and left as the school's all-time leader in home runs with 15.

LaVigne spent the summers of 1977 and 1978 playing for Cotuit in the Cape Cod League. He won the league batting championship and the Sportsmanship Award in his final season with Cotuit.

Randy was a four-year starter on the basketball team and a two-time Academic All-American. His teams twice advanced to the NCAA tournament, peaking in 1976 with a trip to the Sweet 16. The swingman was All New England as a senior, leading his team in assists and free-throw percentage for his final season.

Randy received the Connecticut Baseball Distinguished Alumni Award in 2007.

A son of Hartford, LaVigne played baseball and basketball for the South Catholic Rebels, which won the 1974 state basketball championship. He finished fifth in his class academically and graduated in 1975.

Morhardt spent seven years at Hartford, the last two as its head coach. He is the only person to be involved with the program both times it was one win away from reaching the NCAA tournament. The Hawks lost twice to Northeastern on May 22, 1994, in the North Atlantic Conference finals. Morhardt won 42 games as Hartford's head coach.

After Hartford, Morhardt was the head coach for three seasons at Division III Western Connecticut (1997-1999) and spent seven seasons guiding the Danbury Westerners in the summer New England Collegiate Baseball League (NECBL), a wooden-bat league.

After retiring from baseball, Randy LaVigne worked for two years at Price Waterhouse Coopers before taking the University of Hartford job. He spent two years with the Hawks before moving to Acme Auto as its comptroller for four years. After that he spent more than two decades as the office and business manager for his wife's veterinary business. Along the way, he forged a career as a basketball announcer with the University of Hartford men (15 years over two separate spans) and Connecticut women (five years).

The coaching staff was very much a cohesive unit. "Dan (Gooley) was a great pitching coach and leader, while Moe put an incredible amount of thought in everything he did and had a unique way of conveying his teachings to the players," LaVigne said. "There were no egos on the staff. I would put our staff up against anyone I've ever dealt with in baseball as among the most knowledgeable."[24]

"Our strength as coaches was what we were as a group," said Gooley. "We never questioned each other and we were loyal. We also respected the players as young men and baseball players. We had a special bond that still exists today. Moe and Randy are two of the finest people I have ever met."[25]

SOURCES

In addition to the sources cited in the Notes, the author also consulted:

University of Hartford, press releases/media materials, Spring 1988.

Randy LaVigne, the baseballcube.com, minor-league stats.

University of Connecticut, "LaVigne to Receive Distinguished Alumni Award," uconnhuskies.com, January 16, 2007.

University of Hartford, 1994 Baseball Media Guide.

NOTES

1. Dan Gooley, phone interview, December 4, 2017.
2. Ibid.
3. Randy LaVigne, phone interview, December 6, 2017.
4. Gooley interview.
5. Moe Morhardt, phone interview, November 29, 2017.
6. LaVigne interview.
7. Chris Petersen, email exchange, November 21, 2017.
8. Moe Morhardt, phone interview, November 29, 2017.
9. Ibid.
10. Gary Gallagher, email exchange, November 20, 2017.
11. Bob Casey, "Hitting an Art Few Can Teach," *New Haven Register*, Spring 1988, from the University of Hartford SID clip files.
12. Ibid.
13. Ibid.
14. George Smith, "Hartford's Crunch Bunch: 'Coach Moe Provides Momentum for a Fearsome Foursome,'" *Hartford Courant*, May 4, 1988.

A CONSISTENT LAD IN THE LAND OF STEADY HABITS

15 Ibid.
16 Morhardt interview.
17 Brian Crowley, phone interview, November 20, 2017.
18 Morhardt interview.
19 Ibid.
20 Ibid.
21 Ibid.
22 Ibid.
23 LaVigne interview.
24 Ibid.
25 Gooley interview.

Bill Denehy

By Alan Cohen

"He's a heck of a guy. He's enthusiastic and great for the (University of Hartford) program. He's the reason why a lot of us are here. He is a man with big dreams. His dreams became our dreams. We believed in him."

> – University of Hartford player Brian Crowley in the aftermath of Bill Denehy's termination as head baseball coach at the University of Hartford in 1987.[1]

"He got me to spread my feet farther apart and moved my hands into my body. It shortened my swing and got me on the ball better."

> – University of Hartford player Jeff Bagwell in 1989.[2]

This is a story about a man whose talent was unfortunately compromised by equal doses of rage and addiction. Along the way there were moments of exhilarating success accompanied by episodes of debilitating pain. His moment in the sun has become a time of darkness as he enters old age. And it is the story of some enduring friendships.

Bill Denehy never knew his paternal grandfather, James Denehy, but his grandmother, Anne Frances Denehy, related that grandpa was prone to display his temper. Bill Denehy, like his grandfather, had his moments of anger, including an early one that caused him to be kicked off his high-school baseball team in his junior year.

William Francis Denehy was born on March 31, 1946, in Middletown, Connecticut, the only child of Frank "Stretch" Denehy and Anna Zawisa Denehy. Bill's father had been born Francis Joseph Denehy on April 11, 1912, and died on April 11, 1996. He was director of shipping at International Silver.[3] As with many of his generation, baseball started in Little League and Bill, in 1958, pitched his Moose Little League All-Stars to the District Nine Little League title.[4]

He pitched for his high-school varsity team beginning in his sophomore year, but his control was nonexistent. In his junior year, after he purposely hit a batter, his coach, Gene Pehota, dropped him from the squad. Nevertheless, scouts had begun to take notice. One scout, Bots Nekola of the Boston Red Sox, counseled Denehy in 1963 and urged him to change his delivery from directly overhand to three-quarters.

With the new delivery, Denehy resurfaced that summer in American Legion ball, hurling two no-hitters. In the second, on July 10, he struck out 16 in the seven-inning game, and the only batter to reach base safely did so when he was hit by a pitch.[5] Bill starred in basketball and baseball at Woodrow Wilson High School in Middletown and was named to the *Middletown Press* All-Star basketball team in his junior year. He had dreams of going to St. Bonaventure to play basketball and baseball. However, St. Bonaventure discontinued its baseball program, and Denehy concentrated on the sport, especially after the success he had enjoyed in the summer of 1963. In his final basketball game with Woodrow Wilson, he scored 18 points as his team fell to Middletown, 48-38, in an early-round game in the State Class B tournament.[6]

Denehy reverted to his old overhand style the following spring and led his baseball team to the 1964 Class B championship. Although the team was rated only 15th in its division, it had won its last four conference games before the state tournament and raced through the tournament. During the season, Denehy won his last eight decisions after being the tough-luck loser in two early-season starts. He struck out 10 batters or more seven times.[7]

His season had several highlights. In a 2-1 14-inning win over cross-town rival Middletown at Palmer Field in front of 1,500 fans on May 30, "Baseball Bill" pitched all 14 innings, striking out 23 batters. The large crowd was there because the game was a benefit for Denehy's basketball teammate Stan Kosloski, who had suffered severe back injuries in a traffic accident on February 24, 1963.[8] In the semifinals of the state tournament on June 10, Denehy was matched up against John Lamb of Housatonic Regional. Through the regulation seven innings, the game was scoreless and Denehy had not allowed a hit. He allowed a hit in the eighth inning, but the game remained scoreless until the 11th inning, when Woodrow Wilson pushed across three runs to win the game.[9] Lamb went on to pitch parts of three seasons with the Pittsburgh Pirates. In the championship game on June 15, 1964, Denehy pitched his team to the title with a three-hitter, striking out 10, and hitting a triple in the 8-1 win over Seymour High School.[10]

Denehy graduated from high school on June 17, 1964, and pitched American Legion ball again that summer. His Middletown Post 75, with his father, Stretch, then 52, as the assistant coach, dominated its zone, going 16-1, and went on to compete in the state championship tournament. The team fell one game short of qualifying for the championship game; it was eliminated from the tournament on August 8.[11] During the regular season, on July 5, he struck out 26 Niantic batters in a 15-inning game, winning, 1-0.[12] By the end of the August, Denehy was sought by each major-league club, and it came down to a choice between the Red Sox, the Yankees, and the Mets, all of whom were offering modest bonuses. He signed with Mets scout Len Zanke on September 8, 1964, for a package in the range of $20,000, and because he felt there was more of an opportunity to move up quickly in the organization. Denehy was assigned in the fall to the Mets team in the Florida Instructional League, The Mets director of player development, Eddie Stanky, looked at Denehy's 220-pound frame and told him that losing weight was a must. Denehy dropped 20 pounds, appeared in 11 games (five starts), and went 2-3 with a 2.91 ERA.

In his first full season in the minors, Denehy played with Auburn, the Mets' Class-A affiliate in the New York Penn League. He was an all-star selection, tying for the team lead in wins with 13 and leading the team with 10 complete games. He led the starters with a 2.78 ERA. He pitched a team-leading 194 innings as Auburn under manager Clyde McCullough finished second in the six-team league with a 73-55 record. McCullough praised the youngster, saying, "Denehy's a real hustler. Of the six games he's lost (through August 10), he's been in all the way. Binghamton beat him the other night, 2-0, on two unearned runs. It was the best game he's pitched all year. … He's a thinking pitcher, not a thrower."[13]

With the escalation of the war in Vietnam, Denehy joined the National Guard in the fall of 1965 and spent four months at Fort Dix, New Jersey, getting out of basic training just in time to report to spring training with the Mets in 1966.[14]

At the beginning of the 1966 season, Denehy was promoted to Williamsport of the Double-A Eastern League and his success continued. Playing for Bill Virdon, he went 9-2 to post the highest winning percentage on the team (.818) and led the starters with a 1.97 ERA. In early July, when his record at Williamsport was 7-2, he was promoted to Triple A but did not perform well at Jacksonville in 10 appearances (0-4, 6.30 ERA). He was sent back to Williamsport on August 13 and won his final two decisions of the season. He was sent to the Instructional League at season's end. Among those giving him instruction was Mets special field assistant Whitey Herzog. Denehy went 2-2 with a 2.50 ERA in 10 appearances.

In spring training in 1967, there were raves about Denehy and it appeared that he would be destined for long relief in the Mets bullpen in 1967. Under the tutelage of pitching coach Harvey Haddix, he changed his grip with positive results. Joe Donnelly of *Newsday* observed, "[H]is fastball takes off and his curve dives. They come out of a tangle that straightens six feet four inches and 200 pounds, delivered in the classic overhand manner."[15] Denehy had struck out 20 batters in 20 spring innings, and his ERA for the spring was 0.53. When Topps issued its set of cards for the season, his picture was on a card titled "Mets 1967 Rookie Stars." His picture was on the left. In the picture on the right side of the card was Tom Seaver. Bill Denehy's rookie card has grown in value over the years.

Denehy had earned a spot as the fifth man in the Mets five-man pitching rotation. His first appearance came in the Mets' fifth game of the season, on April 16 in Philadelphia. There was only one bat in the lineup that worried Denehy—the same bat that worried every other pitcher in the National League not wearing a Philadelphia uniform. Dick Allen was called Richie Allen in those days and, in his first two at-bats did not see anything resembling a strike from Denehy. In the fifth inning, after a walk to Dick Groat, Allen stepped in. Denehy's first pitch was high and tight for ball one. The second pitch was a slider, low and away, but it was tailing back toward the batter as it reached home plate. Allen swung, and the ball headed to deep left-center field, where it was intercepted in flight by a Coca-Cola sign atop the left-field roof, above the 357-foot sign.[16] The two-run homer was all the Phillies would need. The Mets were unable to put any runs on the board. When Denehy left the game with one out in the seventh inning, he had eight strikeouts to his credit. The Mets lost the game, 2-0, and Denehy's first career decision was a loss. After the game, Groat said, "We won, he lost, but that could be quite a kid."[17] The eight strikeouts tied the franchise record for a debut, equaling the total collected by Tom Seaver only three days earlier. That mark would hold for 45 years, until Matt Harvey fanned 11 in his debut with the Mets on July 26, 2012.

Denehy was fully entitled to file suit against his mates for lack of support during his first four starts. In his second start and first appearance in front of a home crowd, Denehy allowed three runs in eight innings. He was victimized once again by the home-run ball. He yielded a solo homer to Tony Gonzalez in the second inning and after the Mets tied the score in the bottom of the inning, the Phillies manufactured a run on three singles (two of them bunts) in the fourth to take a lead they would not relinquish. An eighth-inning homer by Allen was the stuff of legend. *Newsday*'s Steve Jacobson wrote, "Allen hit it over the fence, over the grass behind the fence, and onto the path where the buses park."[18] Denehy had become the first pitcher in the Mets' six-year history to lose his first two major-league starts despite quality outings. The Mets managed one hit off Cincinnati's Gerry Arrigo in Denehy's third start, and three errors led to only two of the six runs he allowed being earned. After the 7-0 loss to the Reds, he was 0-3.

"It was like that one bad breakup in your lifetime you don't ever get over."

– (Daughter) Kristin Denehy April 2005[19]

Start four was against San Francisco's Juan Marichal, who had never lost to the Mets in 17 decisions.[20] Before the game, Denehy was given a "black beauty" by a teammate. It was an amphetamine said to add three feet to a pitcher's fastball. Whether or not it was due to the amphetamine, Denehy threw in pain from that day forward.

In the fourth inning he began to feel intense pain in his shoulder, particularly after throwing a hard slider[21] and walking Willie Mays (whom he had struck out in the first inning) with two outs and none on. He then loaded the bases before yielding a two-run double to Hal Lanier. Denehy escaped the inning without further damage but the two runs in four innings resulted in his being tagged with his fourth loss. The Giants extended their lead after Denehy left and won, 8-0. In Denehy's first four starts, the Mets lost by a cumulative score of 20-1.

After a stint on the disabled list, the first of many cortisone shorts, and a couple of relief outings, Denehy took the mound at Shea Stadium in the first game of a doubleheader on May 28 in front of 48,548, the largest crowd of the young season. The Mets were facing the Atlanta Braves and Denehy for the first time had run support, principally from Tommy Davis, who had a career day with 5 RBIs. He banged out a first-inning three-run homer, hit an RBI single in the third, and had RBI doubles in the fifth and seventh. Denehy was victimized by a two-run shot by Clete Boyer and a solo shot by Joe Torre but was leading 5-3 when he left the game with two outs in the sixth inning, Jack Hamilton shut down the Braves the rest of the way, and the 6-3 victory was Denehy's first major-league win.

After going 1-7 with the Mets, Denehy was demoted to Triple-A Jacksonville on June 28. With Jacksonville he was 3-3 in 11 appearances (10 starts) and had a 4.19 ERA in 58 innings. On August 7 he threw his last pitch of the season. It was a fifth-inning RBI single with two outs off the bat of Richmond's Tommie Aaron that plated the third run in a 3-1 loss to the Braves' farm club.[22] Denehy was pitching in pain and "they took a series of 20 pictures and found a torn muscle in the rear of my arm near the armpit." He rehabbed at home during the winter, doing much in the way of running, basketball, exercise, and swimming.[23]

In November 1967 it was announced that Denehy would be sent, along with $100,000, to the Washington Senators in exchange for manager Gil Hodges. While with the Senators, Denehy roomed with Mike Epstein. The pair was very much into self-help nutritional supplements and were very well-read, making their way through Ted Williams's *How to Be a Better Hitter* and *Psycho-Cybernetics* by Dr. Maxwell Maltz.[24]

The Senators wasted little time in checking to see if there was any residual damage in Denehy's arm. In the first 1968 spring-training game, on March 7, he went up against the Yankees. In three innings, the only hit he allowed was a wind-blown single by Tom Tresh.[25]

But Denehy's time with the Senators would be brief. Despite a good spring,[26] he was not in the Senators' starting rotation, and he was used sparingly. He appeared in three April games. Of the 13 batters he faced in two innings pitched, four got hits and four were walked. On April 29 Denehy was sent to Triple-A Buffalo, where, starting every fourth day,[27] he went 9-10 with a 4.87 ERA in 25 appearances, all as a starter. His ninth loss of the season, to Syracuse on August 30, was perhaps his best start of the season. In the 2-0 defeat, he pitched the first eight innings and struck out 17 batters.

On February 1, 1969, the 24-year-old Denehy married 20-year-old Marilyn Waylock. They had two daughters, Kristin and Heather, before divorcing in 1987. He had met Marilyn, who was also from Middletown, after playing with the Mets in the Instructional League in 1965. Marilyn is the younger sister of John Waylock, Denehy's teammate from the 1964 Middletown American Legion team. Daughter Kristin grew up to be a choreographer, and has had twin daughters.

After playing under new manager Ted Williams during spring training in 1969 and absorbing lessons from the master of hitting, learning "as much about pitching from Ted as I did from all of my pitching coaches combined,"[28] Denehy began the season back at Buffalo and got off to a good start exemplified by pitching the first eight innings of a 3-0 shutout against Rochester on May 27. He was pitching in pain and receiving more and more cortisone shots, and by June 20 he was 2-4 with a 4.58 ERA. At that point Denehy moved on to Portland in the Pacific Coast League when he was traded by Washington to Cleveland for Lee Maye. With Portland he was 1-3 (4.37).

After the 1969 season, Denehy was assigned to the Indians' Double-A club in Waterbury, Connecticut, and was drafted by the Mets Tidewater farm club on December 1. He went to spring training with his original organization, and he was assigned to Double-A Memphis at the start of the season. His arm was feeling better; he had found a new doctor and a new drug to ease the pain. Toward the end of Denehy's time in Portland, Dr. Stanley Jacob administered dimethyl sulfoxide (DMSO) and the results had him feeling better than he had since the injuries began in 1967.

(Jacobs has been referred to as the father of DMSO. In the mid-1970s, DMSO was approved for horses only.[29])

After spending two months with Memphis, going 3-4 and striking out 49 batters in 46 innings, Denehy was promoted to Triple-A Tidewater. On August 4 he was the Denehy of old, striking out 13 batters in a 5-1 win over Louisville. He scattered seven hits and didn't lose his shutout until the eighth inning.[30] With Tidewater, he was 7-4 with a 3.29 ERA, and at the end of the season he was put on the Mets 40-man roster.

That winter Denehy was sent to Puerto Rico and played for Roberto Clemente with the San Juan Senadores.

Spring training went well for Denehy in 1971 and he thought he had a good chance to go north with the Mets, especially after his performance on March 13 when he pitched four no-hit innings against the Dodgers in relief.[31] In what was to be his swan song for the Mets, he pitched one inning against the Yankees on March 28, allowing no runs and one hit. But as the exhibition season concluded, Denehy was traded to the Detroit Tigers along with veteran Dean Chance for pitcher Jerry Robertson and

$75,000. He was assigned to Toledo, but after pitching in three games, he joined the Tigers and appeared for the first time on May 1. He relieved in 30 of his 31 appearances, and pitched batters high and tight. For the season, Denehy was 0-3 with a 4.22 ERA. He was credited with a save and three (retroactive) holds as the Tigers went 91-71 under Billy Martin, finishing second in the AL East.

> *"That fight brought our club together. It was one of the closest-knit clubs I had played with during my years in professional baseball."*
>
> – Bill Denehy about the 1971 Tigers.[32]

Denehy hit four batters during the season, and the second hit batsman proved memorable. In the opener of a doubleheader at Cleveland on June 18, the Indians' Sam McDowell hit two Detroit batters, Willie Horton and Bill Freehan, as Detroit won, 4-3. Balls kept going in the direction of Detroit batters in the second game, and three Tigers (Freehan, Jim Northrup, Ed Brinkman) were hit in the first seven innings. Denehy entered the game in the bottom of the seventh inning with the Tigers trailing, 3-0. Cleveland scored another run that inning, and the score was 4-0 when Ray Fosse led off for Cleveland in the bottom of the eighth. Denehy hit Fosse in the ribs with a pitch.[33] Whether or not this was intentional was of little concern to Fosse, who charged the mound. Denehy, with equal components of rage and smarts, defended himself. Per Watson Spoelstra, "Slender Bill Denehy ... repelled Fosse with a kangaroo-style kick with his spikes and this way he could keep pitching and not be sitting in the trainer's room with a sore hand."[34] As *Sports Illustrated*'s Ron Fimrite explained, "[T]he battle was joined, and the diamond was soon as warm with flailing ballplayers."[35] Denehy got the rest of the day off along with Horton and Ike Brown of the Tigers and Fosse and Gomer Hodge of the Indians.

Although hitting Fosse was not intentional, Denehy was not immune from throwing at batters at the behest of manager Billy Martin. On August 9, the Tigers were playing the Red Sox at Fenway Park. Denehy entered the game in the bottom of the sixth inning with the Tigers trailing, 10-7. The first batter up was Reggie Smith. Denehy drilled him and expected to be thrown out of the game. The umpires let him continue and he pitched two innings, allowing one run, before coming out for a pinch-hitter.

Otherwise, the season proved uneventful for Denehy. After the season he was assigned to the Toledo roster. He had faced his last major-league batter. He finished his 49-game major-league career with a 1-10 record and a 4.56 ERA.

Denehy spent the 1972 season wandering the minor leagues. He went to spring training with the Cardinals but was released before the season began. He signed in May with the Tucson Toros of the Pacific Coast league. His rage got the better of him on May 20, when he tagged Kurt Bevacqua in the mouth during a rundown play, precipitating a brawl reminiscent of what happened in Detroit the prior season.[36] Denehy was released by Tucson on June 3 and hooked up with Kinston, the Yankees affiliate in the Class-A Carolina League. While there, in one of his two appearances, he pitched five no-hit innings with 5 walks and 5 strikeouts.

On June 19, for one day only, Denehy joined Triple-A Syracuse and pitched an inning of relief in an exhibition against the Yankees. In July he signed with the Double-A Reading Phillies in the Eastern League, with whom he spent the balance of the season.

The offseason in Connecticut was but a blur punctuated by equal parts of rage and addiction to drugs and alcohol. Denehy's major-league career had fallen short of its initial promise and the stress of his deteriorating behavior was beginning to take a toll on his marriage. However, there was a glimmer of hope on the horizon.

In the spring of 1973 Denehy was back in Florida to give it another try with the Phillies. He was released but hooked on with the Double-A Bristol Red Sox. Bristol was not far from his Connecticut home and he got to spend the summer with Marilyn. On June 17 of that season, his family grew with the birth of his first child, Kristin. But on the field, it was not a good season. He went 1-5 with a 4.73 ERA before being released. In the spring of 1974, Denehy was briefly in the Giants' spring camp and was released for the last time.

Life after baseball was a roller-coaster of opportunities wasted, addictions encountered, and mischievous behavior. Denehy's first venture (he was still only 28 years old) was real estate in Arizona. Although he had some success, the principal result of his time in Arizona was a cocaine habit. Baseball, however, was not out of his system entirely and he pitched semipro ball in the Southern Arizona Association. While Bill and Marilyn were in Arizona, baby number two, Heather Lynn Denehy, entered the world on October 27, 1977.

A new career began for Denehy in 1981 when he joined the staff of the fledgling Enterprise Radio, based in Connecticut, and was on the air as a weekend radio talk-show host from 1:00 A.M. to 4:00 A.M. Soon, he became "Wild Bill" Denehy, cowboy hat and all. He covered spring training and college basketball and learned his craft working with producer John Chanin. However, his addictions to alcohol and drugs were still in play and there were nights when Denehy's behavior was unacceptable, especially when he arrived home late to his distraught wife.

On June 12, 1981, major-league ballplayers had gone on strike and Denehy was not too sure of the status of the broadcast network. He contacted the Bristol Red Sox and while still with Enterprise, joined the Bristol Red Sox as pitching coach in August. Enterprise Radio ran into difficulties and shut down after the baseball season. Denehy remained with Bristol as the pitching coach. He stayed with the team through 1983, its first year in New Britain, and coached future Red Sox Oil Can Boyd, Al Nipper, and Roger Clemens. After the 1982 season, Denehy taught a course in baseball at Middlesex Community College in his hometown of Middletown. In Baseball 101, he discussed theories on the art of baseball.[37] He and the New Britain Red Sox parted ways after the 1983 season.

> *"Buy a brick, build a stadium. Sprinkle some seed and then go out and hustle. I'm a salesman, but I've never had the opportunity to sell baseball. That would really be fun."*
>
> – Bill Denehy, August 16, 1984.[38]

Denehy was out of baseball as the 1984 season began, and although he found a job with a bank, he was miserable and ached to get back in the game. He was hired in August as the head baseball coach at the University of Hartford. The school had not won a game in two seasons, had lost 29 consecutive games, and its facilities were subpar. Home games were played off-campus.[39] Denehy hired three assistants to help him for the 1985 spring season, friends Don "The Grog" Lombardo, Don's brother Ted, and Paul LaBella. Under the stewardship of university vice president Bob Chernak, the school was moving to Division I in basketball and baseball, even without a playing field for baseball. Denehy's first players were willing, but not quite able, and the losses continued to pile up. It would be a bit of time before the most talked-about player on the team was someone other than a 5-foot-1-inch second baseman named Tom McVetty whom his mates called "Dirt."[40]

There was a game that first year in which Denehy could not contain his rage. The opponent was Amherst. Amherst scored seven runs in the first inning and in the second inning a brawl broke out with Denehy not playing the peacemaker role. Amherst went on to win, 13-1, and the streak was up to 32. The streak grew to 38[41] before the Hawks defeated Bridgeport on April 9. They won only two games that season, but Denehy was convinced he could turn the program around. One note of encouragement was that his top pitcher, John Tuozzo, had been drafted by the New York Mets. Although Tuozzo made it only as far as Class A and won only six minor-league games, Hartford was being noticed. Tuozzo was the second player from the University of Hartford to be drafted and the sixth to play professionally. Those numbers would increase substantially over the next several years, and two of Denehy's recruits would be the first University of Hartford players to perform at the major-league level.

To build Hartford into a winner, it would take great recruiting, and Denehy set out to get the best recruits available. With a blend of blarney and craziness, he not only recruited but set about to raise funds for his ambitious goals. The recruiting began during the 1985 season, and by the time the 2-24 season was over, the Hawks had grabbed off several top players from Connecticut. One of them was catcher Rick Murray of Xavier High School in Middletown, but it would be another player from Xavier, recruited the following year, who would jump-start the Hartford program to prominence. The goals included an expanded schedule. On November 20, 1985, a dinner was held to raise funds for the baseball program. It was "The First Annual Baseball Dinner: An Evening with George Steinbrenner," and "The Boss" came to West Hartford.[42] The team, whose bus broke down en route to Yale for the opener in 1985, would be jetting to Arizona in March 1986. On board were 19 prized freshman recruits.[43]

The Arizona trip in 1986 produced losing results but a couple of the recruits left their mark. One was right fielder Brian Crowley, who homered on the first pitch he saw and gave the Hawks an early lead. Also homering in a 21-3 loss was Pat Hedge.[44] The two would be the first of Denehy's recruits drafted by major-league teams. Through their first 29 games, the Hawks had five wins, including a 15-4 drubbing of Central Connecticut, and were in the process of rewriting the school's record books as team members scored more runs, hit more homers, and batted for higher averages than ever before.[45]

Hartford which joined the Eastern Collegiate Athletic Conference in 1986, got its first ECAC win (after eight losses) in the first game of a doubleheader against Vermont on April 26, but it was one of those "step forward, step back" days for Denehy and his Hawks. A bench-clearing brawl broke out in the second game and by the time the dust settled, Denehy was ejected and the game ruled a forfeit.[46]

Although the team put up another losing record (8-34), there was more help on the horizon. The list of recruits was headed by Jeff Bagwell of Xavier High School. Denehy's assistants were familiar with Bagwell from American Legion play, and Denehy had already recruited two Xavier players.

The first time Denehy saw Bagwell was in Bagwell's junior year at Xavier. The pro baseball scouts had not been impressed with Bagwell, but Denehy saw something. He remembered in 1994 that "I saw him as a junior for the first time and the thing that impressed me the most was that he had an awful lot of power to the opposite field."[47] Hartford assistant coach Paul LaBella headed the charge to entice Bagwell. The only issue was that Bagwell wanted to continue to play soccer, where he had been an All-State selection. By 1986, the years of a college athlete playing two sports were over, especially in baseball, for which many schools had both fall and spring programs. Denehy insisted that Bagwell commit to baseball alone, and Bagwell first played baseball for Hartford in the fall of 1986.

During the summer of 1986, Denehy got back into radio, hosting a show on WGAB Radio. A seemingly positive change for Denehy was made at Hartford in the autumn of 1986 when Don Cook was named athletic director. On January 31, 1987, Denehy put together a baseball clinic at which former major leaguers Tom House and Lou

Piniella participated. However, Denehy would not be at Hartford long enough to see his most famous recruit emerge as a star. By then Denehy's argumentative nature was established, and when he did not attend the annual baseball dinner in the fall of 1986, the establishment at the University of Hartford was disturbed.

With Bagwell and other new recruits, the Hawks took to the field in 1987, but they were still a young team and still prone to mistakes. On their Florida trip, they made 27 errors to the opponents' 10, and their pitchers allowed a staggering 55 walks to the opposition's 33.[48] Through their first 10 games, they were 1-9. Then the squad, which included 18 freshmen and sophomores on the 22-man roster,[49] began to jell. Although the team was only 6-14 in its first 20 games, it got off to a good start in the ECAC, taking two of three games from Maine. The team was improving, and Bagwell's bat was as good as expected. His fielding at shortstop, however, was not helping the team and this was evident after just a few games. Denehy moved Bagwell to third base. It would prove to be Denehy's last role in the development of Bagwell.

Denehy's dream of a stadium for Hartford would happen, but by the time it did, in 2017, his eyesight had diminished to the point that he would not see it. Indeed, he would leave the University of Hartford scene before many of his recruits completed their education at the school.

Denehy's run-ins with authorities, on the field or at the university, would continue and be his undoing. On April 14, 1987, the Hawks played the UConn Huskies and the mood was tempestuous. Brawls erupted in both the fifth and sixth innings and Hartford players Pat Hedge and Tony Franco were in the middle of things. The game was stopped by umpire Barry Chasen, and UConn, leading, 2-1, at the time, was declared the winner.[50] In the aftermath of this game, Denehy was reported to have made comments detrimental to personnel at UConn. Speaking with writer George Smith of the *Hartford Courant*, athletic director Don Cook said, "The alleged comments made by our coaching staff … do not convey a message which is representative of the athletic department or the university and for that reason we apologize. I [personally] [disassociate] myself from such statements as does the university because they certainly don't reflect the general philosophy of the university."[51]

On April 16, Denehy and his coaches were fired. The most damning of the statements attributed to Denehy in an article printed in the *Norwich Bulletin* indicated that he had particularly harsh views toward UConn assistant coach Mitch Pietras and indicated that the next time Pietras (who was also a soccer referee) went to the Hartford campus, he hoped "somebody bombs his car."[52]

Cook, once considered a blessing by Denehy when he arrived, now was the person who fired Denehy. He took over as coach of the 7-15 squad, and the firing hit the players hard. Rick Murray was particularly distraught, calling the firing "a major setback," and adding, "We were just learning how to win. There was a different feeling coming back on the bus from Maine Sunday after winning two of three games. Now this. Now what?"[53]

The Hartford program would continue its upward climb. Despite the turbulence as the team stumbled to an 11-27 record in 1987, Jeff Bagwell went on to complete his freshman season with a .402 batting average with university records in homers (7), RBIs (32), hits (51), total bases (86), and doubles (12).[54] The next season, with Denehy recruits Hedge and Crowley serving as co-captains and Bagwell continuing his hitting surge, the team advanced to postseason play in the ECAC Tournament.

Of the players recruited by Denehy, four played professionally. Pitcher Mark Czarkowski was undrafted but signed with Seattle and played seven seasons of professional ball. Three players were drafted. Pat Hedge and Brian Crowley fell short of making it to the majors, but Jeff Bagwell went on to a Hall of Fame career. Denehy's impact on the Hartford program was not lost on his successor, Dan Gooley, who said, "I give Bill a lot of credit. He's a friend and we are all coaching brothers. He did a great job here. I feel for him."[55]

Denehy, however, would have issues over the coming years. His marriage was coming apart at the time of the firing and he and Marilyn were divorced in November 1987. His ongoing drug use escalated, and his rage did not dissipate. He worked in construction for a while, played some semipro baseball, and in 1988, through an attorney, he wrote to the University of Hartford to try to reach a "settlement" that would have the university share in the responsibility for the events of April 1987 and not have the "dark cloud hang solely over Bill's head on the issue."[56]

Over the next couple of years, Bill found his way in and out of jobs in radio in Connecticut, and he relocated to Florida. He had hoped to play in the Senior Professional Baseball Association in the fall of 1989, but injuries sustained in a car accident kept him off the field. He returned to broadcasting and again, starting in November 1990, became a talk-show host, this time at WFNS in Tampa.[57] Differences with management over the firing of a production assistant led to his dismissal from that position in March 1991.[58] He also became more abusive of drugs during his time in Florida, and although he found some work broadcasting games on television with the Sunshine Network, his life was without any meaningful direction.

On June 15, 1992, Bill Denehy's life reached a turning point. He had been in Connecticut visiting his daughters, who were participating in the Connecticut Interscholastic Athletic Conference softball tournament. Heather was a sophomore star pitcher at Mercy High School in Middletown and pitched a one-hitter on May 29.[59] Her coach was Paul LaBella, who had been Bill's assistant during his time at the University of Hartford.[60] Her team was eliminated on June 8,[61] but Bill stayed on through Father's Day. Bill still had a drug habit. He was about to depart for Florida. At breakfast, in a moment of introspection, he asked his daughters, "Is there something we didn't do this time that you'd like to do the next time we're together?" His younger daughter, Heather, said, "I'd like to play catch." As Denehy remembered in his book *Rage*, "[H]er words hit me like a ton of bricks that weighed heavily on my heart. I was an ex-major leaguer [who should have been playing catch with his daughters all along], yet I was so screwed up [from the alcohol and drug abuse] ... that I couldn't spend fifteen minutes playing catch with my daughter." At that point, he committed to turning his life around.[62]

He returned to Florida and sought to rehabilitate his life. A month after his talk with Heather, he enrolled as an outpatient at Glenbeigh Hospital in Orlando, where he was counseled by Dr. Irving Kolin and executive director John Brandenburg. It was to them that he first came clean about his problems and they set him on the path to recovery. In group and individual therapy sessions led by Vicky O'Grady, he came to grips with his disease, the roots of his disease, and the need to address the issue of rage that had imprisoned him since his days in Little League.[63]

Denehy stayed in broadcasting and hosted a program called *Comeback*, which focused on people, mostly sports figures, who had overcome various addictions and afflictions.[64] He went on to form, with Ryne Duren, the National Association of Recovering Professional Athletes (NARPA), whose purpose is "to educate the young about the dangers of drugs and alcohol and provide support for pro athletes who have had and may still have addictions."[65]

As it turned out, the goals of NARPA and Glenbeigh could not be fully realized. Both organizations failed to survive, with Glenbeigh going bankrupt in March 1995 and NARPA folding its tent in 1994. But Bill Denehy did survive, found other work, and was sober.

He was inducted into the Middletown Sports Hall of Fame in 1995. For a time, he worked with Edwin Watts Golf in Florida but was fired in 1998 over various incidents at work, some related to his ongoing rage issues. Despite his sobriety, he still had issues with rage. But he found his calling, taking to the lecture circuit to warn people about the dangers of alcohol and drug abuse.

Denehy's father had died on April 11, 1996, after relocating to Florida in 1995. In 2000, his mother, who was living with him in Florida, was stricken with Alzheimer's and died on March 1, 2004, at the age of 89.

Over the next years, Denehy was in and out of jobs, including a position at Universal Studios in 2003. That year, he co-authored a book, *Intrinsic Golf: It's Within You*.[66] But all the rage and all the cortisone and all the drugs took their toll.

Denehy's life entered a new phase on January 19, 2005. He woke up that day unable to see out of his right eye.[67] His retina was damaged and, even with surgery, he lost sight in the eye. Ultimately, there would be problems in his left eye as well, leaving him virtually blind. He maintained that the many cortisone injections he received during his days in the majors were a major contributor to his vision difficulties.

In December 2013 Denehy was able to partner with Kane, a Guide Dog provided by Fidelco, a group headquartered in Bloomfield, Connecticut, not far from Denehy's boyhood home. In August 2014, Denehy and Kane returned to Middletown for the 50th reunion of the Woodrow Wilson High School Class of 1964.[68]

In recent years, Denehy has reconnected with Marilyn, Kristin, and Heather. He wrote his memoirs in *Rage: The Legend of "Baseball Bill" Denehy*, and he still follows University of Hartford baseball—and yes, before his eyes failed him, he did have that catch, on Thanksgiving Day in 1992, with Heather![69]

SOURCES

In addition to the sources shown in the notes, the author used Baseball-Reference.com, Ancestry.com, and the following:

Canfield, Owen. "From Middletown to the Majors Through Hell and Back," *Hartford Courant*, March 7, 1993: A1, A12.

Karmel, Terese. "'Wild Bill' Denehy Finds Plate in Job as Brisox Pitching Coach," *Hartford Courant*, May 15, 1982: C3.

Lang, Jack. "Potent Potion for Bum Arm—Denehy Ready Now," *The Sporting News*, March 13, 1971: 44.

Post, Fred. "Black Beauty Set Pitcher Off in Wrong Direction," *Hartford Courant*, March 31, 1999: 8.

Schmitz, Brian, "Former Pitcher Denehy Was in Howe's Shoes," *Orlando Sentinel*, December 12, 1992: B1.

Sears Campbell, Diane. "An Inspired Speaker Gets Some Motivation," *Orlando Sentinel*, June 13, 1999: H-4.

Trecker, James. "Legion Baseball," *Hartford Courant*, July 12, 1964: 8C.

NOTES

1 George Smith, "Hartford Fires Denehy for Post-Fight Comments," *Hartford Courant*, April 17, 1987: E 10.

2 Smith, "They're Hawking Hartford's Hitter," *Hartford Courant*, June 4, 1989: E4.

3 "Francis Denehy Obituary," *Orlando Sentinel*, April 12, 1996: 46.

4 "Moose Little Leaguers Win District Nine Title," *Hartford Courant*, August 3, 1958: 5D.

5 "Upset Wins Enliven Legion Races: Denehy Hurls No-Hit Gem in Zone 4," *Hartford Courant*, July 11, 1963: 14.

6 "Middletown Tops Wilson by 48 to 38 Before 2,500 Fans," *Hartford Courant*, February 29, 1964: B-14.

7 *Hartford Courant*, 1964 (Games in which Denehy struck out 10 or more batters were 4/17, 4/29, 5/05, 5/15, 5/30, 6/10, and 6/15.

8 "Woodrow Wilson Nips Middletown," *Hartford Courant*, May 31, 1964: C-4; "Youth Hurt in Wrecker Accident," *Hartford Courant*, February 25, 1963: 18.

9 "Denehy's Gem Wins for Wilson," *Hartford Courant*, June 11, 1964: 18.

A CONSISTENT LAD IN THE LAND OF STEADY HABITS

10. Bill Newell, "Bill Denehy Hurls Wilson to Class-B Title with 8-1 Win," *Hartford Courant*, June 16, 1964: 22.
11. James Trecker, "Bristol Defeats Middletown to Gain Final," *Hartford Courant*, August 9, 1964: 2C.
12. Trecker, "Legion Baseball," *Hartford Courant*, July 12, 1964: 8C.
13. "Mets Think Bill Denehy is Top Pitching Prospect," *Hartford Courant*, August 11, 1965: 22.
14. Bill Denehy (with Peter Golenbock), *Rage: The Legend of "Baseball Bill" Denehy* (Las Vegas: Central Recovery Press, 2014), 52-53.
15. Joe Donnelly, "Westrum May Make a Point with Denehy," *Newsday*, April 4, 1967: 21A.
16. Red Foley, "Jax Strings Along Mets, 2-0, Richie Ruins Denehy's Debut," *New York Daily News*, April 17, 1967: 54.
17. Joe Donnelly, "Denehy Reminds People of Rohr: Allen Spoils Met Rookie's Debut," *Newsday*, April 17, 1967: 21A.
18. Steve Jacobson, "Right Up Allen's Alley," *Newsday*, April 24, 1967: 32A.
19. Emily Badger, "Pitcher's 'World Fell Apart' the Day He Injured His Arm," *Orlando Sentinel*, April 10, 2005: C-13.
20. Joseph Durso, "Denehy is Picked to Face Marichal," *New York Times*, May 4, 1967: 46.
21. Fred Post, "Black Beauty Sent Pitcher Off in Wrong Direction," *Hartford Courant*, March 31, 1999: Middletown Section: 8.
22. Shelley Rolfe, "R-Braves Defeat Suns, 3-1," *Richmond Times Dispatch*, August 8, 1967: B6.
23. George Minot Jr., "Nats Denehy Faces Yanks Today: Newcomer Eager to Face Challenge," *Washington Post*, March 7, 1968.
24. *Washington Post*, March 1, 1968: D1.
25. Merrell Whittlesey, "It was a Great Day for Pitchers," *Washington Evening Star*, March 8, 1968: A17.
26. Morris Siegel, "Senators Eye Fourth," *Washington Evening Star*, April 6, 1968: 14.
27. Whittlesey, "Humphreys Recalled, Denehy Farmed Out," *Washington Evening Star*, April 29, 1968: 18.
28. Denehy and Golenbock, 104.
29. nytimes.com/1982/05/15/us/mistrial-called-in-conspiracy-case-involving-wonder-drug-approval.html.
30. Ron Coons, "Denehy Whiffs 13, Tides Win," *Courier Journal* (Louisville, Kentucky), August 5, 1970, B-7.
31. Bill Lee, "Bill Denehy Challenges for Mets Bullpen Job," *Hartford Courant*, March 14, 1971: C-1.
32. Denehy with Golenbock, 132.
33. Vito Stellino (Associated Press), "Angels Boil—Cleveland Explodes," *Jersey Journal*, June 19, 1971: 15.
34. Watson Spoelstra," Great in the Clutch, Gates Wants a Regular Job," *The Sporting News*, July 10, 1971: 11.
35. Ron Fimrite, "Billy the Kid as Peacemaker," *Sports Illustrated*, June 28, 1971: 18.
36. Russell Schneider, "Aspro: Tribe Has mark of Winner," *Cleveland Plain Dealer*, May 23, 1972: 3-C.
37. Terese Karmel, "Middlesex Offers Baseball 101," *Hartford Courant*, August 28, 1982: C4.
38. Owen Canfield, "Hartford Needs a Stage to Showcase Baseball," *Hartford Courant*, August 17, 1984.
39. Canfield, "Crazy Like a Hawk: Sky's the Limit at U of H," *Hartford Courant*, July 17, 1985: C1.
40. Smith, "Hawks Struggling to Halt Draught," *Hartford Courant*, April 2, 1985: C1.

41 Smith, "Rocky Hawks Sitting on 2 Milestones," *Hartford Courant*, April 20, 1985: C5.

42 Tom Yantz, "U of H Gets Steinbrenner for Dinner," *Hartford Courant*, October 11, 1985: C2

43 Smith, "Frosh-Filled Hawks Leaping Into Big Time Baseball," *Hartford Courant*, March 2, 1986: E19.

44 Jack Magruder, "UA Uses Hartford for Batting Practice," *Arizona Daily Star* (Tucson), March 12, 1986: C2.

45 Smith, "Hawks End Nine-Game Skid," *Hartford Courant*, April 16, 1986: D7.

46 Don Fillion, "Forfeit Gives Vermont Split," *Burlington* (Vermont) *Free Press*, April 27, 1986: 3C

47 Smith, "He'll Always Be Player from the Old School," *Hartford Courant*, October 28, 1994: C1.

48 Smith, "Yale Sweeps Slumping Hartford," *Hartford Courant*, March 29, 1987: 33

49 Smith, Hawks Go Bear Hunting, Get a Pair," *Hartford Courant*, April 14, 1987: D2.

50 Smith, "Brawls Halt UConn-UH Game," *Hartford Courant*, April 15, 1987: D1.

51 Smith, "UConn and U of H Say No Rematch," *Hartford Courant*, April 16, 1987: D2.

52 Smith, "Hawks' Ax Falls," School Fires Baseball Coach, Staff," *Hartford Courant*, April 17, 1987: E1.

53 Smith, "Hartford Fires Denehy for Post-Fight Comments," *Hartford Courant*, April 17, 1987: E 10.

54 Smith, "Hawks Turn a Page in Baseball program, *Hartford Courant*, August 27, 1987: D3.

55 Canfield, "Give Gooley a Letter 'S' for Success," *Hartford Courant*, April 28, 1988: G-1, G-6.

56 Tom Yantz, "The Sporting Look.," *Hartford Courant*, June 9, 1988: D2.

57 "WTKN Evens the Score," *St. Petersburg Times*, November 16, 1990: 17.

58 Steve Persall and Roger Fischer, "Q-105 May Be on the Rebound," *St. Petersburg Times*, March 29, 1991: 19.

59 "Mercy's Denehy Pitches One-Hit Shutout," *Hartford Courant*, May 30, 1992: E4.

60 Chris Sheridan, "Pitcher Near Top as School Year Winds Up," *Hartford Courant*, June 7, 1992: H4.

61 "Holy Cross Turns Back Mercy, 8-1," *Hartford Courant*, June 9, 1992: D5.

62 Denehy with Golenbock, 255-256.

63 Canfield, "From Middletown to the Majors Through Hell and Back," *Hartford Courant*, March 7, 1993: A1, A12.

64 Catherine Hinman, "Radio Waves," *Orlando Sentinel*, November 7, 1992: E2.

65 Canfield, "November Is Season to Hunt Autographs," *Hartford Courant*, November 12, 1993: E3.

66 Bill Denehy with Bob Gold, *Intrinsic Golf: It's Within You: How to Play Better Golf When You Don't Have Time to Practice or Take Lessons* (Bloomington, Indiana: Trafford Publishing, 2003).

67 Badger, "Before There Were Steroids: Former Players Say Cortisone Abuse Once Was Rampant in Big Leagues," *Orlando Sentinel*, April 10, 2005: C12.

68 Steven Goode, "Former Major Leaguer Bill Denehy Says He's Thankful for Fidelco Guide Dog," *Hartford Courant*, August 22, 2014.

69 Brian Schmitz, "Former Pitcher Denehy was in Howe's Shoes," *Orlando Sentinel*, December 12, 1992: B1.

Gary DiSarcina Recalls Bagwell, College Foe

*Interview with Gary DiSarcina by Bill Nowlin
at Fenway Park on August 4, 2017*

BN: You played against him when you were in college, in 1987 and 1988?

GD: Right. And then we were supposed to be on the same Cape League team in Chatham. We were together for about three days but then I got drafted and I left.

BN: Well, that was good news for you.

GD: Yeah.

BN: But you played against him when you were in college. You were a shortstop.

GD: At UMass.

BN: A year ahead of him in school?

GD: I believe I was a year ahead of him. I would have got out in '89 so, yeah, a year ahead of him.

BN: The editor of the book sent me a couple of boxscores. I don't know if you remember this 6-5 game, a 10-inning game. You got a couple of doubles, it looks like.

GD (looking at printout): And I hit a rare home run.

BN: Two doubles and a home run. No wonder you got drafted.

Did Jeff stand out in any way?

GD: Yeah, he did. I think he was a little bit raw at the time, but his batting stance really didn't change much from the time he was in college to the time of seeing him in Houston. Unfortunately, we didn't have interleague played where the Angels played the Astros at the time, and the Astros were not in the American League back then. But I'd see him on TV, see him from afar, but his batting stance was always wide. As he got older, he got stronger and the power came with it. I didn't remember him really having a ton of power in college. He was more of a…I think he might have hit .400 one year. He was more of a gap-to-gap singles hitter, not yet developed into his body. I believe he played third base, too, in college. Good third baseman.

BN: He was born in Boston and you were born in Malden, here in Greater Boston. He'd moved to Connecticut but I don't know if you ever talked about both being from the same general area.

GD: I think my junior year, his sophomore year, we were supposed to be teammates together down in Chatham and I got drafted in the sixth round. He wasn't eligible for the draft yet. He played third and I was playing short, and one of our jobs was to pick rocks from the infield dirt before the season started. We had like two or three workouts before the season.

We were just kind of talking about playing pro ball, coming from this area and having the opportunity. He actually made a couple of comments that stuck with me. He said, "Hey, it's not worth holding out for a couple of thousand dollars. Go get your career started. Look at you right now. We're both picking rocks on the field on the Cape. Go get your career started."

BN: Of course, he ended up with this organization [drafted by the Red Sox the next year, in 1989].

GD: Yeah. Yeah.

BN: Probably no one ever guessed that he'd end up in the Hall of Fame. You can't ever guess that about anyone that early.

GD: No, but I just thought…I always admired his career track from afar. In college, he did command the zone. He didn't swing at many bad pitches. As he grew older and grew up into who he became—he also played in that big ballpark, too. That's a huge park. So for him to hit some home runs, the way he hit them, he hit them really high and he hit line drives that had a high arc.

I used to keep pace with Tommy Glavine. I always would admire those guys. We didn't play interleague so I didn't play the Braves (of Billerica, MA), but I always watched those guys on TV. I obviously cared about them because they came from the area and that was a connection.

Jeff was great. He was scrappy in college. A little bit younger guy with a really different swing, different batting stance—but it worked.

BN: It did work.

Freshman Bagwell Had Remlinger's Number

By Alan Cohen

During his time at the University of Hartford, Jeff Bagwell faced Mike Remlinger, who went on to pitch in the major leagues.

Mike Remlinger hailed from Middletown, New York and attended Dartmouth College. He was more concerned with winning than who he faced in his college years and doesn't remember much of the game on April 1, 1987 when Dartmouth visited the University of Hartford. However, his friends did remind him, correctly, that he yielded a couple of home runs to Bagwell, then a freshman, that day. Remlinger was more concerned that his team came out victorious as, despite Jeff's big day, the Hartford Hawks came out on the short end, losing 10-4. On the day, Bagwell had a double, in addition to the homers, in four at bats, and was credited with three RBI's. Lost in Remlinger's memory, and perhaps everyone else's is the fact that, with his team trailing 10-2, Bagwell pitched a scoreless ninth inning. Remlinger pitched the first six innings for Dartmouth and was credited with the win, bringing his record to 3-1. The loss brought the Hawks' record to 3-10. At season's end, Remlinger was selected by the Giants in the first round of the draft (16th overall), and pitched in the majors for parts of 14 seasons. In 2002, when he went 7-3 with a 1.99 ERA for Atlanta, he was named to the NL All Star team.

The author interviewed Mike Remlinger on November 8, 2017.

NEW BRITAIN RED SOX 1990

(Collection of Karl Cicitto)

Last Stop for Bagwell in Connecticut — The 1990 New Britain Red Sox

By Alan Cohen

"In 1990, when the Red Sox sought Houston reliever Larry Andersen for their stretch drive, (longtime Houston scout and former major-league ballplayer Stan) Benjamin, (then 76 years old), and scouting colleague Tom Mooney of Pittsfield, Massachusetts, recommended that the Astros ask for outfielder Jeff Bagwell in return. They hesitated, because Bagwell had only four homers in 136 games for the Double-A New Britain Red Sox. 'Babe Ruth couldn't hit home runs in that ballpark,' Benjamin said of New Britain's Beehive Field."

— Garry Brown. "Remembering Greenfield Coach and Major League Baseball Scout Stan Benjamin," Springfield Republican, January 1, 2010

"I knew he was going to hit. I couldn't ask any more or less from him in the second half. Jeff Bagwell is a manager's player, any manager's player."

—Butch Hobson *during the 1990 Eastern League All-Star break*[1]

Seldom has the climax to a story overshadowed the story as it did on the last day of Jeff Bagwell's time with the New Britain Red Sox. The pictures and emotions of a baseball trade (the first and only one of his professional career) having put an end to his dreams of playing for the Boston Red Sox—those would be lasting. They would form the substance of memories about that time.

But that time was not about a trade but about a wonderful ride in what, even before the 1990 season began, was known to be Bagwell's baseball farewell to Connecticut. The hometown boy, a boy no longer, had returned to the place of his upbringing for a minor-league season that could, if things went right, catapult him to big-league stardom.

JEFF BAGWELL IN CONNECTICUT

In 1990, Bagwell was in his second season of professional ball and was on a fast track to the majors. A fast track that would pass through the Eastern League and bus rides in a league that crisscrossed its way from Connecticut to Ohio with six other stops, including one in Canada, in between.

The opening game of the season was played on a soggy April 10 in front of 767 onlookers at New Britain's Beehive Field. The game had two long rain delays and didn't end until 12:20 A.M.[2] Although the Britsox lost 9-3 to the visiting London Tigers, Bagwell had his first two hits in a New Britain uniform.

On Saturday night April 14, only 841 fans braved the cool evening at Beehive Field and witnessed Bagwell's first big hit as a member of the Britsox. It came in a 7-4 win over the Albany-Colonie Yankees. His fifth-inning RBI double broke a 2-2 tie. The double brought his average to .250 (4-for-16), according to the *Hartford Courant* game story, but Bagwell was just warming up. After his first big hit he said, "I'm trying to swing at better pitches. [The double] was the first good pitch to hit I had seen, and I just swung."[3]

But the team was playing unevenly in the early going. The bats were slumping (the team batting average was .227) until one night in Hagerstown, Maryland. Against the Suns on April 23, the Britsox exploded for 14 hits and Bagwell had his best game to date. The third baseman went 4-for-5 with three singles and a double, scoring two runs and batting in a pair. The 10-6 win brought the Britsox' record to 7-5, and brought Bagwell's batting average to .348.[4]

The Britsox hit a hot streak, as did Bagwell in early May, and on May 11 at Reading, with Bagwell going 3-for-5 with a triple, his first homer of the season, two runs scored, and two RBIs, New Britain defeated Reading, 7-5 (their seventh win in 10 games) to stretch their record to 17-11 and take over first place.[5] The Britsox remained in first place through the end of the month, and on June 1 took the field at New Britain when the unbelievable happened—a season-high 3,775 fans jammed themselves into the Beehive for a doubleheader against Albany. The teams split the two games and New Britain's league lead was now 3½ games. And the crowds kept coming—the next night, the crowd was 4,525 (the second-highest in franchise history) as the Britsox lost.[6]

When the Britsox took to the road for an 11-game trip to Harrisburg, Hagerstown, and Williamsport, they won only three games and stumbled back to New Britain having lost five in a row. They had slipped to third place. Bagwell came up big against Hagerstown and Williamsport when the team returned to the Beehive, going 11-for-16 over four games as New Britain took three of the first four games on the home stand. He even had his first stolen base of the season, against Williamsport. The skid was stopped and, after a 3-2 win over Williamsport, Bagwell said, "We're getting better. This was a big win, it will give us some confidence. We're not getting everything perfect, but there is a long way to go."[7] During the home stand, they drew more than 3,000 in four consecutive games for the first time in New Britain franchise history.

At the All-Star break, Bagwell was batting .312, and the team was in a fight for the league lead. The Britsox had slipped out of first place but were only one game behind Harrisburg. For the All-Star game, the eight-team league was split into two divisions. The Giamatti Division included the league's older clubs, and the Eshback division, named for the league's president, represented its newer franchises.[8] Britsox manager Butch Hobson headed up the Giamatti Division (New Britain, Reading, Albany, Williamsport) squad. Bagwell, who was named as a starter for the June 25 game in London, Ontario, batted fourth, and went 2-for-4 as the Giamatti Division lost, 8-4, to the Eshbach Division squad, which mounted a five-run rally in the seventh inning to take the lead.

After the All-Star Game, Bagwell went on a tear. On June 27, having traveled from New Britain to London and then on to Canton, Ohio, Bagwell met up with his teammates who took on the Canton-Akron Indians in a series during which Bagwell feasted. In the first game, a Britsox loss, Bagwell had three hits. In the second game, the Britsox came away with a 12-2 win as Bagwell's first inning bases-loaded single brought in the game's first run. He had three hits as New Britain (39-33) pulled into a virtual second-place tie with the AA-Indians.[9] His six hits in the first two games of the series raised his average to .322, and he was far from finished. For the last week of June, Bagwell was awarded player of the week honors with a 13-for-23 performance.

During the spurt, Gary Grabowski of the *New Britain Herald* told his readers that Bagwell was "plodding a path to the majors." Bagwell said, "I'm starting to get my head on straight a little bit. I feel pretty comfortable right now with my game. Hopefully, the same things will continue to happen for me this second half as it did in the first half. Still, I want to get better. I want to solidify my defense. I want to be more consistent and to do the things that will help the team win."[10]

Grabowski caught up with Bagwell's college coach, Dan Gooley of the University of Hartford. Gooley said, "He has great work habits and a great heart. Those are two intangible things about Jeff Bagwell that are the most impressive to me. He was the best offensive player I've ever coached to hit a slider. I've had kids run better than Jeff Bagwell. I've had kids with better gloves, but I've never had a player with better work habits or with a greater heart to play the game of baseball."[11]

When Canton-Akron visited New Britain in early July, Bagwell feasted on the Indians again, at least when they pitched to him. In the first three games of the series, he came to the plate 15 times and had only seven at-bats. He was walked seven times and hit by a pitch once. In those seven at-bats, he had four hits, including a single and triple on July 5, bringing his batting average to a league-leading .338. This all moved the Canton manager, Ken Bolek, to say, "We told him that when they send him the batting champion's trophy at the end of the year, we want half of it."[12] Bagwell hit safely in nine of the first 10 games after the All-Star break. This included three three-hit games.

As June turned into July, the Britsox hit a snag. Other than Bagwell, the team was not hitting and it fell a couple of notches in the standings. As play concluded on July 21, the Britsox, losers of five straight, were only one game above .500, but in the coming days, they turned things around. One of the team's fans, a little girl, understanding the team's plight, gave Bagwell a rabbit's foot.[13] After New Britain defeated Albany, 10-2, on July 23, Bagwell, whose average was up to .335 with two hits in the rout, said, "A lot of people got big hits tonight who really needed them. We got nervous when we started to lose some games, and we got tight at the plate."[14] But the team was six games out of the league lead.

As the July 31 trading deadline approached, Bagwell was one of those prospects on whom an "off-limits" sign had been placed. At the time, Bagwell, then living in Killingworth, had been labeled the best hitting prospect in the Eastern League and was batting .335.

The presence of Bagwell and a winning team in New Britain in 1990 boosted attendance at Beehive Field, the city's wooden grandstand reminiscent of old-time minor-league venues. After disappointing crowds in the early going, attendance picked up in June and the Britsox, for the first time in New Britain history, had crowds of more than 3,000 in four successive games (June 20-June 24). For the season, they drew 123,017, the best since their first season in New Britain, seven years earlier, when they drew 130,433.

The team went into a slump in late July that extended into August, but Bagwell went on a tear, putting together a 17-game hitting streak that extended from July 22 through August 8. On August 2, despite Bagwell's going 2-for-4 and raising his average to .337 in front of a Thursday night crowd of 2,058 at Beehive, the team lost its sixth in a row. The Britsox were 7½ games out of first place with a 53-56 record. They were 3½ games out of the fourth and final playoff spot, causing Dom Amore of the *Hartford Courant* to write, "The Eastern League playoffs are starting to look like a speck on the horizon for the New Britain Red Sox."[15]

But the Britsox came back to life. They put together a modest winning streak and got back to .500 after defeating Williamsport, 3-2, on August 5, for their third straight win. In the game, Bagwell hit his first and only Beehive Field homer, a fourth-inning blast that put New Britain in front, 1-0.

That season would prove to be Bagwell's last as a third baseman, and it was probably destined to be that way early on, as the parent Red Sox were stocked with third basemen. Bagwell's play at third base was not equal to this offensive prowess, especially in the early part of the season when he made 15 errors in his first 41 games. He showed improvement as the season wore on, but on August 15 at Canton, his throwing error allowed the tying run to score with two out in the ninth inning and the Britsox lost, 6-5 in extra innings. That put the team back into a fourth-place tie.

During the Britsox' final home stand, Bagwell hit safely in each of the first six games, bringing his league-leading batting average to .343. The team was in fourth place and although Bagwell went 0-for-5 in his final game at New Britain, the team took to the road in fourth place (the final playoff spot), finishing up with series at London and Albany.

As August rushed to a close, and a place in the Eastern League playoffs loomed, it was reasonable to speculate that Bagwell might be called up to the Red Sox for the September drive and miss the Eastern League playoffs.

But there would be no playoffs for Bagwell and no late-season call-up. By the time the team clinched a playoff spot in Albany on August 31, Bagwell had been traded to the Houston Astros for Larry Andersen. The trade had been announced one hour before the game, leaving Bagwell to say, "I'm happy (at being selected team MVP by his teammates). I had a pretty good year. I just wish I could be here with these guys the rest of my life. I guess that's baseball. I've got to learn the reality of it. It's a business."[16]

Without Bagwell, the Britsox advanced to the playoffs, winning the first round against the regular-season champion Albany-Colonie, 3 games to 2, before being swept by London (3-0) in the final.

Bagwell, who appeared in each of his team's first 136 games, left his mark on the New Britain Red Sox and the Eastern League. He was named the league's All-Star third baseman and was chosen the league's Most Valuable Player. His .333 batting average was second in the league only to Luis Mercedes of Hagerstown. Mercedes passed Bagwell on the day of the trade (going 3-for-5 in a doubleheader), and sat out the last two games of the season, his team having been eliminated from playoff consideration.[17] Bagwell led the league with 34 doubles and was second in triples with seven. His league-leading 160 hits set a New Britain franchise record.

After it was all over, Robert Bagwell, Jeff's father, who had been at virtually every game, said, "It's a disappointment in a way. He's loved it here in New Britain. It's his hometown, friends were able to come out to see him. We were really fortunate to have that opportunity. He could've been drafted by the Dodgers and played out in LA. We've just got to be thankful we saw him play here one year."[18]

On September 6, Jeff Bagwell returned to Beehive Field, a face in the crowd watching the fourth game of the playoffs between Albany-Colonie and New Britain. New Britain won the game to tie the series at two games apiece. The next day they would win again to move onto the finals against London. Bagwell said, "Day by day, I feel better about (the trade). I know I have a better chance to make the major leagues sooner with Houston than I did with the Red Sox. I know the trade could be a blessing in disguise. At first, I felt unwanted, I guess. But obviously Houston wanted me real bad because they gave up a major-league pitcher just for me."[19]

SOURCES

The author consulted numerous New Britain game stories/standings in the *Hartford Courant* and the *New Britain Herald*.

In addition to the sources cited in the Notes, the author used Baseball-Reference.com and the following:

Bernstein, Viv. "Bagwell Hits the Top (.337) with the Britsox," *Hartford Courant*, July 8, 1990: E-11.

Bowman, Phil. "Britsox Collect 21 Hits in 12-2 Rout," *Hartford Courant*, June 29, 1990: E-6.

NOTES

1. Dom Amore, "Hobson and His Britsox Living the Good Life," *Hartford Courant*, June 27, 1990: F-8.
2. Gary Grabowski, "Tigers Rain Runs in Soggy Beehive Opener," *New Britain Herald*, April 11, 1990: 9
3. Don Amore, "Bagwell, Masse Make Adjustments," *Hartford Courant*, April 16, 1990: C-5.
4. Scott Reinardy, "Britsox Top Hagerstown," *Hartford Courant*, April 24, 1990: D-3
5. "Britsox Beat Reading, 7-5, Take Over First Place," *Hartford Courant*, May 12, 1990: E-7.
6. Don Amore, "Britsox Lose in Ninth, 7-2," *Hartford Courant*, June 3, 1990: C-12.
7. Don Amore, "Britsox Win on Kelly's Single in Ninth: Wedge's Hit-and-Run Single Keys 3-2 Victory Over Williamsport," *Hartford Courant*, June 23, 1990: C-6.
8. David Assad, "Carrick's Wehner Eastern League All-Star; Jelic at .300," *Pittsburgh Post-Gazette*, June 28, 1990:17.
9. Red Nichols, "Red Sox Clobber AA Indians, 12-2," *Cleveland Plain Dealer*, June 29, 1990: 3-D.
10. Gary Grabowski, "Bagwell's Plodding a Path to the Majors," *New Britain Herald*, June 30, 1990: 21-22.
11. Ibid.
12. Viv Bernstein, "Bagwell Leads Britsox," *Hartford, Courant*, July 6, 1990: C-6.
13. Viv Bernstein, "Baseball America Rates Bagwell as League's Top Prospect," *Harford Courant*, July 29, 1990: D-6
14. Don Amore, "Britsox Rout Albany, 10-2," *Hartford Courant*, July 24, 1990: E4.
15. Don Amore. "Britsox Lose to Williamsport in Ninth, 4-3," *Hartford Courant*, August 3, 1990: E-3.
16. Sean Horgan, "Bagwell Traded for Andersen," *Hartford Courant*, September 1, 1990.
17. Don Amore, "Bagwell Gives Hobson a Boost," *Hartford Courant*, September 9, 1990: K-11.
18. Viv Bernstein, "Hobson Won't Dwell on Loss of Bagwell," *Hartford Courant*, September 2, 1990: C-9, C11.
19. Don Amore, "Britsox Force Game Five," *Hartford Courant*, September 7, 1990: E-13.

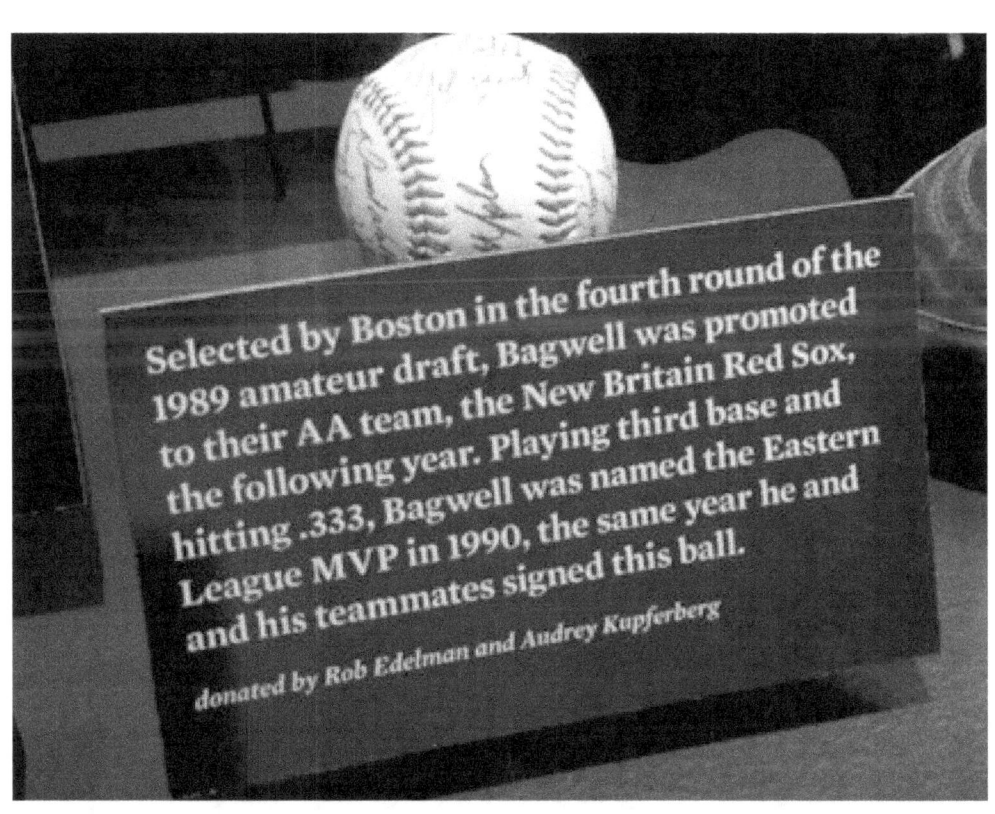

A 1990 New Britain Red Sox team signed baseball on display at the Hall of Fame in 2017. Husband and wife, Rob Edelman and Audrey Kupferberg, were regulars at the New Britain games in 1990 and were given the ball during that season by a team employee. In the wake of Bagwell's Hall election, Rob and Audrey donated the ball to the Cooperstown museum. On a visit to the Hall of Fame in May that same year they were delighted to see their ball on display. (Courtesy of Rob Edelman and Audrey Kupferberg.)

New Britain Red Sox Game Log

Jeff Bagwell and the New Britain Red Sox - 1990

Date	Opponent	Score	Record	Place	AB	R	H	RBI	2B	3B	HR	Avg.	AB	R	H	RBI	2B	3B	HR
10-Apr	London	3-9	0-1	8	4	0	2	0	0	0	0	0.500	4	0	2	0	0	0	0
11-Apr	London	4-1	1-1	4T	2	1	0	0	0	0	0	0.333	6	1	2	0	0	0	0
12-Apr	London	4-6	1-2	6	3	1	1	1	0	0	0	0.333	9	2	3	1	0	0	0
13-Apr	Albany-Colonie	6-0	2-2	3T	5	0	0	0	0	0	0	0.214	14	2	3	1	0	0	0
14-Apr	Albany-Colonie	7-4	3-2	3	5	1	1	2	1	0	0	0.211	19	3	4	3	1	0	0
16-Apr	Harrisburg	6-0	4-2	1-T	4	0	1	0	0	0	0	0.217	23	3	5	3	1	0	0
18-Apr	Harrisburg	4-3	5-2	2	4	0	1	1	0	0	0	0.222	27	3	6	4	1	0	0
19-Apr	Harrisburg	0-5	5-3	2	3	0	2	0	1	0	0	0.267	30	3	8	4	2	0	0
20-Apr	Harrisburg	2-1	6-3	2	3	0	0	0	0	0	0	0.242	33	3	8	4	2	0	0
21-Apr	at Harrisburg	2-4	6-4	2	5	0	2	0	0	0	0	0.263	38	3	10	4	2	0	0
22-Apr	at Harrisburg	2-8	6-5	4	3	0	2	1	0	0	0	0.293	41	3	12	5	2	0	0
23-Apr	at Hagerstown	10-6	7-5	3-T	5	2	4	2	1	0	0	0.348	46	5	16	7	3	0	0
24-Apr	at Hagerstown	2-13	7-6	3-T	2	0	0	0	0	0	0	0.333	48	5	16	7	3	0	0
25-Apr	at Hagerstown	2-5	7-7	4-T	4	0	0	0	0	0	0	0.308	52	5	16	7	3	0	0
27-Apr	Williamsport	3-2	8-7	5	4	1	1	0	0	1	0	0.304	56	6	17	7	3	1	0
28-Apr	Williamsport	8-7 (10)	9-7	4-T	4	0	1	1	0	0	0	0.300	60	6	18	8	3	1	0
29-Apr	Williamsport	1-6	9-8	4-T	4	0	1	0	0	0	0	0.297	64	6	19	8	3	1	0
30-Apr	Hagerstown	3-1	10-8	3	4	0	1	0	0	0	0	0.294	68	6	20	8	3	1	0
1-May	Hagerstown	1-5	10-9	5	4	0	1	0	0	0	0	0.292	72	6	21	8	3	1	0
2-May	Hagerstown	2-0	11-9	4	4	0	0	0	0	0	0	0.276	76	6	21	8	3	1	0
3-May	Hagerstown	2-1	12-9	3	4	1	1	0	1	0	0	0.275	80	7	22	8	4	1	0
6-May	at Williamsport	1-0 (13)	13-9	4	5	0	1	0	0	0	0	0.271	85	7	23	8	4	1	0
6-May	at Williamsport	4-0	14-9	2	2	0	0	0	0	0	0	0.264	87	7	23	8	4	1	0
7-May	at Canton	5-3	15-9	2	4	0	2	1	0	0	0	0.275	91	7	25	9	4	1	0
8-May	at Canton	5-2	16-9	1	4	1	2	1	1	0	0	0.284	95	8	27	10	5	1	0

Date	Opponent	Score	Record	Place	AB	R	H	RBI	2B	3B	HR	Avg.	AB	R	H	RBI	2B	3B	HR
9-May	at Canton	2-4	16-10	1	3	0	0	0	0	0	0	0.276	98	8	27	10	5	1	0
10-May	at Canton	5-15	16-11	2	3	2	1	0	0	0	0	0.277	101	10	28	10	5	1	0
11-May	at Reading	7-5	17-11	1	5	2	3	2	0	1	1	0.292	106	12	31	12	5	2	1
12-May	at Reading	7-5	18-11	1	5	0	2	1	0	0	0	0.297	111	12	33	13	5	2	1
14-May	Canton	6-3	19-11	1	2	1	1	1	1	0	0	0.301	113	13	34	14	6	2	1
15-May	Canton	3-1	20-11	1	3	0	0	0	0	0	0	0.293	116	13	34	14	6	2	1
18-May	Reading	1-4	20-12	1	4	1	2	0	0	0	0	0.300	120	14	36	14	6	2	1
19-May	Reading	7-4	21-12	1	4	1	2	2	1	0	0	0.306	124	15	38	16	7	2	1
20-May	Reading	5-0	22-12	1	3	1	0	0	0	0	0	0.299	127	16	38	16	7	2	1
21-May	at London	4-2	23-12	1	4	1	3	0	1	0	0	0.313	131	17	41	16	8	2	1
22-May	at London	2-6	23-13	1	4	0	1	0	0	0	0	0.311	135	17	42	16	8	2	1
23-May	at London	10-6	24-13	1	5	2	1	3	1	0	0	0.307	140	19	43	19	9	2	1
24-May	at London	0-2	24-14	1	4	0	1	0	0	0	0	0.306	144	19	44	19	9	2	1
25-May	at Albany	9-2	25-14	1	5	1	1	0	0	0	0	0.302	149	20	45	19	9	2	1
26-May	at Albany	3-4	25-15	1	5	0	0	0	0	0	0	0.292	154	20	45	19	9	2	1
27-May	at Albany	3-5	25-16	1	4	0	1	1	0	0	0	0.291	158	20	46	20	9	2	1
28-May	London	2-0	26-16	1	2	0	1	2	1	0	0	0.294	160	20	47	22	10	2	1
30-May	London	2-6	26-17	1	4	0	0	0	0	0	0	0.287	164	20	47	22	10	2	1
31-May	London	10-1	27-17	1	4	1	1	1	0	0	0	0.286	168	21	48	23	10	2	1
1-Jun	Albany-Colonie	1-2	27-18	1	3	1	2	0	0	0	0	0.292	171	22	50	23	10	2	1
1-Jun	Albany-Colonie	5-1	28-18	1	3	1	1	0	0	0	0	0.293	174	23	51	23	10	2	1
2-Jun	Albany-Colonie	2-7	28-19	1	4	0	0	0	0	0	0	0.287	178	23	51	23	10	2	1
3-Jun	Albany-Colonie	1-6	28-20	1	3	0	2	1	0	0	0	0.293	181	23	53	24	10	2	1
4-Jun	Harrisburg	10-3	29-20	1	4	1	2	0	2	0	0	0.297	185	24	55	24	12	2	1
5-Jun	Harrisburg	1-3	29-21	1	2	1	1	0	1	0	0	0.299	187	25	56	24	13	2	1
5-Jun	Harrisburg	0-11	29-22	1	3	0	0	0	0	0	0	0.295	190	25	56	24	13	2	1
6-Jun	Harrisburg	4-1	30-22	1	4	1	1	0	0	1	0	0.294	194	26	57	24	13	3	1
7-Jun	Harrisburg	3-7 (12)	30-23	1	5	1	1	0	0	0	0	0.291	199	27	58	24	13	3	1
8-Jun	at Harrisburg	1-3	30-24	2	3	0	2	1	0	0	0	0.297	202	27	60	25	13	3	1
9-Jun	at Harrisburg	5-4	31-24	1	5	0	3	1	0	0	0	0.304	207	27	63	26	13	3	1
10-Jun	at Harrisburg	2-5	31-25	2	3	0	0	0	0	0	0	0.300	210	27	63	26	13	3	1
11-Jun	at Hagerstown	3-4	31-26	2	4	0	1	2	1	0	0	0.299	214	27	64	28	14	3	1
12-Jun	at Hagerstown	9-4	32-26	2	5	2	2	2	1	0	0	0.301	219	29	66	30	15	3	1
13-Jun	at Hagerstown	9-7	33-26	2	4	1	0	0	0	0	0	0.296	223	30	66	30	15	3	1
14-Jun	at Hagerstown	0-11	33-27	2	4	0	0	0	0	0	0	0.291	227	30	66	30	15	3	1
15-Jun	at Williamsport	3-7	33-28	2	4	1	1	1	0	1	0	0.290	231	31	67	31	15	4	1

Date	Opponent	Score	Record	Place	AB	R	H	RBI	2B	3B	HR	Avg.	AB	R	H	RBI	2B	3B	HR
16-Jun	at Williamsport	6-7	33-29	3	3	0	2	1	0	0	0	0.295	234	31	69	32	15	4	1
16-Jun	at Williamsport	1-6	33-30	3	3	0	1	0	1	0	0	0.295	237	31	70	32	16	4	1
17-Jun	at Williamsport	0-5	33-31	4	4	0	0	0	0	0	0	0.290	241	31	70	32	16	4	1
18-Jun	Hagerstown	3-2 (10)	34-31	3	4	1	3	1	1	0	0	0.298	245	32	73	33	17	4	1
19-Jun	Hagerstown	15-3	35-31	3	4	2	3	0	0	0	0	0.305	249	34	76	33	17	4	1
20-Jun	Hagerstown	0-1	35-32	2	4	0	2	0	0	0	0	0.308	253	34	78	33	17	4	1
22-Jun	Williamsport	3-2	36-32	3	4	1	3	0	0	0	0	0.315	257	35	81	33	17	4	1
23-Jun	Williamsport	4-3	37-32	3	3	0	1	0	0	0	0	0.315	260	35	82	33	17	4	1
24-Jun	Williamsport	1-0	38-32	3	3	0	0	0	0	0	0	0.312	263	35	82	33	17	4	1
27-Jun	at Canton	4-6	38-33	3	4	2	3	1	0	2	0	0.318	267	37	85	34	17	6	1
28-Jun	at Canton	12-2	39-33	3	6	0	3	1	0	0	0	0.322	273	37	88	35	17	6	1
29-Jun	at Canton	2-3	39-34	3	4	0	1	0	0	0	0	0.321	277	37	89	35	17	6	1
30-Jun	at Reading	15-3	40-34	2	3	2	3	0	1	0	0	0.329	280	39	92	35	18	6	1
1-Jul	at Reading	0-2	40-35	4	3	0	1	0	0	0	0	0.329	283	39	93	35	18	6	1
1-Jul	at Reading	2-5	40-36	4	3	0	2	0	0	0	0	0.332	286	39	95	35	18	6	1
2-Jul	at Reading	6-4	41-36	3	3	1	1	1	0	0	1	0.332	289	40	96	36	18	6	2
3-Jul	Canton	0-5	41-37	4	3	0	2	0	1	0	0	0.336	292	40	98	36	19	6	2
4-Jul	Canton	5-4 (11)	42-37	3	2	1	0	0	0	0	0	0.333	294	41	98	36	19	6	2
5-Jul	Canton	7-3	43-37	3	2	1	2	1	0	1	0	0.338	296	42	100	37	19	7	2
6-Jul	Canton	1-5	43-38	3	2	0	1	0	0	0	0	0.339	298	42	101	37	19	7	2
6-Jul	Canton	3-2	44-38	3	3	0	0	0	0	0	0	0.336	301	42	101	37	19	7	2
7-Jul	Reading	8-2	45-38	3	2	2	1	1	1	0	0	0.337	303	44	102	38	20	7	2
8-Jul	Reading	1-0	46-38	3	3	0	1	0	0	0	0	0.337	306	44	103	38	20	7	2
9-Jul	Reading	0-1	46-39	3	4	0	1	0	0	0	0	0.335	310	44	104	38	20	7	2
11-Jul	at London	1-5	46-40	2	4	0	0	0	0	0	0	0.331	314	44	104	38	20	7	2
12-Jul	at London	4-1	47-40	2	4	1	2	0	0	0	0	0.333	318	45	106	38	20	7	2
13-Jul	at Albany	0-9	47-41	3	4	0	2	0	0	0	0	0.335	322	45	108	38	20	7	2
14-Jul	at Albany	1-7	47-42	3	4	0	1	0	0	0	0	0.334	326	45	109	38	20	7	2
15-Jul	at Albany	5-3	48-42	3	4	0	3	0	1	0	0	0.339	330	45	112	38	21	7	2
16-Jul	at Albany	0-2	48-43	3T	4	0	1	0	1	0	0	0.338	334	45	113	38	22	7	2
17-Jul	London	1-0	49-43	3T	1	0	0	0	0	0	0	0.337	335	45	113	38	22	7	2
17-Jul	London	2-5	49-44	3T	2	0	0	0	0	0	0	0.335	337	45	113	38	22	7	2
18-Jul	London	3-6	49-45	4	3	0	0	0	0	0	0	0.332	340	45	113	38	22	7	2
19-Jul	London	1-8	49-46	4	4	0	1	0	1	0	0	0.331	344	45	114	38	23	7	2
20-Jul	Albany	3-6	49-47	4	4	0	2	1	1	0	0	0.333	348	45	116	39	24	7	2
21-Jul	Albany	4-5	49-48	4	3	0	0	1	0	0	0	0.330	351	45	116	40	24	7	2

Date	Opponent	Score	Record	Place	AB	R	H	RBI	2B	3B	HR	Avg.	AB	R	H	RBI	2B	3B	HR
22-Jul	Albany	3-1	50-48	4	4	0	2	0	1	0	0	0.332	355	45	118	40	25	7	2
23-Jul	Albany	10-2	51-48	4	3	1	2	3	0	0	0	0.335	358	46	120	43	25	7	2
24-Jul	Harrisburg	5-11	51-49	4	4	0	1	1	0	0	0	0.334	362	46	121	44	25	7	2
25-Jul	Harrisburg	2-7	51-50	5	3	1	1	0	0	0	0	0.334	365	47	122	44	25	7	2
26-Jul	at Harrisburg	5-1	52-50	4	4	1	2	0	1	0	0	0.336	369	48	124	44	26	7	2
27-Jul	at Harrisburg	10-2	53-50	4	3	2	1	3	0	0	1	0.336	372	50	125	47	26	7	3
28-Jul	at Harrisburg	1-6	53-51	4	4	0	1	0	0	0	0	0.335	376	50	126	47	26	7	3
29-Jul	at Harrisburg	2-4	53-52	5	4	0	1	1	0	0	0	0.334	380	50	127	48	26	7	3
30-Jul	at Hagerstown	3-6	53-53	6	4	0	1	0	0	0	0	0.333	384	50	128	48	26	7	3
31-Jul	at Hagerstown	0-7	53-54	6	3	0	2	0	0	0	0	0.336	387	50	130	48	26	7	3
1-Aug	at Hagerstown	2-3	53-55	6	4	1	1	1	1	0	0	0.335	391	51	131	49	27	7	3
2-Aug	Williamsport	3-4	53-56	6	4	1	2	0	1	0	0	0.337	395	52	133	49	28	7	3
3-Aug	Williamsport	5-1	54-56	6	3	0	2	1	0	0	0	0.339	398	52	135	50	28	7	3
4-Aug	Williamsport	4-3	55-56	6	3	0	1	0	0	0	0	0.339	401	52	136	50	28	7	3
5-Aug	Williamsport	3-2	56-56	6	4	1	1	1	0	0	1	0.338	405	53	137	51	28	7	4
8-Aug	Hagerstown	4-0	57-56	6	2	0	1	0	0	0	0	0.339	407	53	138	51	28	7	4
8-Aug	Hagerstown	1-0	58-56	5T	3	1	1	0	0	0	0	0.339	410	54	139	51	28	7	4
9-Aug	at Williamsport	7-3	59-56	5T	2	2	0	0	0	0	0	0.337	412	56	139	51	28	7	4
10-Aug	at Williamsport	2-3	59-57	5	4	0	1	0	0	0	0	0.337	416	56	140	51	28	7	4
11-Aug	at Williamsport	5-3	60-57	5	3	1	2	2	0	0	0	0.339	419	57	142	53	28	7	4
12-Aug	at Williamsport	1-3	60-58	5	3	0	0	0	0	0	0	0.336	422	57	142	53	28	7	4
13-Aug	at Canton	4-2	61-58	4	3	0	0	0	0	0	0	0.334	425	57	142	53	28	7	4
14-Aug	at Canton	3-4	61-59		4	0	1	0	0	0	0	0.333	429	57	143	53	28	7	4
15-Aug	at Canton	5-6 (10)	61-60	4	4	1	2	2	2	0	0	0.335	433	58	145	55	30	7	4
16-Aug	at Reading	6-3	62-60	4	3	0	2	3	0	0	0	0.337	436	58	147	58	30	7	4
17-Aug	at Reading	4-1	63-60	4	2	1	2	1	0	0	0	0.340	438	59	149	59	30	7	4
18-Aug	at Reading	6-8	63-61	4	4	1	2	0	1	0	0	0.342	442	60	151	59	31	7	4
19-Aug	at Reading	1-2	63-62	4	4	0	0	0	0	0	0	0.339	446	60	151	59	31	7	4
20-Aug	Canton	5-3	64-62	4	2	1	1	0	0	0	0	0.339	448	61	152	59	31	7	4
21-Aug	Canton	1-0	65-32	4	3	0	1	0	0	1	0	0.339	451	61	153	59	32	7	4
22-Aug	Canton	2-1	66-62	4	3	0	2	1	1	0	0	0.341	454	61	155	60	33	7	4
23-Aug	Reading	3-1	67-62	4	2	0	1	0	0	0	0	0.342	456	61	156	60	33	7	4
25-Aug	Reading	1-0	68-62	4	3	0	1	0	1	0	0	0.342	459	61	157	60	34	7	4
25-Aug	Reading	5-1	69-62	4	2	1	1	0	0	0	0	0.343	461	62	158	60	34	7	4
26-Aug	Reading	1-3	69-63	4	5	0	0	0	0	0	0	0.339	466	62	158	60	34	7	4

Date	Opponent	Score	Record	Place	AB	R	H	RBI	2B	3B	HR	Avg.	AB	R	H	RBI	2B	3B	HR
27-Aug	at London	0-3	69-64	4	3	0	0	0	0	0	0	0.337	469	62	158	60	34	7	4
29-Aug	at London	11-7	70-64	4	5	1	1	1	0	0	0	0.335	474	63	159	61	34	7	4
29-Aug	at London	1-5	70-65	4	3	0	0	0	0	0	0	0.333	477	63	159	61	34	7	4
30-Aug	at London	2-0	71-65	4	4	0	1	0	0	0	0	0.333	481	63	160	61	34	7	4
								DNP - Traded											
31-Aug	at Albany	3-0			481	63	160	61	34	7	4								

Butch Hobson

Manager, 1990 New Britain Red Sox

By Andrew Blume

Before Curt Schilling and the bloody sock in 2004, one player who personified toughness in a Boston Red Sox uniform was Butch Hobson. Hobson's legacy is that of a power-hitting third baseman who brought a football mentality to the diamond in the way he played through pain and gave every ounce of effort on the field that his body could muster.

Clell Lavern Hobson Jr. was born on August 17, 1951, in Tuscaloosa, Alabama. An American Legion and Bessemer (Alabama) High School Most Valuable Player, he followed in his father's footsteps to play football and baseball at the University of Alabama. His father, a three-year letterman at quarterback for Alabama, was Hobson's football coach at Bessemer High. Butch was named to the All-Jefferson County team as a quarterback. He was a safety and backup quarterback at Alabama under legendary coach Paul "Bear" Bryant. In the 1972 Orange Bowl national championship game, won by Nebraska over Alabama, 38-6, Hobson ran the wishbone offense for the Crimson Tide after starting quarterback Terry Davis was injured in the fourth quarter. Alabama's most successful offensive options in that game were the option running and draw plays executed by their quarterback tandem. According to Herb Crehan in *Red Sox Heroes of Yesteryear*, Hobson carried the ball 15 times in the game, rushing for 59 yards.

Entering his senior year at Alabama, Hobson decided to concentrate solely on baseball. In 2004 he said, as reported to Kevin Glew in *Baseball Digest*, "I told Coach Bryant my decision and he told me, 'Well, Butch, from what I've seen of you on the baseball field, you'll be playing football for me next year.'"[1] Hobson's choice proved to be a wise one. In 1973 he was the team leader in hits (38), home runs (13), and RBIs (37), and tied for the team lead in runs (20). The 13 home runs were a Southeastern Conference record. He was named to the ABCA All-South Region Team and was a First Team All-SEC selection. Hobson lettered in baseball at Alabama in 1970, 1972, and 1973, playing for coaches Joe Sewell and Hayden Riley. He hit .250 for his collegiate career (80-for-320) with 18 homers and 54 RBIs. In 1993 Hobson was named to Alabama's All-Century baseball team in commemoration of the school's 100th anniversary of baseball.

Hobson was selected by the Red Sox in the eighth round of the 1973 amateur draft and was signed to a contract by Red Sox scout Milt Bolling on August 1. He was assigned to Winston-Salem, where he hit a mere .179 in 17 games. His numbers improved over a full season at Winston-Salem; he hit .284 with 14 homers and 74 RBIs in 1974 and they earned him a promotion to Bristol of the Eastern League. His 15 homers, 73 RBIs, and .265 batting average at Bristol in 1975 helped secure him a call-up to Boston in September.

Hobson made his major-league debut on September 7, 1975, in the second game of a doubleheader against the Brewers at Milwaukee's County Stadium, pinch-running for Cecil Cooper in the fifth inning. In his only other 1975 appearance in the Red Sox lineup, he started at third base at Fenway Park on September 28 in an 11-4 loss to the Cleveland Indians. Hitting eighth in the order, he struck out twice and flied out to center field before getting his first major-league hit, a single off left-hander Jim Strickland in the eighth inning.

After beginning the 1976 season at Triple-A Pawtucket (in an attempt to appeal to a broader audience, the club was briefly named the Rhode Island Red Sox, but changed back to the Pawtucket Red Sox in 1977), Hobson made his 1976 debut at Fenway Park on June 28 in a 12-8 victory over the Baltimore Orioles. Getting the start at third base and batting second, he went 2-for-5, doubling off Jim Palmer and hitting his first major-league homer in the sixth, off Rudy May. Centerfielder Paul Blair missed catching Hobson's drive to center, allowing Hobson to circle the bases with Cecil Cooper ahead of him for the inside-the-park home run.

Hobson played 76 games at third base in 1976 for the Red Sox as the successor at the hot corner to Rico Petrocelli. Petrocelli was winding down a 13-year career with the Red Sox, hitting only .213 in 85 games in his final season. Hobson, made the everyday third baseman by new manager Don Zimmer (who replaced Darrell Johnson after the All-Star break), hit .234, contributing 8 homers and 34 RBIs.

The 1977 season was Hobson's breakout year and also his finest as a major leaguer. He smashed 30 round-trippers, establishing a Red Sox record for third basemen. It has often been printed that Hobson set this standard. In fact, in 159 games in 1977, he hit third in five games, sixth in 12 games, seventh in 47 games, eighth in 89 games, and ninth in only six games. He hit no homers in the nine spot. Twenty-eight of his 30 homers were hit in the seventh or eighth spot in the batting order. The 1977 Red Sox offensive juggernaut, affectionately known as the Crunch Bunch, hit a then team-record 213 home runs, 21 more than the White Sox, who were second in the major leagues. Five Red Sox hit more than 25 homers, with Jim Rice leading the American League with 39.

The Red Sox hit five or more homers in eight games. They slugged 33 home runs in a 10-game stretch from June 14 through June 24 (establishing a major-league record) and 16 in three games against the New York Yankees June 17-19 (also a major-league record). On July 4 the Red Sox hit a then-record eight home runs (still a Red Sox team high), including seven solo shots (still a single-game record) in a 9-6 pounding of the Toronto Blue Jays in Boston. Hobson's free-swinging ways combined to produce a career-best .265 batting average, 30 homers, 33 doubles, 112 RBIs, and 162 strikeouts in 159 games at third base. Hobson put together an 18-game hitting streak. He was named the BoSox Club Man of the Year for 1977 for his contributions to the success of the team and for his cooperation in community projects.

Old football injuries sustained on the artificial turf at Alabama contributed to a nightmarish 1978 season defensively for Hobson. Bone chips floating around in his right elbow made every throw from third base an adventure. His impairment would often cause his arm to lock up, disrupting his throws. A familiar sight in 1978 was Hobson making a play and then rearranging the bone chips in his elbow. In addition to his sore arm, Hobson was hobbled by cartilage damage in both knees and a torn hamstring muscle. He played 133 games at third base in 1978 (he also served as the DH in 14 games), and he drove in 21 runs in a 10-game stretch from April 14 through 23. Hobson's 43 errors yielded a fielding percentage of .899, the first time since 1916 that a regular player's defensive average registered below .900 for the season.

Manager Zimmer, accurately characterizing Hobson as a "gamer," refused to pull him out of the lineup. While his defense suffered, he would manage to be a productive hitter, belting 17 homers and driving in 80 runs. He finally asked out of the lineup on September 22 in preparation for postseason elbow surgery, with Jack Brohamer filling in at third and Hobson still serving as a DH. In the 5-4 playoff loss to the Yankees on October 2, Hobson was 1-for-4 (a single) in the number-seven spot in the order while serving as the designated hitter.

Hobson came back in 1979 to play 142 games at third base. He slugged a career-high .496, batting .261 with 28 homers and 93 RBIs. Shoulder problems in 1980 prompted Zimmer to replace him at third with rookie Glenn Hoffman, who hit .285 in 110 games, while Hobson's batting average dropped to .228 (with 11 homeruns and 39 RBIs) in 93 games, 57 of them at third base. On May 31 the Red Sox hit six home runs, including a back-to-back-to-back trio by Tony Perez, Carlton Fisk, and Hobson, in a 19-8 loss to the Brewers. On June 12, 1980, Hobson had the only multi-homer game of his career, swatting a pair in a 13-2 win over the Angels in Anaheim.

On December 10, 1980, Hobson was traded with Rick Burleson to the California Angels for third baseman and future 1981 batting champion Carney Lansford, outfielder Rick Miller, and pitcher Mark Clear. He was limited to 85 games with the Angels in the strike-shortened 1981 season as a result of elbow injuries and a separated shoulder, hitting .235 with 4 homers and 36 RBIs. On March 24, 1982, Hobson was traded to the Yankees for pitcher Bill Castro. He hit only .172 in 30 games with New York, his final major-league stop as a player. In eight years as a player in the majors, Hobson had a career average of .248 with 98 home runs and 397 RBIs. He drove in four runs in a game seven times in his career with Boston and once with the Angels.

The way Hobson threw his body around on the field for the good of the team contributed to a shortened major-league career. It also helped make him a fan favorite. In a 2002 interview, Hobson explained his popularity: "Boston Red Sox fans are supportive. ... Whether a guy goes 0-for-20, as long as you are out there and giving 110 percent every day, that's all they care about. They're rooting for that blue-collar guy that runs through walls. They want that guy who will dive into the stands for a ball because they know, in the long run, it's going to be what helps them come out on top. As long as you can continue that when you play [in Boston], you're going to be very well accepted."[2]

After playing one partial and three full seasons in Columbus, the Yankees' Triple-A farm club and ending his playing career, Hobson returned in a manager's role. In 1987 and 1988 he managed the New York Mets' team in Columbia in the Class-A South Atlantic League. He joined the Red Sox system in 1989, managing New Britain of the Double-A Eastern League. His 1990 squad advanced to the final round of the Eastern League playoffs. Around this time, Hobson also served a stint as manager of the Winter Haven Super Sox in the short-lived Senior Professional Baseball League. In his fifth season as a minor-league manager, in 1991, Hobson guided the Triple-A Pawtucket Red Sox to a 79-64 record and a first-place finish in the International League East Division. His Paw Sox lost in the Governor's Cup Championship, getting swept, 3-0, by his last minor-league team as a player, the Columbus Clippers. Hobson was honored by *Baseball America* as its Minor League Manager of the Year and by the International League as its Manager of the Year. He was viewed by the Red Sox front office as a rising star as a manager.

On October 8, 1991, the Red Sox fired manager Joe Morgan and named Hobson as his replacement. "We couldn't risk losing such a talent in our organization," said general manager Lou Gorman.[3] The Red Sox hoped they would be getting a managerial version of the tough player Hobson had been. But Hobson's toughness as a player was not evident in his performance as a manager as perceived by the media. (*Boston Globe* columnist Dan Shaughnessy often referred to manager Hobson as "Daddy Butch.") This did not bode well during a three-year period in which the Red Sox seriously underachieved.

Hobson lost his first two games as manager in 1992 in New York. The season opener on April 7 was lost by a 4-3 score with Roger Clemens on the mound for the Red Sox. His first win was a 19-inning, 7-5 decision over the Indians at Cleveland Municipal Stadium on April 11. The Red Sox, at 73-89, were seventh and last in the American League East, their worst finish since 1966 — and their first last-place finish since 1932. After Roger Clemens (18-11), Frank Viola (13-12) was the only pitcher with a won-lost percentage over .500. Offensively, the team hit .246, 13th out of the 14 American League teams. Jack Clark, after hitting 28 homers in 1991, hit only five in 1992 and hit .210 in the final season of his career. Wade Boggs hit a career-low .259 and left for the Yankees after the season. Mike Greenwell hit .233. Tom Brunansky led the team with 15 homers and 74 RBIs.

The 1993 season saw the batting average improve to .264 with the emergence of Mo Vaughn (29 homers, 101 RBIs). However, Roger Clemens had his worst season as a professional (11-14, 4.46 ERA, a season in which he had been bitten on the pitching hand by his dog) and the team was again mired in the second division, finishing fifth in the AL East with a mediocre 80-82 record.

The players strike shortened the 1994 season, and the Red Sox compiled a 54-61 record and finished fourth in the AL East. Clemens led the staff with a 9-7 record. The offense, led by Vaughn and John Valentin, hit a combined .263 (12th in the AL) while the team ERA of 4.93 (ninth in the AL) is the only other fact one needs to figure out what happened with this team. New general manager Dan Duquette shipped players in and out trying to light a fire under the Red Sox. After the season he decided to ship out his manager as well, firing Hobson and bringing in Kevin Kennedy to manage the team.

Don Zimmer served as Hobson's bench coach in 1992 and theorized in his book *Zim* that substance abuse, alcohol in particular, played a role in Hobson's failure as a Red Sox manager. His substance-abuse problem was exposed to all in May 1996. After his dismissal from the Red Sox, Hobson became the manager of the Triple-A Scranton/Wilkes-Barre Red Barons. On May 4, 1996, his team was in Pawtucket to play the PawSox. Hobson was arrested in his hotel room on a felony charge of cocaine possession. Approximately 2.6 grams of cocaine (about $120 in value) were alleged to have been found in Hobson's shaving kit, having been sent to him in a Federal Express package by a former friend from Alabama named Jerry Poe. Poe owed Hobson money and sent the supposedly unsolicited drugs in payment of that debt. On August 8, 1996, Hobson was fired by the Philadelphia Phillies, Scranton's parent club. He was able to resolve the drug charge without a guilty finding in exchange for entering a first-offender program and performing approximately 60 hours of community service. He denied ever using cocaine while managing the Red Sox or the Red Barons. He has acknowledged a past history with the drug that began when he was a player. "I came up in an era when (using drugs) was what you were supposed to do. As a good old boy from Alabama, I thought that was the way to fit in. It probably cost me three or four years of baseball," he said.[4]

After his termination from the Red Barons, it was the Red Sox who gave Hobson another chance. In February 1997 he was hired as a special-assignment scout. In 1998 he continued his comeback as manager of the Sarasota Red Sox in the Class-A Florida State League. Finally, on December 2, 1999, Hobson returned to New England as the manager of the Nashua (New Hampshire) Pride of the independent Atlantic League. As the third manager in the team's history, Hobson led the 2000 Pride to the Atlantic League title. The championship was New Hampshire's first professional sports title in more than 50 years. Hobson's 2001 squad was eliminated in the first round of the playoffs. In 2003 the Pride returned to the championship series before they lost in five games to the Somerset Patriots, the team they had swept for the 2000 title.

In 2007 Hobson led the Pride to another championship, the Can-Am League crown. In 2011, he became manager of the independent Atlantic League's Lancaster (Pennsylvania) Barnstormers. In 2014 the Barnstormers won the league championship.

Hobson has three grown daughters, Allene, Libby, and Polly, from his first marriage, and three boys, K.C., Hank, and Noah, and a daughter, Olivia, from his second marriage, to his wife, Krystine.

Note

A version of this biography was originally published in *'75: The Red Sox Team That Saved Baseball*, edited by Bill Nowlin and Cecilia Tan, and published by Rounder Books in 2005. Republished by SABR in 2015.

SOURCES

Ashmore, Mike. "Ten Questions With Butch," AtlanticLeagueBaseball.com, September 14, 2004.

Boston Red Sox 1977, 1978, 1979 Yearbooks.

Boston Red Sox 1976 Press-TV-Radio Guide.

Boston Red Sox 2005 Media Guide.

Brooks, Scott. "Hobson's Choice: Pride Boss Staying in Nashua," *New Hampshire Union-Leader* (Manchester), November 23, 2004.

Comey, Jonathan. "Hobson Finally Back Where He Belongs," *South Coast Today*, February 8, 1997.

Complete Baseball Record Book, 2004 Edition, *The Sporting News*, 2004.

Courtney, Will. "The Fall and Rise of Butch," *Eagle-Tribune* (Lawrence, Massachusetts), August 10, 2000. Accessed via eagletribune.com,

Crehan, Herb. *Red Sox Heroes of Yesteryear* (Cambridge, Massachusetts: Rounder Books, 2005).

A CONSISTENT LAD IN THE LAND OF STEADY HABITS

Dewey, Donald, and Nicholas Acocella. *The New Biographical History of Baseball* (Chicago: Triumph Books, 2002).

Gammons, Peter. *Beyond the Sixth Game* (Boston: Houghton Mifflin Company, 1985).

Golenbock, Peter. *Red Sox Nation* (Chicago: Triumph Books, 2005).

Halvatgis, Jenna. "Hobson's Hope," *South Coast Today*, May 11, 1998.

Hickling, Dan. "Hobson's Choice," minorleaguenews.com, May 6, 2005.

Kahn, Roger. *October Men* (New York: Harcourt Inc., 2003).

Linn, Ed. *The Great Rivalry* (New York: Ticknor & Fields, 1991).

Malinowski, W. Zachary, and John Castellucci, New England Sports Service, "Butch Gets Busted," *South Coast Today*, May 9, 1996.

McDonald, Joe. The *Independent* Interview: Butch Hobson, alindependent.com, July 9, 2004.

Petraglia, Mike. "Where Have You Gone, Butch Hobson?" mlb.com, February 19, 2002.

Smith, Curt. *Our House* (Chicago: Masters Press, 1999).

Stout, Glenn, and Richard A. Johnson, *Red Sox Century* (Boston: Houghton Mifflin Company, 2000).

Thorn, John, et al. *Total Baseball*, Sixth Edition (Kingston, New York: Total Sports, 1999).

Zimmer, Don, with Bill Madden. *Zim: A Baseball Life* (Chicago: Contemporary Books, 2001).

Websites

baseballlibrary.Com.

nashuapride.com.

retrosheet.org.

rolltide.com.

NOTES

1   Kevin Glew, "Former Third Baseman Butch Hobson: Players Who Left The Game On Their Own Terms," *Baseball Digest*, December 2004.

2   Mike Petraglia, "Where Have You Gone, Butch Hobson?" mlb.com, February 19, 2002.

3   *Boston Globe*, October 9, 1991.

4   Glew.

Beehive Stadium: Grand Canyon East

By Stan Dziurgot

" 'It was a big field, cold all the time,' Bagwell recalled."
David Borges, Connecticut Post.[1]

Beehive Stadium had a repetitive role in the life of Jeff Bagwell. He played at Beehive in high school as a Xavier Falcon, in college as a Hartford Hawk, and in the minors with the New Britain Red Sox.

But for the foiled attempts of a team owner to renege on a verbal commitment, Beehive might not have been built at all.

In 1982 the city of New Britain built Beehive Stadium to complete a verbal agreement to bring a minor-league team to the city. It did so to secure the franchise before the team owner could change his mind.[2]

Although a modern and professional-quality stadium was not built in New Britain until 1982, pro ball has a long history in 'Hard-hitting' New Britain.

Professional baseball in the Hardware City started in 1884 and 1885 when the city had a team in the Connecticut State League. Pro ball would surface again in 1891 and 1898 with the New Britain entry in the Connecticut State League, with that team disbanding in midseason in 1898.[3]

After 1898 a team would not call New Britain home until 1908, when the New London Whalers moved there. The New Britain Perfectos played at Electric Field at White Oak Park on the New Britain-Plainville line. The teams from 1908 to 1912 featured four Cuban players, the first Hispanics to play in an American professional league; thus, the team was dubbed the Perfectos, after the cigar. One of the Cubans, Armando Marsans, played eight major-league seasons with the Reds, Browns, and Yankees. The team tried to play Sunday baseball, forbidden in many cities at the time, without success. On May 17, 1908, one such attempted Sunday game was halted when Deputy Sheriff Myron Rogers stopped the game and arrested the team owner for violating the Sabbath.[4]

The Connecticut State League changed its name in 1913 to the Eastern Association when several teams outside Connecticut joined it. It disbanded after the 1914 season. New Britain was not home to another professional team for almost 70 years. Industrial-league teams played in New Britain at Pioneer Field on Ellis Street in those times.

New Britain is a blue-collar, working-class community, home to the Stanley Works and other manufacturers. Its large Polish population and blue-collar reputation may be at the root of the sobriquettes "Hard-Hittin' New Britain" and "New Britski."[5]

Negotiations for a professional minor-league team go back to the late 1970s, according to the *New Britain Herald*. The Waterbury team playing in the Eastern League at the time had an interest in moving but no move occurred.[6]

In the fall of 1982 negotiations with Bristol Red Sox owner Joe Buzas appeared to make New Britain home to a professional team. He would move his Double-A Eastern League team, the Bristol Red Sox, to New Britain.

New Britain officials would learn that an oral agreement with Buzas was as good as the paper it was written on.[7]

Buzas had been involved in pro baseball since the 1940s. He was signed by Yankees scout Paul Krichell out of Bucknell University and was the Yankees' Opening Day shortstop in 1945. He owned at least one minor-league team in every season going back to 1957.[8]

The Boston Red Sox Triple-A farm team had been in Louisville, Kentucky, until 1972. Wanting to move the team closer to Boston, the Red Sox moved it to Pawtucket, Rhode Island, where the Louisville Colonels became the Pawtucket Red Sox.

In order to make that change, Boston relocated its Double-A affiliate, the Pawtucket Red Sox, to Bristol, where the team, newly the Bristol Red Sox, would play at historic Muzzy Field. Thus, many people may not know that the original PawSox were a Double-A team that would end up in New Britain by way of Bristol. The original PawSox became the BritSox.[9]

Even after securing a deal with New Britain, Buzas continued to look for a better location for his team. A reporter for a local paper told Paul Shaker Sr., New Britain's primary negotiator, that Buzas was investigating a move to Portland, Maine. That potential transfer ended when Portland's City Council failed to approve the move. With nowhere else to move the team for 1983, Buzas left the New Britain deal in place.[10]

Buzas's roving eye would periodically look for better opportunities over the course of his team's time in New Britain.

With the approval of New Britain Mayor William J. McNamara, Paul Shaker, the chairman of the Parks & Recreation board, and Walter Palenski, acting director of Parks & Recreation, went to the homes of the city councilors to make sure they had a unanimous vote of final approval by the City of New Britain. With a team thus secured and approval complete, the city needed to have the stadium ready for the start of the 1983 season.[11]

Willow Brook Park on the New Britain-Berlin line would be the site of the new ballpark. This park already had a football stadium, softball diamond, and a swimming pool. In the early 1950s it had been a Little League field and before that a baseball diamond. Willow Brook Park was made into a city park in the 1920s.[12]

The new ballpark was built on swampland and with its large outfield (400 feet to centerfield/325 feet down the lines) and thick air would be known as a pitcher's park.[13] The *New Britain Herald* called the park Grand Canyon East.[14] Locker rooms and concessions were added, and a contest was held to name the stadium.[15] Two people out of 79 submitted the winning entry—Beehive Stadium. The seal for the town of New Britain was a beehive with the motto, "Industry fills the hive and enjoys the honey."

The ballpark, whose official address is 230 John Karbonic Way[16], has a capacity of 4,700. Though it was symmetrical in its distances to the outfield fences, it was not without its oddities. The press box was down the third-base line instead of behind home plate and the light stands came straight up through the bleachers, creating an obstructed view for some fans. The park was designed to look like a 1930s ballpark with modern features. The look of Beehive Stadium and other Eastern League parks such as Quigley Stadium in West Haven are in stark contrast to the major- and minor-league stadiums built a decade later. These 1990s ballparks had brick and concrete façades like Baltimore's Camden Yards and New Britain Stadium, the ballpark that would replace Beehive in the Eastern League in 1996.

One problem remained. Joe Buzas owned the Reading team in the Eastern League and because league rules forbade a person owning two teams, he put the New Britain team in the name of his daughter, Dr. Hillary Buzas Bonner.

Opening Day for the new ballpark was April 23, 1983, with Mayor William J. McNamara throwing out the first pitch as the Red Sox lost to the Waterbury Reds, 6-4.[17]

Ironically, Waterbury was the same franchise that Paul Shaker had talked about moving to New Britain in the late 1970s.[18]

When the ballpark opened, Buzas was asked about parking at the facility. He told the city that parking was their problem, so $1.00 per car was charged for parking and the money went to the city, not Buzas.[19]

The team bounced back quite well after its Opening Day loss. In fact, it won its only Eastern League Double-A championship in New Britain in 1983, the season that Roger Clemens was brought up from Winter Haven and had a 4-1 record with a 1.38 ERA. The merry ring of the coins was heard by Buzas at Beehive. From 1973 to 1982 the highest attendance figure in Bristol was just over 77,000 people or just over 1,000 per game. New Britain drew more than 140,000 to Beehive in 1983.[20]

Many players who would one day play at Fenway Park also played at Beehive. Those major leaguers in the making include Brady Anderson, Ellis Burks, Oil Can Boyd, Curt Schilling, Matt Stairs, Aaron Sele, Jody Reed, Paul Quantrill, Al Nipper, John Marzano, Sam Horn, Todd Benzinger, and Glenn Hoffman.

Infielder Steve Lyons played in Bristol in 1982 and hit 13 home runs for the BritSox at Muzzy Field. Seeing Beehive Stadium for the first time, he assumed he would hit as many if not more. When Lyons initially saw the field, there were eight-foot-high walls in the outfield, but for advertising purposes the height of the walls was soon raised to 16 feet. With the higher walls and heavy air in the ballpark, Lyons mustered only seven homeruns in 1983, his only year at Beehive.[21]

Kevin Romine (who later had two sons play major-league baseball), Scott Hatteberg (of *Moneyball* fame), and Hall of Famer Jeff Bagwell also played in New Britain. The manager of Bagwell's 1990 New Britain team was former Red Sox third baseman Butch Hobson.

A game at Beehive Stadium featured between-innings entertainment like those still done today at minor-league games, such as the dizzy bat race. Adults could check out future Red Sox players while younger fans also had their own form of fun.

In 1985 a local man, Ralph Chunt, was introduced to Beehive crowds while wearing a yellow and black costume with an antenna on his head. The BritSox now had a mascot; the New Britain Bee, later called Buddy Bee. A young child racing Buddy Bee around the bases became a ballpark tradition.[22]

In January of 1985 the *New Britain Herald* reported that Joe Buzas was looking to move the team to Warminster, Pennsylvania, about 20 miles north of Philadelphia and closer to his Reading team. Buzas denied it and the team remained in New Britain.[23]

In 1984 Beehive had been in the running to be the location for shooting some baseball scenes for the Robert Redford movie *The Natural*. That didn't pan out, but according to Paul Shaker a Pringles potato-chip commercial was filmed at Beehive around that time.[24]

Willow Brook Park, a nearby city park, had summer concerts with acts such as the Charlie Daniels Band and Gregg Allman. When concert ticket sales exceeded Beehive's capacity, the concerts were held at Willowbrook's football venue, Veterans Memorial Stadium.[25]

In April 1988 an inebriated fan fell to his death from the top of the bleachers during a Red Sox game; from that point on, beer was sold in 12-ounce cups instead of 16-ounce cups and no more than two beers at a time could be bought.

In May 1988 the ECAC Division Baseball Tournament was held at Beehive. Teams in the tournament were C.W. Post College, Fairleigh Dickinson University, Fordham, Le Moyne College, the University of Maine, and the University of Hartford. Hartford and Fordham met in the tournament final with Fordham prevailing 10-8 after Hartford had opened up an 8-4 lead in the seventh inning. Future New Britain Red Sox third baseman Jeff Bagwell was the University of Hartford's third baseman.

The Eastern League All-Star Game was played at Beehive Stadium on June 29, 1987. It was the American League affiliates against the National League affiliates with the NL winning 6-0 in front of a crowd of 3,106. Dwight Smith, who was batting .359, scored two runs and drove in another and was named the game's MVP. Smith and first baseman Mark Grace represented the Pittsfield Cubs in the game. National League President Bart Giamatti was present. "I was just telling Bobby Brown that I never see enough games," Giamatti said, according to Tom Yantz in the June 30 *Hartford Courant*. Though the AL was shut out, it did turn an unusual 8-6-2-5-6 double play, according to the *Courant*.

Despite occasional upgrades to the ballpark like the installation of some pricier armchair seats, Joe Buzas complained about Beehive.[26] Although the ballpark was only a decade old, Buzas wanted the city to build him a new one. He had an ally in Boston Red Sox general manager Dan Duquette. Duquette wanted to have more of a presence for the Red Sox in Western Massachusetts and suggested moving the BritSox to Springfield, Massachusetts. A ballpark could be built off Route 141 on the Springfield/Chicopee line. Springfield promised Buzas a big season-ticket base. To Duquette's dismay, Buzas decided to keep the team in New Britain.

After the 1994 season Duquette moved the Red Sox' Double-A affiliate from New Britain to Trenton, New Jersey. In 2003 that affiliate was renamed the Portland Sea Dogs and played in the Maine city that Buzas had tried to move it to in 1982.

After the BritSox moved to Trenton, the Minnesota Twins moved their Double-A team to New Britain for the start of the 1995 season. This team employed the city's nickname for its first two seasons. It was called the Hardware City Rock Cats, eschewing the Twins name. Because major-league teams often switched minor-league affiliates at the time, many minor-league teams used their own team name and team colors while merely wearing a patch on the uniform top to show their major-league affiliation.

The 1995 season was the last year for minor-league baseball at Beehive because the city built a new ballpark for the Rock Cats' 1996 season. New Britain Stadium holds about 2,000 more people than Beehive. It has a brick and concrete façade with more concessions. It has a covered concourse for fans to shelter from the rain, unlike Beehive's concourse, which is open to the elements. The Hardware City Rock Cats began play in the new ballyard in 1996. In 1997 its name became the less unwieldy New Britain Rock Cats.[27]

Joe Buzas sold the team in 1998. He battled prostate cancer beginning in 1994. Despite his wandering eye and despite his complaints about Beehive, Buzas was praised for his loyalty to New Britain and for not moving the team to Springfield.

He was known to be frugal on matters regarding the team and the stadium. He was, however, known to be generous to some of his employees. He wanted his generosity to be kept private. In that regard, he had a little George Steinbrenner in him.

Beehive Field still stood as of 2018 and was used for a variety of events. The field was home to the New Britain High School baseball team. The New Britain Little League Juniors Division and American Legion teams have played their games there. Central Connecticut State University has played home games there and the University of Hartford played at Beehive in 2006 when its ballpark, Fiondella Field, was being built. Upgrades were done at Beehive in 2015 to make it handicapped-accessible.[28]

Often when a new ballpark like New Britain Stadium is built, the old one is torn down and the space is used for something practical like a parking lot, à la the Joni Mitchell song. It is unusual to have two facilities that hosted minor-league baseball continue to stand next to each other and both be in continued use. New Britain, the city that claims to have invented the wire coat hanger in 1869, also has that unusual distinction.[29]

At the end of the 2015 season, the New Britain Rock Cats relocated to Hartford as the Hartford Yard Goats. An independent team from the Atlantic League played at New Britain Stadium in 2016, 2017, and 2018; their name: the New Britain Bees.[30]

Had the city not built the new ballpark in 1996, the Bees could have played at Beehive.

It would have made perfect sense.

SOURCES

In addition to the sources cited in the Notes, the author also consulted BaseballReference.com, BaseballStadiumReviews.com, intheballparks.com, Charliesballparks.com, Ballparkreviews.com, and the following:

Malan, Douglas S. *Muzzy Field—Tales from a Forgotten Ballpark* (Bloomington, Indiana: iuniverse, 2009).

NOTES

1 David Borges, "Jeff Bagwell, Headed to Hall of Fame, Proud of His Connecticut Roots," July 21, 2017. ctpost.com/sports/article/Jeff-Bagwell-headed-to-Hall-of-Fame-proud-of-11306443.php.

2 Interview with Bill Demaio, formerly of New Britain Parks & Recreation, October 10, 2017.

3 baseball-reference.com/bullpen/New_Britain,_CT.

4 Ken Lipshiz, "A New Tradition—The Bees Become Part of New Britain Baseball History," *New Britain Bees Program*, 2016.

5 Patrick Thibodeau, *New Britain: The City of Invention* (Chatsworth, California: Windsor Publications, 1989). 60.

6 .Demaio interview.

7 Interviews with Paul Shaker Jr. formerly of New Britain Parks & Recreation, October 10 and 20, 2017.

8   Jack Cavanaugh, "Minor Leagues '86: Joe Buzas a Baseball Man Who Is in a League All by Himself," *New York Times*, August 10, 1986.

9   funwhileitlasted.net/2013/09/10/1973-1982-bristol-red-sox/.

10 Shaker interviews.

11 Ibid

12 Ibid.

13 Byron Bennett, "Beehive Field: Still Abuzz With Baseball in New Britain," April 26, 2015. deadballbaseball.com/?p=6547.

14 Gary Grabowski, "You Gotta Bee-lieve," *New Britain Herald*, April 9, 1985.

15 Shaker interviews.

16 In 1990, the road leading into the athletic complex was renamed for John Karbonic to honor his long service to New Britain youth and the Boys Club, according to his Jan. 17, 2010 obituary. https://www.legacy.com/obituaries/hartfordcourant/obituary.aspx?n=john-henry-karbonic&pid=138641194&fhid=4099

17 Owen Canfield, "The Beehive's Ready," *Hartford Courant*, April 23, 1983.

18 Shaker interviews.

19 Ibid.

20 baseball-reference.com/bullpen/New_Britain,_CT.

21 Ibid.

22 Shaker interviews.

23 Ibid.

24 Ibid.

25 Demaio interview.

26 Shaker interviews.

27 Lipshiz.

28 Demaio interview.

29 Thibodeau, 45.

30 Lipshiz.

STATISTICS

Retrieved by Tom Monitto

Jeff Bagwell's Statistical Legacy

By Steve Krevisky

For the Houston Astros, 2017 was a good year: They won the World Series and Jeff Bagwell was elected to the Hall of Fame. In March 2017, the Connecticut SABR chapter celebrated Bagwell with a panel discussion involving his coaches and teammates from Xavier High School, the University of Hartford, and the New Britain Red Sox.

Bagwell retired in 2005 with a career .297 batting average in the major leagues, a .408 on-base average, and a .540 slugging average. He led the National League three times in runs scored, once in doubles, once in RBIs, and once in walks. He won the National League Most Valuable Player Award in the strike-shortened 1994 season, with 39 home runs, a league-leading 116 RBIs, a .368 batting average, a .451 on-base average, and a league-leading .750 slugging average. He also led in OPS, and OPS+.

Career wise, in the regular season Jeff scored 1,517 runs, drilled 488 doubles, and had 449 home runs. He is 40th all-time in career home runs, tied with 2018 inductee Vladimir Guerrero. Also, according to the Jay Jaffe JAWS system, which is a WAR scoring system using a seven-year average of a player's peak WAR scores, Bagwell ranks sixth all-time among first basemen. He is in select company. The five ahead of him are Lou Gehrig, Albert Pujols, Jimmie Foxx, Cap Anson, and Connecticut's own Roger Connor. In this system, Bagwell is ahead of such luminaries as Dan Brouthers, Johnny Mize, Frank Thomas, and Jim Thome. All of these players are Hall of Famers except for Pujols, who stands a good chance of being inducted one day.

Bagwell had eight consecutive years of 30-plus homers and was a four-time All-Star. He enjoyed seven consecutive years of drawing 100-plus walks.

Based upon a measure called Similarity Scores, Bagwell is comparable to Carlos Delgado (879.9), Frank Thomas (874.6), with whom he shares the same birthday, Fred McGriff (865.9), Vladimir Guerrero (860.4), Todd Helton (859.7), and Willie Stargell (842.9). Similarity Scores compare the performance of two players. The higher the score, the more similar the two players are. For batters, the score starts at 1,000 points and requires graduated deductions for differences in the number of games played, at-bats, runs, hits, doubles, triples, home runs, RBIs, walks, strikeouts, stolen bases, batting average, and slugging percentage. The results are in a measured context and can help draw conclusions about the relative value of a player's performance. You can read more about calculating Similarity Scores at baseball-reference.com/about/similarity.shtml.

Again, Bagwell is in very good company. By age, Jeff compares favorably to Thomas from ages 32 to 35. He also compares to Paul Goldschmidt from ages 27 to 29. Bagwell's BFW[1] value of 52.9 (from the *ESPN Baseball Encyclopedia*) compares favorably to most of the first basemen on this list.

You can be sure that the Red Sox wish they had kept him instead of trading him to the Astros (that team again) for Larry Andersen in 1990. We should consider that the Astrodome was very favorable to the pitcher and that should enhance the appreciation of Bagwell's stats even further. He could have been elected to the Hall of Fame sooner had his home field been a different one. It did not help Bagwell's chances of getting into the Hall of Fame that the Astros didn't get to the World Series until 2005, his final season. He also fell short of the hallowed 500-home-run plateau, which he probably would have reached in a more favorable home park.

Overall, Bagwell is a very good choice for the Hall of Fame, and Connecticut should thus be proud of him.

SOURCES

Baseball-reference.com.

Jaffe, Jay. "First Base JAWS leaders," from Baseball-reference.com(baseball-reference.com/leaders/jaws_1B.shtml).

Gillette, Gary, and Pete Palmer, eds. *ESPN Baseball Encyclopedia*(New York: Sterling Publishing, 2008).

NOTES

1. Batter-Fielder Wins" are the sum of a player's batting wins, base stealing wins, and fielding wins. The figure indicates how many games a player won or lost for his team compared with an average player. (*ESPN Baseball Encyclopedia*, 6.)

Batting

Year	Age	Team	Lg	G	PA	AB	R	H	2B	3B	HR	RBI	SB	CS	BB
1991	23	HOU	NL	156	650	554	79	163	26	4	15	82	7	4	75
1992	24	HOU	NL	162	697	586	87	160	34	6	18	96	10	6	84
1993	25	HOU	NL	142	609	535	76	171	37	4	20	88	13	4	62
1994	26	HOU	NL	110	479	400	104	147	32	2	39	116	15	4	65
1995	27	HOU	NL	114	539	448	88	130	29	0	21	87	12	5	79
1996	28	HOU	NL	162	719	568	111	179	48	2	31	120	21	7	135
1997	29	HOU	NL	162	717	566	109	162	40	2	43	135	31	10	127
1998	30	HOU	NL	147	661	540	124	164	33	1	34	111	19	7	109
1999	31	HOU	NL	162	729	562	143	171	35	0	42	126	30	11	149
2000	32	HOU	NL	159	719	590	152	183	37	1	47	132	9	6	107
2001	33	HOU	NL	161	717	600	126	173	43	4	39	130	11	3	106
2002	34	HOU	NL	158	691	571	94	166	33	2	31	98	7	3	101
2003	35	HOU	NL	160	702	605	109	168	28	2	39	100	11	4	88
2004	36	HOU	NL	156	679	572	104	152	29	2	27	89	6	4	96
2005	37	HOU	NL	39	123	100	11	25	4	0	3	19	0	0	18
15 Yrs	Totals			2150	9431	7797	1517	2314	488	32	449	1529	202	78	1401

A CONSISTENT LAD IN THE LAND OF STEADY HABITS

SO	BA	OBP	SLG	OPS	OPS+	TB	GDP	HBP	SH	SF	IBB	Pos	Awards
116	0.294	0.387	0.437	0.824	139	242	12	13	1	7	5	*3	RoY-1
97	0.273	0.368	0.444	0.812	135	260	17	12	2	13	13	*3	MVP-19
73	0.32	0.388	0.516	0.903	145	276	20	3	0	9	6	*3	MVP-20
65	0.368	0.451	0.75	1.201	213	300	12	4	0	10	14	*3/9	AS MVP-1GGSS
102	0.29	0.399	0.496	0.894	143	222	9	6	0	6	12	*3	MVP-15
114	0.315	0.451	0.57	1.021	178	324	15	10	0	6	20	*3	AS MVP-9
122	0.286	0.425	0.592	1.017	168	335	10	16	0	8	27	*3/D	AS MVP-3SS
90	0.304	0.424	0.557	0.981	158	301	14	7	0	5	8	*3	
127	0.304	0.454	0.591	1.045	164	332	18	11	0	7	16	*3/D	AS MVP-2SS
116	0.31	0.424	0.615	1.039	152	363	19	15	0	7	11	*3/D	MVP-7
135	0.288	0.397	0.568	0.966	140	341	20	6	0	5	5	*3	MVP-7
130	0.291	0.401	0.518	0.919	135	296	16	10	0	9	8	*3/D	
119	0.278	0.373	0.524	0.897	128	317	25	6	0	3	3	*3	MVP-14
131	0.266	0.377	0.465	0.842	116	266	12	8	0	3	6	*3/D	
21	0.25	0.358	0.38	0.738	94	38	2	1	0	4	1	3	
1558	0.297	0.408	0.54	0.948	149	4213	221	128	3	102	155		

Ballpark Splits

Park	G	GS	PA	AB	R	H	2B	3B	HR	RBI	SB	CS	BB	SO
3 Rivers Std	57	54	247	213	38	68	19	1	11	43	4	2	27	44
3Com Park	21	20	94	66	13	22	7	0	3	11	3	3	27	18
Astrodome	661	645	2832	2324	465	704	164	11	126	469	71	23	444	441
Atl-Fulton	32	31	138	114	26	36	4	0	8	20	0	2	19	22
Bank One Bpk	24	24	112	98	16	24	3	0	3	10	4	0	14	17
Bp Arlington	11	11	47	42	6	7	2	0	1	6	1	0	3	11
Busch Stad	94	92	417	342	60	101	32	0	13	60	9	4	61	61
Candlestick	32	30	146	119	34	50	10	1	9	32	1	0	22	23
Cinergy Fld	48	48	220	181	33	54	13	1	15	37	8	1	35	33
CitizensBank	2	2	9	9	1	1	1	0	0	0	0	0	0	0
Comerica Pk	3	3	14	8	2	1	1	0	0	0	0	0	6	1
ComiskeyPk 2	6	6	29	25	7	10	1	0	5	11	1	1	2	6
Coors Fld	40	40	189	156	34	37	7	1	10	40	3	1	25	29
County Stad	18	18	87	69	19	21	2	0	4	9	3	1	18	10
Dodger Stad	71	70	318	265	36	78	10	0	15	46	11	5	43	50
Enron Field	161	159	707	587	153	193	44	3	49	144	9	5	106	126
Fenway Pk	3	3	15	14	2	4	2	0	1	1	0	0	1	4
GreatAmer BP	18	17	81	60	18	19	2	0	6	17	1	0	16	10
JackMurphySt	38	38	164	136	24	42	6	1	8	25	7	4	23	27
Jacobs Fld	6	6	29	25	4	6	1	0	1	2	0	1	4	8
JoeRobbieStd	17	17	76	62	6	13	2	0	0	7	1	1	11	14
KauffmanStad	9	9	41	28	10	9	3	0	3	17	2	1	12	9
Metrodome	6	6	28	22	6	9	3	0	3	4	1	0	6	2
MileHigh Std	6	6	26	22	2	7	1	1	1	3	1	0	4	2
Miller Pk	39	38	173	149	20	38	8	0	9	30	3	0	22	35
MinuteMaidPk	261	254	1105	919	188	264	39	4	59	166	12	5	158	198
NetworkAssoc	3	3	13	13	1	3	0	0	0	1	0	0	0	6
PacBell Park	12	12	53	47	11	17	6	1	2	5	1	0	6	10
Petco Pk	3	3	13	9	0	3	0	0	0	1	0	0	4	4
PNC Pk	38	33	149	124	15	32	6	0	3	15	1	1	22	24
ProPlayerStd	30	30	140	106	21	29	8	1	7	19	2	2	29	21
Qualcomm St	29	29	134	113	25	41	5	0	11	27	5	2	17	20
RiverfrontSt	31	31	134	117	14	34	6	0	6	22	4	2	15	22
Safeco Fld	3	3	12	9	2	2	1	0	0	1	0	0	3	3
SBC Park	3	3	12	12	2	2	0	0	1	1	0	0	0	4
Shea Stad	66	64	290	262	35	77	12	2	14	57	6	3	24	47

A CONSISTENT LAD IN THE LAND OF STEADY HABITS

BA	OBP	SLG	OPS	TB	GDP	HBP	SH	SF	IBB	ROE	BAbip	tOPS+
0.319	0.393	0.573	0.965	122	8	2	0	5	3	4	0.350	102
0.333	0.532	0.576	1.108	38	1	1	0	0	2	0	0.422	137
0.303	0.421	0.546	0.966	1268	56	43	2	19	64	36	0.325	104
0.316	0.409	0.561	0.970	64	2	1	1	3	4	1	0.322	104
0.245	0.339	0.367	0.707	36	2	0	0	0	0	2	0.269	51
0.167	0.234	0.286	0.520	12	1	1	0	1	0	0	0.194	10
0.295	0.403	0.503	0.906	172	12	6	0	8	5	4	0.319	92
0.42	0.521	0.748	1.268	89	4	4	0	1	4	0	0.466	166
0.298	0.418	0.630	1.048	114	6	3	0	1	6	1	0.291	119
0.111	0.111	0.222	0.333	2	1	0	0	0	0	0	0.111	-32
0.125	0.500	0.250	0.750	2	0	0	0	0	1	0	0.143	69
0.4	0.448	1.040	1.488	26	0	1	0	1	0	0	0.333	202
0.237	0.360	0.487	0.847	76	7	6	0	2	3	1	0.227	78
0.304	0.448	0.507	0.956	35	0	0	0	0	0	1	0.309	104
0.294	0.390	0.502	0.892	133	6	3	0	7	2	5	0.304	89
0.329	0.434	0.664	1.099	390	22	8	0	6	11	6	0.344	129
0.286	0.333	0.643	0.976	9	1	0	0	0	0	0	0.333	101
0.317	0.444	0.650	1.094	39	1	1	0	4	1	1	0.271	129
0.309	0.409	0.544	0.953	74	4	2	0	3	2	3	0.327	101
0.24	0.345	0.400	0.745	10	0	0	0	0	0	0	0.313	59
0.21	0.316	0.242	0.558	15	2	0	0	3	0	1	0.255	22
0.321	0.537	0.750	1.287	21	0	1	0	0	3	0	0.375	171
0.409	0.536	0.955	1.490	21	0	0	0	0	0	0	0.353	208
0.318	0.423	0.591	1.014	13	0	0	0	0	0	3	0.316	113
0.255	0.358	0.490	0.848	73	5	2	0	0	0	3	0.276	78
0.287	0.398	0.531	0.929	488	23	18	0	10	10	14	0.305	96
0.231	0.231	0.231	0.462	3	0	0	0	0	0	0	0.429	-1
0.362	0.434	0.660	1.094	31	1	0	0	0	0	0	0.429	129
0.333	0.538	0.333	0.872	3	0	0	0	0	2	0	0.600	94
0.258	0.369	0.379	0.748	47	6	1	0	2	4	6	0.293	61
0.274	0.414	0.566	0.980	60	2	0	0	5	3	1	0.265	106
0.363	0.455	0.699	1.154	79	6	3	0	1	3	2	0.361	141
0.291	0.366	0.496	0.861	58	2	0	0	2	3	1	0.308	82
0.222	0.417	0.333	0.750	3	0	0	0	0	0	0	0.333	64
0.167	0.167	0.417	0.583	5	1	0	0	0	0	0	0.143	18
0.294	0.352	0.515	0.867	135	12	1	0	3	0	5	0.309	82

Park	G	GS	PA	AB	R	H	2B	3B	HR	RBI	SB	CS	BB	SO
Stade Olymp.	61	61	284	237	55	67	15	0	10	44	10	2	38	55
Tiger Stad	3	3	14	9	4	0	0	0	0	0	0	0	4	2
Turner Fld	26	26	120	101	13	27	4	2	5	17	5	1	18	10
VeteransStad	59	59	272	224	37	70	18	1	13	56	4	1	38	48
Wrigley Fld	96	92	433	345	58	89	18	1	14	53	8	4	74	79
Yankee Stad	3	3	14	14	1	3	2	0	0	0	0	0	0	2

BA	OBP	SLG	OPS	TB	GDP	HBP	SH	SF	IBB	ROE	BAbip	tOPS+
0.283	0.391	0.473	0.863	112	7	6	0	3	0	1	0.326	83
0	0.357	0.000	0.357	0	0	1	0	0	2	0	0.000	-13
0.267	0.375	0.495	0.870	50	2	0	0	1	3	2	0.253	84
0.313	0.415	0.576	0.991	129	3	5	0	5	3	4	0.339	108
0.258	0.395	0.438	0.833	151	14	8	0	6	11	3	0.291	78
0.214	0.214	0.357	0.571	5	1	0	0	0	0	0	0.250	19

Home Away

Split	G	GS	PA	AB	R	H	2B	3B	HR	RBI	SB	CS	BB	SO
Home	1083	1058	4644	3830	806	1161	247	18	234	779	92	33	708	765
Away	1067	1044	4787	3967	711	1153	241	14	215	750	110	45	693	793

A CONSISTENT LAD IN THE LAND OF STEADY HABITS

BA	OBP	SLG	OPS	TB	GDP	HBP	SH	SF	IBB	ROE	BAbip	tOPS+
0.303	0.417	0.560	0.978	2146	101	69	2	35	85	56	0.323	106
0.291	0.398	0.521	0.919	2067	120	59	1	67	70	55	0.310	94

Left-Right Batting Splits

	AB	R	H	2B	3B	HR	RBI	BB	IBB	SO	HBP	SH
vs RHP	6000	1106	1737	363	25	342	1154	988	96	1250	118	2
vs LHP	1797	411	577	125	7	107	375	413	59	308	10	1

Day-Night Batting Splits

	G	AB	R	H	2B	3B	HR	RBI	BB	IBB	SO
Day	649	2327	438	692	146	6	139	456	421	42	462
Night	1501	5470	1079	1622	342	26	310	1073	980	113	1096

A CONSISTENT LAD IN THE LAND OF STEADY HABITS

SF	XI	ROE	GDP	SB	CS	AVG	OBP	SLG
81	0	95	164	141	59	0.29	0.396	0.529
21	0	28	57	61	19	0.321	0.446	0.577

HBP	SH	SF	XI	ROE	GDP	SB	CS	AVG	OBP	SLG
36	0	33	0	30	66	61	21	0.297	0.408	0.544
92	3	69	0	93	155	141	57	0.297	0.408	0.539

Minor Leagues

Year	Age	AgeDif	Team	Lg	Lev	Aff	G	PA	AB	R	H	2B	3B
1989	21		2 Teams	2 Lgs	A-Rk	BOS	69	262	229	30	71	14	2
1989	21	-1.3	Winter Haven	FLOR	A	BOS	64	240	210	27	65	13	2
1989	21	1.8	Red Sox	GULF	Rk	BOS	5	22	19	3	6	1	0
1990	22	-1.6	New Britain	EL	AA	BOS	136	569	481	63	160	34	7

A CONSISTENT LAD IN THE LAND OF STEADY HABITS

HR	RBI	SB	CS	BB	SO	BA	OBP	SLG	OPS	TB	GDP	HBP	SH	SF	IBB
2	22	1	1	26	25	0.310	0.386	0.415	0.801	95	7	3	3	1	0
2	19	1	1	23	25	0.310	0.384	0.419	0.803	88	7	3	3	1	0
0	3	0	0	3	0	0.316	0.409	0.368	0.778	7		0	0	0	0
4	61	5	7	73	57	0.333	0.422	0.457	0.880	220		6	3	6	12

Postseason

Year	Age	Team	League	Series	Opp	Rslt	G	PA	AB	R	H	2B	3B	HR
1997	29	HOU	NL	NLDS	ATL	L	3	13	12	0	1	0	0	0
1998	30	HOU	NL	NLDS	SDP	L	4	16	14	0	2	0	0	0
1999	31	HOU	NL	NLDS	ATL	L	4	19	13	3	2	0	0	0
2001	33	HOU	NL	NLDS	ATL	L	3	12	7	0	3	0	0	0
2004	36	HOU	NL	NLDS	ATL	W	5	25	22	5	7	2	0	2
2004	36	HOU	NL	NLCS	STL	L	7	31	27	1	7	2	0	0
2005	37	HOU	NL	NLDS	ATL	W	2	2	2	1	1	0	0	0
2005	37	HOU	NL	NLCS	STL	W	1	1	1	0	0	0	0	0
2005	37	HOU	NL	WS	CHW	L	4	10	8	1	1	0	0	0
		Total Post Season (6 Years)					33	129	106	11	24	4	0	2
		6 NLDS					21	87	70	9	16	2	0	2
		2 NLCS					8	32	28	1	7	2	0	0
		1 WS					4	10	8	1	1	0	0	0

RBI	SB	CS	BB	SO	BA	OBP	SLG	OPS	TB	GDP	HBP	SH	SF	IBB
0	0	0	1	5	0.083	0.154	0.083	0.237	1	0	0	0	0	0
4	0	0	1	6	0.143	0.250	0.143	0.393	2	0	1	0	0	0
0	0	0	5	4	0.154	0.421	0.154	0.575	2	0	1	0	0	2
0	0	1	5	1	0.429	0.667	0.429	1.095	3	0	0	0	0	0
5	0	0	3	3	0.318	0.400	0.682	1.082	15	1	0	0	0	0
3	1	1	4	5	0.259	0.355	0.333	0.688	9	1	0	0	0	0
1	0	0	0	0	0.500	0.500	0.500	1.000	1	0	0	0	0	0
0	0	0	0	0	0.000	0.000	0.000	0.000	0	0	0	0	0	0
0	0	0	0	1	0.125	0.300	0.125	0.425	1	0	2	0	0	0
13	1	2	19	25	0.226	0.364	0.321	0.685	34	2	4	0	0	2
10	0	1	15	19	0.229	0.379	0.343	0.722	24	1	2	0	0	2
3	1	1	4	5	0.250	0.344	0.321	0.665	9	1	0	0	0	0
0	0	0	0	1	0.125	0.300	0.125	0.425	1	0	2	0	0	0

Team Splits

Split	G	GS	PA	AB	R	H	2B	3B	HR	RBI	SB	CS	BB
Inter-League	115	114	507	421	92	118	30	1	29	86	11	5	71
Los Angeles Angels of Anaheim	3	3	13	10	3	4	1	0	2	2	0	0	2
Arizona Diamondbacks	49	49	218	197	34	52	6	0	9	28	10	1	20
Atlanta Braves	126	125	547	464	72	136	24	3	21	67	12	4	73
Baltimore Orioles	3	3	14	10	3	4	1	0	0	0	0	0	4
Boston Red Sox	3	3	15	14	2	4	2	0	1	1	0	0	1
Chicago Cubs	199	191	864	707	124	192	40	4	37	131	13	5	128
Chicago White Sox	12	12	56	46	14	15	1	0	9	19	2	1	7
Cincinnati Reds	197	194	860	701	152	216	42	2	49	154	26	5	138
Cleveland Indians	15	15	68	59	9	17	4	0	3	7	1	3	9
Colorado Rockies	102	101	465	375	84	105	21	2	28	88	8	3	80
Detroit Tigers	9	9	42	29	9	6	2	0	2	4	1	0	11
Florida Marlins	100	99	449	354	66	101	22	2	17	63	7	3	83
Kansas City Royals	15	15	66	50	16	17	5	0	5	23	2	1	14
Los Angeles Dodgers	131	129	573	473	76	129	22	1	26	77	16	5	86
Milwaukee Brewers	113	111	499	412	84	112	19	1	25	79	10	2	79
Minnesota Twins	14	14	60	51	11	17	4	0	5	10	2	0	8
New York Mets	125	121	543	470	78	139	18	3	25	95	11	3	61

SO	BA	OBP	SLG	OPS	TB	GDP	HBP	SH	SF	IBB	ROE	BAbip	tOPS+
94	0.28	0.394	0.563	0.957	237	7	11	0	4	9	2	0.295	101
1	0.4	0.538	1.1	1.638	11	0	1	0	0	0	0	0.286	236
40	0.264	0.335	0.431	0.766	85	2	1	0	0	1	5	0.291	62
76	0.293	0.388	0.494	0.882	229	11	3	1	6	17	6	0.308	87
2	0.4	0.571	0.5	1.071	5	0	0	0	0	0	0	0.5	133
4	0.286	0.333	0.643	0.976	9	1	0	0	0	0	0	0.333	101
145	0.272	0.39	0.496	0.887	351	25	17	0	12	17	6	0.289	87
11	0.326	0.429	0.935	1.363	43	1	2	0	1	0	0	0.222	178
126	0.308	0.426	0.583	1.009	409	17	12	0	9	23	9	0.312	112
14	0.288	0.382	0.508	0.891	30	0	0	0	0	2	1	0.333	88
84	0.28	0.415	0.571	0.986	214	14	8	0	2	7	7	0.291	107
6	0.207	0.452	0.483	0.935	14	1	2	0	0	3	0	0.19	100
75	0.285	0.416	0.503	0.919	178	9	3	0	9	7	4	0.31	95
12	0.34	0.485	0.74	1.225	37	0	1	0	1	4	0	0.353	156
93	0.273	0.386	0.488	0.874	231	8	6	0	8	5	10	0.285	85
82	0.272	0.393	0.505	0.898	208	15	5	0	3	1	7	0.282	90
7	0.333	0.433	0.706	1.139	36	0	1	0	0	0	0	0.308	137
92	0.296	0.379	0.506	0.886	238	15	6	0	6	6	9	0.318	87

Split	G	GS	PA	AB	R	H	2B	3B	HR	RBI	SB	CS	BB
New York Yankees	3	3	14	14	1	3	2	0	0	0	0	0	0
Oakland Athletics	3	3	13	13	1	3	0	0	0	1	0	0	0
Philadelphia Phillies	119	118	532	444	86	132	37	2	24	91	6	3	71
Pittsburgh Pirates	190	178	807	668	138	210	50	5	35	139	14	7	125
San Diego Padres	138	136	601	495	93	158	31	2	35	93	19	8	89
Seattle Mariners	6	5	20	17	2	4	1	0	0	2	0	0	3
San Francisco Giants	136	133	604	483	113	168	39	3	32	115	9	8	100
St. Louis Cardinals	192	188	844	700	135	223	63	1	38	139	15	8	122
Tampa Bay Devil Rays	3	3	13	10	3	3	2	0	0	0	0	0	3
Texas Rangers	23	23	100	87	17	20	5	1	2	16	1	0	9
Washington Nationals	121	118	531	444	91	124	24	0	19	85	17	8	75
WP lt .500	1183	1155	5224	4280	928	1314	286	22	266	952	115	37	807
WP of .500+	967	947	4207	3517	589	1000	202	10	183	577	87	41	594

SO	BA	OBP	SLG	OPS	TB	GDP	HBP	SH	SF	IBB	ROE	BAbip	tOPS+
2	0.214	0.214	0.357	0.571	5	1	0	0	0	0	0	0.25	19
6	0.231	0.231	0.231	0.462	3	0	0	0	0	0	0	0.429	
91	0.297	0.401	0.552	0.953	245	6	10	1	6	6	8	0.322	101
125	0.314	0.42	0.561	0.981	375	27	4	0	10	14	16	0.338	107
111	0.319	0.431	0.602	1.033	298	18	12	0	5	14	8	0.347	117
5	0.235	0.35	0.294	0.644	5	0	0	0	0	0	0	0.333	40
104	0.348	0.465	0.64	1.105	309	16	13	0	8	13	2	0.383	132
123	0.319	0.422	0.574	0.997	402	22	11	1	10	12	6	0.337	110
2	0.3	0.462	0.5	0.962	5	0	0	0	0	0	0	0.375	106
21	0.23	0.31	0.379	0.689	33	3	2	0	2	0	1	0.273	46
98	0.279	0.39	0.462	0.852	205	9	8	0	4	3	6	0.317	81
847	0.307	0.421	0.571	0.991	2442	126	76	1	60	83	75	0.325	109
711	0.284	0.391	0.504	0.895	1771	95	52	2	42	72	36	0.307	89

University of Hartford

Year	Team	League	Level	Org	Age	G	AB	R	H	2B	3B	HR	RBI	SB
1987	Hartford	NCAA	College	fr	19	38	127	31	51	12	1	7	32	0
1988	Hartford	NCAA	College	so	20	41	161	49	66	12	1	14	58	1
1989	Hartford	NCAA	College	jr	21	33	112	45	48	7	0	10	36	1

CS	BB	SO	AVG	OBP	SLG	OPS	ISO	secA	Babip	K/BB	AB/HR	TB	PA
1	14	18	0.402	0.524	0.677	1.201	NA	NA	NA	1.29	18.1	86	142
0	26	10	0.410	0.492	0.758	1250	0.348	0.516	0.380	0.380	11.5	122	187
1	31	11	0.429	0.552	0.759	1311	0.330	0.607	0.418	0.350	11.2	85	143

Contributors

ANDREW BLUME has long been obsessed with all things baseball and Red Sox. A SABR member since 2001 along with his dad, Murray, and a contributing author to several SABR publications, including *The 1967 Impossible Dream Red Sox* "Pandemonium on the Field" and *The Red Sox Team That Saved Baseball* [1975], he lives in Natick, Massachusetts, with his wife, Nancy, daughters Emily and Abigail, and felines Velvet, Brady and Holly. In his spare time, he practices law.

JIM BRANSFIELD was born, raised and lived in Middletown (Connecticut), commonly known to locals as the Center of Western Civilization. An alumnus of Middletown High School and Central Connecticut State University, he spent 36 years teaching social studies at the high-school level, first for 10 years at Hale-Ray High in East Haddam, then the rest in Middletown, mostly at Middletown High School. He fell into sportswriting accidentally. In 1966 lights were installed at Palmer Field, the local ballyard, and he asked if he could announce the American Legion games. Until his passing in February of 2018, he announced Xavier High football and basketball, Middletown High football, soccer, and state track meets held at MHS, the high-school baseball championship games, plus Legion ball in the summer. He announced countless state and regional Legion tourneys and two World Series held at Palmer Field. He was a Yankee fan. He wasn't much of a baseball fan until his aunt took him to see the Yankees play the Red Sox at Fenway Park in 1961. The Yankees hit seven home runs that day, including two each by Mickey Mantle and Roger Maris, and won 12-4. He was a Yankee fan ever since that game and had a season package for 21 years. He was in Yankee Stadium for both David Wells's and David Cone's perfect games, was there for the Aaron Boone home-run game in 2003, and was there for the World Series clinchers in 1999 and 2009. He covered countless high-school games in just about all sports and wrote a sports column every Monday in the *Middletown Press* called Monday Musings. "I figure I keep doing this because they can't find anybody else," he said in the autobiography he wrote for this book.

KARL CICITTO is the communications manager for the Connecticut Smoky Joe Wood Chapter of SABR. As a rule he doesn't like tattoos but sports a modest Boston "B" and "Mom" on his left shoulder. The tatty is in loving memory of his late mom,

Mary Ann, who first took the family to Fenway Park in 1968. Karl has led several chapter events. He co-edited and contributed to the 2016 SABR biography on Mike Sandlock. He is the content manager for the chapter newsletter and its Facebook page. He is a co-editor and contributor to this book. His kind and tolerant wife, Lisa, and their three daughters consider Fenway Park their baseball home.

ALAN COHEN has been a member of SABR since 2011, and is vice president/treasurer of the Connecticut Smoky Joe Wood Chapter. He has written more than 38 biographies for SABR's bio-project, and has contributed to several SABR books. His first game story, about Baseball's Longest Day, May 31, 1964, has been followed by 16 other game stories. His research into the Hearst Sandlot Classic (1946-1965), an annual youth all-star game that launched the careers of 88 major-league players, first appeared in the Fall 2013 edition of the *Baseball Research Journal*, and has been followed with a poster presentation at the SABR Convention in Chicago. He is currently expanding his research and is looking forward to having a book published. He serves as the datacaster (stringer) for the Hartford Yard Goats, the Colorado Rockies affiliate in the Double-A Eastern League. A native of Long Island, he now resides in West Hartford, Connecticut, with his wife, Frances, two cats and a dog.

STANLEY DZIURGOT joined SABR in the early 1980s and has always enjoyed SABR historical publications. After a hiatus, Stan rejoined SABR after learning there was a chapter with local activities. He attended his first chapter meeting in 2006 and his first national convention in 2008. Stan is a Yankees fan whose first game was the Bombers' pennant clincher in September of 1962. His father was a Brooklyn Dodgers fan who knew someone with Yankees season tickets, and was thus able to secure seats for Stan's first few games right behind the Yankees dugout. Stan is a graduate of the Connecticut School of Broadcasting and worked at stations in Hamden and Waterbury. After leaving radio he worked for the *New Haven Register*. Since 1991 he has worked at Medtronic. Stan met his wife, Mari Lea, in 1982 at a wedding. They live in Wallingford, Connecticut. They have three sons, Matthew,[wife Melissa], Christopher, and William.

GREG ERION joined SABR in 1980 and was an accomplished author and historian. Since 2015, he served as project leader for the fledgling SABR Games Project and helped this new initiative thrive, building a solid team of editors and contributors, overseeing the production of five SABR Digital Library books, and providing a sense of stability, leadership, and direction for the entire effort. He also contributed many stories of his own to the Games Project and BioProject, including a biography of his favorite player, one-time NL batting champion Debs Garms. He was born August 11,

1947, and was in the first four-year graduating class at El Camino (California) High School. He earned a degree in transportation from San Francisco State University and served with distinction in the US Army in Thailand during the Vietnam War. He worked for many years as an executive with the Western Pacific and Southern Pacific railroads. He earned two master's degrees, one in business and another in history, and taught history classes in recent years at Skyline College.

JIM KEENER is a devout Pittsburgh sports enthusiast whose great loves are baseball and the Pittsburgh Pirates. Roberto Clemente is his hero. Keener, a Pittsburgh native, received a bachelor's degree in athletics administration from Robert Morris University. He has been associated with the University of Hartford since the fall of 1983, spending 30 years in the athletics department before joining the alumni relations office, where he currently serves as assistant director of alumni relations for strategic programs. In athletics, Keener had a variety of roles, the most prominent of which was in sports information. While there, he guided the public-relations efforts surrounding Jeff Bagwell and Vin Baker. Keener's love for the game of baseball is evident in his everyday life. For seven summers during and shortly after college, he was employed at the Ted Williams Camp and counts among his thrills being able to work with the Red Sox legend. Keener is currently the official scorer for the Double-A Hartford Yard Goats and is an avid collector of baseball cards and memorabilia. He lives in Farmington, Connecticut, with his wife, Lesley. They have two children, Alexa and McGwire. Alexa, a young professional, is named after the daughter of Steve Olin, the Cleveland Indian who died in a boating accident in 1993. "Mac," a student at Hartford, is named for Mark McGwire.

STEVE KREVISKY has been President of the Connecticut Smoky Joe Wood chapter of SABR for several years. He has attended the national SABR conventions for 30 years and has often presented, been on winning teams in the trivia contests, and been involved in fantasy/simulations baseball. As a professor of mathematics at Middlesex Community College, Steve often uses baseball to teach and does baseball presentations to the seniors groups on campus. He has made math and baseball presentations at national and international math and statistics conferences. Steve enjoys sabermetrics and baseball history. He is from New York City and follows the Yankees closely. He has the box score of the first game to which his dad took him in 1958 and remembers that the Tigers beat the Yanks, 5-4. Steve has been to Cooperstown many times and enjoys seeing baseball games on road trips.

LEN LEVIN retired as an editor at the *Providence Journal*, and currently has a part-time job editing the decisions of the Rhode Island Supreme Court. He also spends much of his time editing baseball biographies and other material for SABR publications. He has been a passionate Red Sox fan for as long as he can remember.

TOM MONITTO, a resident of Bristol, Connecticut, was born and raised in New Britain. He has worked in IT since 1974. At one point his career landed him in Springfield, Vermont, where he worked for a company from which the father of Carlton Fisk had recently retired. He didn't realize this until he met the Hall of Fame catcher 20 years later. After returning to Connecticut, Tom met his wife, Joneen, at an interoffice softball game. He first took note of her when, as she played catcher, Joneen retired a runner on a tag play at home plate. Tom was a devoted fan of the New York football Giants – "a terrible team" – while growing up in the 1960s. The 1967 Impossible Dream Red Sox team kindled his interest. Around the time of the Joe Pisarcik fumble, football took a back seat to baseball. Tom enjoys the historical and analytic sides of the game. He reads fiction and nonfiction stories about baseball and loves to listen to old broadcasts. A SABR member since December 2013, he was given his SABR membership as a gift from his son and is an active member of the Smoky Joe Wood chapter.

BILL NOWLIN is on the SABR Board of Directors and is author and editor of around 50 baseball books. Fifty is more or less the number of Grammy Awards won by artists on Rounder Records, which he co-founded.

GEORGE PAWLUSH grew up in Wilkes-Barre, Pennsylvania. He received a bachelor's degree and a Master's at Wilkes University. He spent 43 years as a senior public relations practitioner first at his alma mater, Wilkes University, and then at Geisinger-Wyoming Valley Medical Center and hospitals in Connecticut. Now retired, George resides in Cheshire, Connecticut with his wife, Carol. He is the chairman of SABR'S minor league research committee. From 1999-2005, he was the state chairman and tournament director of Connecticut American Legion Baseball. He was inducted in the Connecticut American Legion Baseball Hall of Fame in January 2019. George is a member of the Board of Trustees at Wilkes University. He has written for many SABR publications. He is the author of *Dawn and Dusk of the Colonial League*, which is about a minor league circuit that operated in Connecticut, New York and New Jersey from 1947 to 1950. He is interested in minor league baseball in the Northeast and in Ernest "Duke" Landgraf, who was involved in various capacities organized baseball, from 1898 to 1950.

BILL RYCZEK has written eight books on sports history, concentrating on nineteenth-century baseball, baseball in the 1960s, and professional football in the 1960s. His most recent book is *Baseball on the Brink, The Crisis of 1968*. Bill has also edited or co-edited several collections of nineteenth-century baseball history and was a regular contributor to the National Pastime Museum website.

BRIAN P. WOOD ("Woodie") is an Eagle Scout and a retired naval officer who spent 20 years as an F-14 Tomcat aviator. He is a research associate at the Naval Postgraduate School in Monterey, California, where he and his team conduct field experimentation on new technologies before they are sent to the fleet for operational use. Due to his father also being in the Navy, he has been a fan of several teams as he moved around the country. Brian was a Washington Senators (II) and Texas Rangers fan growing up until he moved to the East Coast in the 1980s and became a staunch Baltimore Orioles supporter – he can still spell out "O-R-I-O-L-E-S" like Wild Bill Hagy, throw in a rousing "O" during the last part of the Star Spangled Banner, and have "Thank God I'm a Country Boy" make him think of baseball and taking a stretch. He has lived in the Monterey area for the past 20 years and is an ardent Giants supporter with his rubber chicken (shown when opposing pitchers would walk Barry Bonds) hanging in a spot of honor in his garage. Woodie has contributed chapters to several SABR books including those on the Expos and Brewers. He has also fact-checked/reviewed several articles for SABR publications. Woodie and his wife, Terrise, live in "America's Last Hometown," Pacific Grove, California, and have three sons, Daniel, Jack, and Nathan, two cats, and a black and orange dog with a large noggin, named Bochy

PETE ZANARDI is a native of Chester, Connecticut, and a graduate of Valley Regional High School, Mitchell College, and Boston University. He spent almost two decades as a sportswriter with the *Manchester Herald, Hartford Times,* and *New Haven Register* covering college sports, pro soccer, minor-league baseball, and auto racing. After another decade spent in manufacturing, he returned to journalism as a free-lance writer and media consultant. While working in media relations for Stafford Motor Speedway and Waterford Speedbowl, Zanardi covered auto racing and baseball for several publications. Among the projects was a history of the Middlesex County Baseball League and a series on Connecticut baseball personalities, both for the *Shoreline Times*. He is also a contributor to SABR's BioProject. A member of SABR since 1983, Zanardi won the Connecticut Sports Writers McGinley Award in 2007. He is a member of the Greater Hartford Twilight League and New England Auto Racers Halls of Fame.

www.ingramcontent.com/pod-product-compliance
Lightning Source LLC
Chambersburg PA
CBHW081719100526
44591CB00016B/2428